CONFRONTING CHILD ABUSE THROUGH RECREATION

CONFRONTING CHILD ABUSE THROUGH RECREATION

By

DAVID L. JEWELL, Ph.D., C. T. R. S.

*Associate Professor of
Recreation and Leisure Studies at
SUNY College at Brockport
Brockport, New York*

CHARLES C THOMAS • PUBLISHER
Springfield • Illinois • U.S.A.

Published and Distributed Throughout the World by

CHARLES C THOMAS • PUBLISHER
2600 South First Street
Springfield, Illinois 62794-9265

© *1989 by* CHARLES C THOMAS • PUBLISHER

ISBN 0-398-05604-8

Library of Congress Catalog Card Number: 89-4580

Printed in the United States of America
SC-R-3

Library of Congress Cataloging-in-Publication Data

Jewell, David L.
Confronting child abuse through recreation / by David L. Jewell.
p. cm.
Bibliography: p.
Includes index.
ISBN 0-398-05604-8
1. Child abuse—United States—Prevention.   2. Abused children—
United States—Recreation.   3. Abused children—United States—
Identification.   4. Recreation—United States—Management.
5. Recreational therapy.   I. Title.
HV741.J45   1989
362.7'68'0973—dc20
89-4580
CIP

To all of those young lives that might have been
and
to all of those that yet may be.

PREFACE

Rarely does a week go by without the issue of child abuse being raised by one or more forms of the news media. In the majority of instances the children have been victimized over long periods of time. Frequently, the victims, particularly those victims five years of age and older, have been identified as having been participants in activities outside of the abusive environment; particularly in school and recreational activities sponsored by various organizations from the governmental, private and commercial sectors.

It would indeed be surprising, even appalling, to find any professional from a human services discipline who would not agree that child abuse must be eradicated from the social scene. It only seems reasonable to expect Recreation and Leisure Service professionals to be committed to such action, since children are and have been a major target population for services. Also, the professional literature has repeatedly expounded the virtues of recreation and meaningful leisure pursuits, professing that they develop character, tolerance of individual differences and social skills; enhance physical, cognitive, and affective development; perpetuate culture; provide opportunities for family solidification; provide balance in life; and so on and so on. Few of us will disagree that recreation can do all of this and much, much more. What is gratifying is that the benefits of recreational activities are not recognized only by recreation professionals but also by physicians, educators, psychologists, social workers, social philosophers, and practically all professionals concerned with human growth and development. Yet, when it comes to recreation's role in the intervention, prevention, and treatment of one of our society's most hideous maladies, definition is lacking. Informally it is agreed that something needs to be done by those of us providing recreation programs for youth. However, our literature does not adequately address the questions of how, what, when, where, and why. This text is an attempt to answer these questions and to expand the recreation professional's role as an advocate for children by sensitizing the reader to the dynamics of the issue.

The decision-making process as to whether or not I should some day assume the task of writing a book addressing the issue of recreation and child abuse began a number of years ago; specifically, I first contemplated the task in 1973. From January 1970 until September 1979 I was the Director of Activity Therapy Services at the Chester Mental Health Center in Illinois. The Center served (and still does) as a maximum security mental health treatment center. The population was comprised of two categories of patients: mittimus and non-mittimus, or those with criminal charges and those without charges. Patients from both categories shared one common characteristic: they demonstrated behavior which labeled them as being dangerous to themselves or others. Oftentimes, this behavior was demonstrated through suicide attempts, self-mutilation, assaultive behavior, rape, homicide, arson, and child sexual abuse. Mittimus patients were placed in the Center for evaluation and treatment until such time they could be remanded to court. Non-mittimus patients were usually transferred to the Center from other state mental health centers after having demonstrated aggressive behaviors endangering the health and welfare of other residents and/or staff. They usually remained at the Center until their behaviors had been adequately controlled by medications and other forms of thera-peutic intervention, including recreation programs.

It was mid-1973 when Activity Therapy Services became active par-ticipants in the treatment planning process, beginning with the initial assessment of the newly admitted resident. As Director of Activity Therapy Services I became an active and frequent member of the in-take team. My role in this activity provided me the opportunity to thoroughly review medical records and case histories of more than 300 newly admitted residents and to interview them with respect to the leisure aspects of their lives. Repeatedly, a common problem would appear regarding their childhoods: child abuse. A conservative estimate is that 85–90 percent of the residents I saw in the admissions unit were either victims of physical abuse, emotional abuse, neglect, or sexual abuse. My interest being spurred by the experience in admissions, I began informally making inquiries of other residents and found the results to be similar. Another alarming fact also appeared with almost the same frequency. Social histories and personal interviews also disclosed that many of the residents had been active in some form of organized recreation program; i.e. Little League, community centers, playground activities, extracurricular school activities, Boy Scouts, Cub Scouts, church youth groups, Boys Clubs, summer camps, YMCA, etc. Several, likewise, indicated that the reasons for terminating participation in activities were either: (1) they were asked not to return due to disruptive behavior; (2) they were ashamed of their own personal appearance; (3) they were lacking the required energy levels; (4) they were frustrated by constantly losing during competition; (5) they perceived the leaders to be uncaring; (6) they were fearful the abuse would "slip out" and that they would get in trouble at home; (7) they perceived the programs as only other means of parental disassociation; (8) they felt the rules were unfair and staff too rigid; (9) they never got to do anything different; or (10) they got bored.

Over the years I asked myself repeatedly, "How could an abused child be in a recreation program and go undetected?" Because of the closeness to the violent consequences of abuse I became angry and disenchanted with my colleagues in the non-institutional settings. I also became angry with the social systems that would allow such a destructive phenomenon as child abuse to continue, seemingly unchecked.

In 1976 I began to seriously pursue my doctorate degree. During the preparation to write my dissertation I reacquainted myself with the recreation and leisure literature. I was gradually enlightened as to one reason why recreation professionals were not addressing child abuse: it was not a topic addressed in the professional literature. It was at this point in early 1977 that I made the decision to someday write a book that may be helpful to recreation professionals and encourage them to join the ranks combating the abuse of children.

In the pages that follow I have attempted to accomplish several tasks. In Chapter One child abuse is defined. One of the major reasons for the difficulties in accumulating current data as to the incidence of abuse and in the reporting of and intervention in abuse has been the lack of understanding what it is.

Chapter Two answers the question, "How Serious is the Problem?" The purpose of Chapter Two is to enlighten Recreation and Leisure Service professionals as to the alarming statistics related to the incidence of abuse. These figures will hopefully demonstrate to the reader that (1) abuse happens more than just occasionally and (2) there is a strong likelihood that he or she will confront the issue.

Chapter Three answers the important question, "Who are Child Abusers?" The chapter will likely result in the reply, "Everyone!" The facts are that no economic, social, or ethnic group is free of suspicion. The chapter will very likely explode numerous myths of child abuse; at least, that is the hope.

Chapter Four will hopefully provide some inspiration to intervene in, prevent, and treat child abuse. The purpose is to make the reader aware of the painful costs of abuse to the abuser, the abused, and society. Some of the personal recollections are explicit or very vivid. The case studies will likely challenge the Recreation and Leisure Services professional's commitment to the very tenets of his or her profession.

Chapters Five through Eight are included to assist the Recreation and Leisure Services professional in the intervention of abuse. Respectively, the chapters provide physical and behavioral indicators for sexual abuse, physical abuse, emotional abuse, and neglect. Hopefully, the chapters will sensitize the reader to the characteristics or signs of abuse and diminish the reluctance to intervene that results from the fear or ignorance of physical and behavioral signals.

Chapter Nine is included to provide insight into how society as a whole, recreation programs included, is guilty of child abuse. Children today are being robbed of the pleasures of childhood as a result of being placed under stress. The co-authors define the problem of stress and also offer some helpful suggestions as to how Recreation and Leisure Service professionals as well as laymen can combat its deleterious effects on our children.

Chapter Ten addresses the need and support for the Recreation and Leisure Services professional's role in a comprehensive community attack on child abuse. It provides some guidelines on how to become a member of the child protective service team. The reader is reminded, as well, of recreation's roots in child advocacy and of how other professionals perceive its role.

Chapter Eleven discusses the basis of action against child abuse. All of the measures that may be taken may have little consequence if the Recreation and Leisure Services agency does not formulate, disseminate, implement, and enforce policies on child abuse. The chapter contains information on policy development, particularly as related to the reporting of suspected abuse and the abusive behavior of agency staff and volunteers. The chapter offers some specific steps and guidelines in policy development.

Chapter Twelve addresses the foundation of confrontation of abuse, the staff; specifically, the selection of staff. Efforts to deal with child abuse are only as effective as the quality and commitment of the staff charged with the responsibility to enforce agency policies and to conduct its programs. The chapter addresses the rationale for careful staff selection, qualities personnel should possess, personal needs of families in crisis, the screening of personnel, recommendations for position advertisement, questions to ask applicants, the structure of the interview process, as well as other steps in the hiring process. The personnel process is also discussed in relation to public perception of the agency and to the courts.

Chapter Thirteen relates to recreation and the law. Specifically, the reader learns who has to report and what some of the criminal and civil consequences are for not reporting suspected abuse. The questions of immunity, mandated personnel screening, and mandated training are also addressed.

Chapter Fourteen suggests some programs, activities, and support services the Recreation and Leisure Service agencies may offer to prevent and treat abuse. The purpose is to (1) provide assistance in program implementation and (2) to kindle creativity or innovative programs within recreation agencies or departments, regardless of their settings. The absence of a program or activity does not diminish its potential value or suggest that it is not applicable to a program of abuse prevention or treatment.

The last chapter, Chapter Fifteen, discusses the results of a study investigating a specific approach to treating abused children. "Adventure Games in the Treatment of Abused Children" relates how such activities as Moon Ball, Go Tag, Blindfold Soccer, etc. compare to traditional recreational games in improving the self-concept of abuse children.

Finally, Appendices A–M serve two purposes. First, to supplement the content of individual chapters or to clarify and expand upon concepts presented. The appendices also provide a substantial amount of resources the reader should find helpful in developing rationale for the agency's role in abuse intervention, prevention, and treatment; reporting abuse; developing abuse policy; understanding some of the terminology of abuse; or interviewing the suspected victim of abuse.

The overriding theme of the text is recreation's role in a comprehensive community approach to the problem of child abuse. A problem of such magnitude extends beyond the boundaries of any single human service and impacts on all elements and strata of society. As dramatic as it may sound, the very existence of our culture as we know it may well depend on our resolve to join forces in the intervention and remediation of the eroding syndrome called child abuse.

D.L.J.

ACKNOWLEDGMENTS

At the risk of confronting tradition I wish to at the beginning recognize and express my gratitude to the individual who more than anyone else made a dream a reality. This text's completion is largely attributed to the support, understanding and encouragement of my wife, Patty. Throughout the lengthier than anticipated writing process it was she that maintained a resemblance of normalcy on the home front. She exhibited monumental tolerance with a dining room table and floor covered with books, brochures, magazines and manuscript pages, with a husband who would excuse himself from numerous family and household obligations using the excuse, "I have to work on the book"; with numerous requests to bring sources home from the college library; and with repeated requests to "listen to how this sounds." Without my wife's strength and support I very likely would not have completed the task.

Two chapters have been contributed by individuals well qualified to address the issues related to the abuse of our children. I would like to formally and publicly express my most sincere gratitude to Doctors Linda and Joseph Balog and Doctor Robert McDonald for their contributions.

The chapter addressing childhood stress was co-authored by Doctors Joseph and Linda Balog. The Balogs are recognized nationally as authorities in the area of stress management. Doctor Linda Balog is presently serving as the Executive Director of the Child and Adolescent Stress Management Institute. For the past seven years she has been intensely involved in helping children who are experiencing high levels of stress. She has personally conducted literally hundreds of workshops and presentations addressing the issue of stress management for children and adolescents. In addition, she serves as a consultant on childhood and adolescent stress management for numerous school districts. She is presently an Associate Professor of Health Science at the State University of New York College at Brockport.

Doctor Joseph Balog is currently the Associate Director of Research and Development for the Child and Adolescent Stress Management

Institute. He has lectured and published extensively in the field of health education. He has served as a national consultant to the American Red Cross on health promotion issues. At the request of corporate officials Doctor Balog recently developed a stress management program for Xerox Corporation. The program, entitled "A Self-Help Guide to Managing Stress," has been distributed nationally to corporation employees. Presently an Associate Professor of Health Science at the State University of New York College at Brockport, Doctor Balog has in excess of 15 years of teaching experience in higher education.

The chapter entitled "Adventure Games in the Treatment of Abused Children" is authored by Doctor Robert McDonald. Doctor McDonald is currently an Assistant Professor in the curriculum of Management of Human Resources at Central Wesleyan College in Central, South Carolina. He is also an experienced Recreation and Leisure Services professional who has more than 20 years of experience as both practitioner and educator. His experience includes that of a Program Director for the YMCA; the Campus Administrator of the Connie Maxwel Children's Home in Greenwood, South Carolina; Research Director on treatment alternatives for abused children at the John de la Howe School in McCormick, South Carolina; Program Director of The South Carolina Department of Mental Retardation's Coastal Center in Charleston, South Carolina; and Associate Director for Student Services at Central Wesleyan College. His contribution describes a study he conducted during 1987 and 1988.

I also wish to acknowledge the contribution made to the text by the numerous state child protection agencies. Without exception, each office responded positively when requested to clarify or to update reporting data. All were very candid in the assessments of the strengths and weaknesses of the child protective services within their respective states. It was rewarding to discover that there are so many people near the apices of bureaucratic, governmental agencies that do in fact care for the welfare of our nation's most precious resource—its children.

I am particularly grateful to "Marge," "Jacob," "Ronnie," "Harold," and "Kyle" for their willingness to share their stories. Their stories vividly demonstrate the need for a comprehensive and energized attack on the contributors and consequences of child abuse and neglect. Their stories had a particularly personal and profound effect on the completion of this book. Like many authors, I reached a point in the writing process when I began to doubt the value of the book, particularly in relationship to other professional responsibilities and interests. After reviewing the stories of these five courageous people my commitment was renewed and some of the other interests lost their appeal. They told their stories in the hope that they would inspire recreation personnel to become stronger advocates for the rights of all children and active agents in the intervention, prevention, and treatment of abuse. "Harold" commented that of all the human service professionals, Recreation and Leisure Service providers perhaps had the most to contribute to the socialization process and the eventual reunification of the family. Hopefully, his and the other personal accounts will motivate our profession to confront the challenge of abuse in a courageous and resolute manner.

The other profound personal effect can best be summarized as guilt—personal and collective. After listening to the tapes of the personal interviews I was consumed by overwhelming guilt for not having been a more militant adversary of child abuse. I also felt the collective guilt as a member of a human service profession that has done little to combat abuse. We have not addressed it in our literature and many of us have very limited or no awareness as to its dynamics. This text is, in part, a response to that guilt.

A project of this nature also requires the cooperation of those with whom you work. I am particularly grateful to Doctor John Phillips, Dean of the School of Professions at the State University of New York College at Brockport, for securing me a one-semester sabbatical to be used for the research and initial writing phase. The leave also meant that my department colleagues had to assume most of my governance and student advisement responsibilities in my absence. I wish to take this opportunity to formally express my gratitude to Doctors M. Joan Davis, Ann Rancourt, and Donald Rith of the Recreation and Leisure Studies faculty. Appreciation is also expressed to Doctor Andrew Brown, Chairperson of the Health Science/Recreation and Leisure Studies Department, for assuming my Coordinator responsibilities during the sabbatical. The cooperation of these four colleagues allowed me to devote a substantial amount of time and energy to the manuscript.

In Chapter Thirteen, reference is made to HB528 enacted by the Maryland General Assembly. I am grateful for the invaluable assistance provided by Mr. Gerald H. Groves and his staff at the Maryland Recreation and Parks Association in making a copy of the bill available for my review and use.

I am likewise appreciative of the equally invaluable assistance provided by Ms. Sarah M. Hanson, Coordinator of Grants and Legislation for the Essex County Department of Parks, Recreation and Cultural Affairs. Ms. Hanson contributed significantly to Chapter Thirteen by providing a copy of the proposed New Jersey legislation, S-2512. As the Maryland bill, the New Jersey bill (if enacted) will have monumental implication on public recreation's responsibility to curb the abuse of children.

Manuscripts do not appear magically. Their preparation requires a great deal of skill and patience. I was extremely fortunate to have available a team of exceptionally skilled and abundantly patient professionals who devoted endless hours to the preparation of the rough drafts and final copy of the manuscript. The staff of the Document Preparation Center at the State University of New York at Brockport were not only highly skilled but gracious beyond all expectations. I wish to express my heartfelt appreciation to Ms. Vicky Willis, Director of the Document Preparation Center and her two able staff members, Ms. Terry Collins and Ms. Loretta Lonnen. From a purely selfish perspective, I hope they remain the best kept secret on the Brockport campus.

CONTENTS

CONFRONTING CHILD ABUSE
THROUGH RECREATION

Chapter One

DEFINING ABUSE AND ITS TYPES

INTRODUCTION

Throughout man's history there is evidence of child abuse. However, it is only since the 1960s that it has been the focus of empirical investigation. A major obstacle in the accumulation of data in the study of the issue has a very fundamental rooting. Namely, "What is child abuse and is it distinctly different from maltreatment?" The effect of such debate and disagreement between individuals in the medical and child care disciplines is evidenced by historical facts. It was not until 1968 that all fifty states had enacted some form of law to mandate the reporting of suspected child abuse cases and it was not until 1974 that the U.S. Congress enacted legislation. It was in 1974 that The Child Abuse Prevention and Treatment Act (PL93-247) was signed into law. This act, which was the result of more than ten years of debate and deliberation, created the first national agency to deal specifically with child abuse, the National Center on Child Abuse and Neglect. As previously stated, one of the major barriers to more immediate action was the lack of consensus on a definition. The absence of concise and accepted definitions impacts our ability to study and deal effectively with the problem. Without clarity in defining child abuse, it is difficult to make inquiries as to its incidence, to intervene, or to specify behaviors needing remediation. Is the parent who raises red welts on his son's buttocks being abusive or only being a strict disciplinarian? Is the parent who deprives her child from participation in all parties and celebrations being emotionally abusive or only complying with religious, denominational doctrine? As pointed out by Mayhall and Norgard, the issue of definition relates directly to the establishment and enforcement of laws pertaining to abuse. This definition-law connection warrants deliberation, since it is the law and its interpretation that determines:

- What is legally considered to be harmful to a child.
- When and what must be reported.

- When is intervention appropriate and/or required.
- Who is to intervene.
- How is intervention to proceed.
- When a child is legally in imminent danger of being harmed.
- When the court is justified in interfering in the privacy of the family, overriding the authority of the parents and their wishes, and possibly severing their parental rights, in order to protect the child.

                                          (Mayhall & Norgard, 1983, p. 71)

Consequently, the recreation worker's role in effective intervention, adjudication, and treatment or his/her capacity to interrupt the cycle of abuse is, in large part, dictated by the comprehension of its definition. Not unlike other social and familial phenomena, the issue of definition is exacerbated by diverse interpretation of key elements of the syndrome. For example, abuse vs. physical discipline, violence vs. roughhousing, accidental vs. intentional, neglect vs. culturally determined child-rearing practices, neglect vs. abuse, harm vs. temporary discomfort, and what determines one's status as a child. With respect to the latter, what is the age frame and is a profoundly retarded or physically disabled offspring over 18 an adult or a child? To say the least, child abuse is very, very difficult to clearly define. The confusion over terminology and aversion to infringe upon the sanctity of parental privilege or family tradition have also contributed to the definition issue. Consequently, there still does not exist a single definition that is accepted by all professionals coping with the child abuse problem. What has resulted is a multitude of definitions, to the extent that each state may have one or more legal definitions. The federal government, namely, the U.S. Congress, has likewise exhibited some indecisiveness as well. Since the critical enactment of CAPTA (The Child Abuse Prevention and Treatment Act) of 1974, the issue of definition has been the cause for almost continual debate and deliberation. Since the initial CAPTA (PL93-247) enacted on January 31, 1974, there have been two other major legislative actions involving definition revision. These two actions are PL95-266, the Child Abuse Prevention and Treatment and Adoption Act and the Child Abuse Amendments Act of 1978 and 1984, respectively (see 92 STAT.205 and 98 STAT.1749). The congressional leadership is in the delicate position of having to enact laws that address mankind's ingenuity and that at the same time do not further dilute an institution already in dire straits, the American family. This confusion has a predictable "trickle-down" effect, particularly in the various state lawmaking bodies. The states have, as a consequence, formulated a number of definitions that are based upon assumptions made about children, families, the predominant cultures, and the resources available. The state lawmaker is in the unenviable position of drafting and enacting laws which will address all of these (and more) factors and be supported if appealed on the basis of national definition and mandate. Added to this confusion is the fact that individual communities and organizations also draft laws and policies containing definitions which may or may not be the same as those drafted at the state and national levels of government. As a result, the Recreation and Leisure Services personnel at the grass roots level should enlighten themselves with the plethora of definitions which may govern their responses to suspected incidence of child abuse or perhaps even cause them to suspect abuse.

It is important, even essential, that Recreation and Leisure Services personnel be cognizant of the various accepted or established definitions in their communities and their governing agencies. These laws can normally be found in

- Criminal Law Definition—those forms of child abuse and neglect which are criminally punishable
- Juvenile Court Act—those forms of child abuse and neglect which authorize the court to provide protective services, and, when necessary, remove children from their parents.
- Reporting Law Definition—those forms of known or suspected child abuse and neglect which require reporting by some persons and permit reporting by others. These reports activate the child protective process which can result in either juvenile court or criminal court action.
(Heindl, Krall, Salus and Broadhurst, 1979, p. 3)

It is important to note that the criminal law definition will likely concentrate on the parent or guardian specific acts or emphasize the particular action that can result in prosecution. The criminal law definition may be more inclusive than parents or guardians and be extended to all adults, particularly those to be considered under the legal concept of loco parentis, i.e. teachers, day care personnel, recreation leaders, etc. In contrast, the juvenile court definition will place less emphasis on the clarification of acts but be more concerned with the resulting harm to the child. In light of the primary purpose of such acts, namely, to protect the child and to address the court's likely concern over the sanctity of the family, the child protective services personnel must be prepared to respond adequately to the court's question of "Why?" Finally, the reporting law definition will likely "describe apparent situations which give rise to sufficient cause for concern ('reasonable cause to believe') to require the investigation of the home situation and the danger to the child by some appropriate investigative agency" (Heindl et al., 1979, p. 3). Such definitions may be the most relevant to the recreation worker, in that they may provide the justification for reporting without the encumbrance of accusation. The emphasis is on outcomes, not process or identification of perpetrators.

As pointed out previously, the syndrome of child abuse is complex. The recreation worker needs to not only have an understanding of child abuse, but of its major forms as well. Beyond being aware of child abuse a knowledge of the definitions of sexual, physical and emotional abuse, and neglect are also critical for informed intervention, reporting, and treatment.

FEDERAL LEVEL

The first definition offered at the federal level was contained in Section 3 of PL93-247. It was as follows (see Appendix E):

> "Child abuse and neglect" means the physical or mental injury, sexual abuse, negligent treatment, or maltreatment of a child under the age of eighteen by a person who is responsible for the child's welfare under circumstances which indicate that the child's health or welfare is harmed or threatened thereby, as determined in accordance with regulations prescribed by the Secretary.

"Secretary" refers to the Secretary of the then Department of Health, Education, and Welfare.

It was only 4 years and 3 months later that leaders in the movement to address child abuse realized that the original 1974 definition was lacking. First, it allowed legal loopholes by not addressing adequately the scope of potential abuses or abusers. Secondly, there seemed to be a consensus that the phrase "under the age of eighteen" was too arbitrary and did not address the mentally, intellectually, and physically disabled child and the obvious potential for their abuse. In addition, the definition did not afford the states the latitude to draft and enforce legislation specific to the issues relevant to their individual regions. As a consequence, the 95*th* Congress on April 24, 1978 enacted PL95-266, also known as the Child Abuse Prevention and Treatment and Adoption Reform Act of 1978. The definition was amended in Section 102 to read:

> Child abuse and neglect means the physical or mental injury, sexual abuse or exploitation, negligentful treatment, or maltreatment of a child under the age of eighteen, or the age specified by the child protection law of the State in question, by a person who is responsible for the child's welfare under circumstances which indicate that the child's health or welfare is harmed or threatened, thereby, as determined in accordance with regulations prescribed by the Secretary.

This definition clearly specifies the responsibility to be aware of State child protection laws. This was a logical progression from PL93-247, since it had made clear to the States that in order to receive federal funding to assist in "developing, strengthening, and carrying out child abuse and neglect prevention and treatment programs" (Section 4, 61) that protection laws would have to be enacted.

PL95-266 remained in force until October 9, 1984 when PL98-247 was enacted by the 98*th* Congress. The act, entitled Child Abuse Amendments of 1984, made sweeping amendments or revisions to the Child Abuse Prevention and Treatment Act. One such revision was the definition of child abuse and neglect. The definition was amended in Section 102 to read:

> Child abuse and neglect means the physical or mental injury, sexual abuse or exploitation, neglectful treatment, or maltreatment of a child under the age of eighteen, or the age specified by the child protection law of the State in question, by a person (including any employee of a residential facility or any staff person providing out-of-home care) who is responsible for the child's welfare under circumstances which indicate that the child's health or welfare is harmed or threatened, thereby, as determined in accordance with regulations prescribed by the Secretary.

This definition has an obvious strong impact on Recreation and Leisure Services personnel, those in residential facilities for the disabled, camps, community centers, playgrounds, and private and public agencies of all types. Prior to this amendment parents or guardians were the individuals receiving the primary attention. This definition is lengthy and to attempt its memorization may be impractical. Yet, the recreation worker concerned with interrupting the cycle of abuse should remind her/himself of the key elements, namely:

(1) sexual abuse or exploitation
(2) physical or mental (emotional) injury
(3) neglectful or maltreatment

(4) age specified by the State in question

(5) perpetrators can be anyone responsible for in-home or out-of-home care

(For information concerning State definitions of child abuse, interested parties should contact the offices specified in Appendix C.)

SEXUAL ABUSE

Though identified in PL93-247 as a form of child abuse, sexual abuse was not defined by the Congress until the revisions contained within PL95-266. Specifically, in Section 104 the Act revised Section 5 of the original Act to include provisions for funding and establishing programs designed to address the issue of sexual abuse. That revision included a definition of sexual abuse as including

> the obscene or pornographic photographing, filming, or depiction of children for commercial purposes, or the rape, molestation, incest, prostitution, or other such forms of sexual exploitation of children under circumstances which indicate that the child's health or welfare is harmed or threatened, thereby, as determined in accordance with regulations prescribed by the Secretary.

As with child abuse, the definition of sexual abuse was likewise amended in the 1984 PL98-457. The revised definition is as follows (see Appendix F):

> The term "sexual abuse" includes the employment, use, persuasion, inducement, enticement, or coercion of any child to engage in, or having a child assist any other person to engage in, any sexually explicit conduct (or simulation of such conduct) for the purpose of producing any visual depiction of such conduct or the rape, molestation, prostitution, or other such form of sexual exploitation of children, or incest with children under circumstances which indicate that the child's health or welfare is harmed or threatened, thereby, as determined in accordance with regulations prescribed by the Secretary....

This definition, particularly in relation to the governing definition of child abuse, expands the scope of sexually abusive behavior and, likewise, allows states to include non-adults as perpetrators as well. The definition is lengthy and by including specific behaviors is exclusive of others, though such is not the intent. It is suggested that to eliminate the potential problems of such an inclusive-exclusive definition that the definition proffered six years earlier by the National Center on Child Abuse and Neglect be adopted by recreation agencies. The Center adopted the following definition of child sexual abuse:

> Contacts or interactions between a child and an adult when the child is being used for the sexual stimulation of the perpetrator or another person. Sexual abuse may also be committed by a person under the age of 18 when that person is either significantly older than the victim or when the perpetrator is in a position of power or control over another child. (*Child Sexual Abuse: Incest, Assault & Sexual Exploitation*, 1978, p. 2).

This definition undoubtedly is more operational or applicable to Recreation and Leisure Service agencies. Behaviors do not require sorting and it also has obvious implications on hiring practices. This will be discussed further in Chapter Twelve when staff considerations are identified.

The 1984 definition was faulted for excluding certain forms of abuse. Another difficulty with the definition is its emphasis on overt, or the more sensational forms of abuse and exploitation. There are sexual acts that are less physical and sensational; for example, those that are categorized by May as non-touching. Specific acts identified by May are:

(1) verbal abuse,
(2) obscene telephone calls,
(3) exhibitionism,
(4) voyeurism, and the
(5) primal scene.

Obscene calls are distinguished from verbal sexual abuse by virtue of the fact that they are made most often by people who are strangers to the child. Also, since they lack the person-to-person contact, they lack the intensity.

Exhibitionism should not be confused with occasional nudity or partial nudity within the household. Self-exposure by a neighbor or someone who is a stranger or a casual acquaintance could have traumatic, abusive effects upon the child, however.

Voyeurism, whether committed by an adult family member or a stranger, can have deleterious effects upon the emotional stability of the child. The sense of being violated may be as strong as if actually being abused physically or touched.

Finally, the primal scene refers to either visual or auditory exposure to adults having sex. It usually refers to the practice of allowing the child to witness sexual intercourse (May, 1984, pp. 5–6).

The complexities of the sexual abuse of children are evidenced by the issues related to definition. As with the general area of child abuse, recreation personnel are urged to contact their respective State and local child protective services authorities to seek further clarification pertaining to the definition of sexual abuse.

PHYSICAL ABUSE

Physical injury as a form of abuse was identified but not discussed in PL93-247. Nor was it defined in either PL95-266 or PL98-457; therefore, there does not exist at the federal level a statutory definition of physical abuse. Such is at the least interesting, since it is physical abuse that is most frequently dealt with by physicians and law enforcement officials. However, it is likely that most states will likely model their definitions after the ones offered by the Kempes and others or the one offered by the NCPCA. The Kempes define physical violence as related to children as "physically harmful action directed against the child; it is defined by any inflicted injury such as bruises, burns, head injury, fractures, abdominal injuries or poisoning" (Kempe and Kempe, 1978, p. 6). Wayne and Avery in *Child Abuse: Prevention and Treatment Through Social Group Work* narrow the scope of the issue when they define physical abuse as "any non-accidental physical injury inflicted on a child by a parent (or other care giver deliberately or in anger" (1980, p. 8). Their definition is somewhat more definitive, in that it stipulates "non-accidental" and by "parent (or other care giver)." Broadhurst, in the 1984 reprint of *The Educator: Role in the Prevention and Treatment of Child Abuse and Neglect*, adds to Wayne and Avery's statement by adding "By definition the injury is not an accident. But neither is it necessarily the intent of the child's caretaker to injure the child. Physical abuse may result from overdiscipline or from punishment which is inappropriate to the child's age or condition" (p. 14). In all instances, physical abuse is an act of commission; it is deliberate, whether the specific physical results are intentional.

EMOTIONAL ABUSE

As with physical child abuse, emotional child abuse is also not defined in federal statutes (Public Laws 93-247, 95-266, or 98-457). In this instance, however, the National Center on Child Abuse and Neglect as a federal entity has in its *Interdisciplinary Glossary on Child Abuse and Neglect* defined psychological/emotional abuse as follows:

> Child abuse which results in impaired psychological growth and development frequently occurs as verbal abuse or excessive demands on a child's performance and results in a negative self-image on the part of the child and disturbed child behavior may occur with or without physical abuse.
>
> (1980, p. 6)

The *Glossary* goes on to define the syndrome further by offering a definition of verbal abuse, the most frequent means of emotional abuse. Verbal abuse is defined as:

> A particular form of psychological/emotional abuse characterized by constant verbal harassment and denigration of a child.
>
> (p. 6)

In the *Glossary,* the note is added that "Many persons abused as children report feeling more permanently damaged by verbal abuse than by isolated or repeated experiences of physical abuse" (p. 6).

Garbarino and Garbarino have formulated an illuminating definition of emotional abuse. They approach this form of abuse from a competency basis, one that incorporates the five categories of emotional abuse (ignoring, terrorizing, rejecting, corrupting, and isolating). They identify four categories of care-giver behavior that can be emotionally deleterious to the youthful recipient. These are as follows:

- Emotional maltreatment is penalizing a child for positive, normal behavior such as smiling, mobility, exploration, vocalization, and manipulation of objects.
- Emotional maltreatment is discouraging care-giver and infant attachment.
- Emotional abuse is penalizing a child for showing signs of positive self-esteem.
- Emotional maltreatment is penalizing a child for using interpersonal skills needed for adequate performance in non-familial contexts such as school and peer groups.

(*Emotional Maltreatment of Children,* 1986, pp. 19–20)

Emotional abuse, as sexual and physical abuse, is an act of commission, as opposed to the remaining type of abuse to be discussed; neglect is an act of omission.

NEGLECT

The National Center on Child Abuse and Neglect offers the only definition at the national level, in that none is statutorily stated by the U.S. Congress. The Center defines neglect as "an act of omission, specifically the failure of a parent or other person legally responsible for a child's welfare to provide for the child's basic needs and proper level of care with respect to food, clothing, shelter, hygiene, medical attention, or supervision" (*Glossary,* p. 6).

The Center has identified and defined five specific forms of neglect. These are as follows:

- Educational Neglect—failure to provide for a child's cognitive development. This may include failure to conform to state legal requirements regarding school attendance.
- Medical Neglect—failure to seek medical or dental treatment for a health problem or condition which, if untreated, could become severe enough to represent a danger to the child.
- Moral Neglect—failure to give a child adequate guidance in developing positive social values, such as parents who allow or teach their children to steal.
- Physical Neglect—failure to provide for a child's basic survival needs, such as food, clothing, shelter and supervision, to the extent that the failure represents a hazard to the child's health or safety.
- Psychological/Emotional Neglect—failure to provide the psychological nurturance necessary for a child's psychological growth and development.

(Glossary, pp. 6–7)

With respect to neglect, particularly the latter form, states may not address it as a form of abuse in the child protective services governing legislation. Even though it is estimated that there are five to six times as many neglectful families as overtly abusive ones, the lack of an act of commission makes intervention and remedial activity difficult to initiate and enforce. Stated another way, the cause-and-effect relationship is difficult to establish.

It may be helpful to define neglect from the perspective of degrees, as well as its types. Such a viewpoint may clarify for Recreation and Leisure Services personnel. Young describes neglect as being either severe or moderate. Following, with permission of the publisher, is Young's enlightening definition of these two degrees of neglect:

Severe Neglect

One characteristic of severe physical neglect is that meals are rarely provided for the children. In these families food comes into the house randomly, and the children must grab it as they can. Rarely is there cooked food; most common are the convenience foods. A typical attitude was expressed by the mother who said, "I don't know what you mean I don't feed my kids. There's always Coca-Cola and potato chips on the table." It is from these families that babies are brought to hospitals suffering from dehydration, from starvation. It is from these families that children can be discovered begging food from neighbors, rummaging through garbage cans.

These are the families where deterioration can be found in every area of life. Substandard housing is common, and often housekeeping is practically nonexistent. Stale food may be left to rot in sinks and on tables. The people may sleep on mattresses without sheets and sometimes without blankets. There is no routine. Children eat as they can, sleep when they must, and wander like lost souls in a world without order, without warmth, without meaning.

What are these parents like who permit such deterioration? How can they live under such conditions, let alone subject their children to them? In the first place, most of them grew up in families almost exactly like these. One such family has been known to the juvenile court and public welfare since 1916, and their living conditions have never changed over the years. From this one family has come perhaps a hundred families, all with the same way of life. Children of such families know no other way of life, so they continue the legacy as they become adults.

In general these families are large—not because the parents are devoted to their children, but because they never plan. Children, like everything else in life, just happen to these people. They see themselves as acted upon, not acting. They live for the day, without regard for past or future, their only continuity the disorder of their lives.

Not surprisingly, there is a high percentage of mental retardation, mental illness, alcoholism, and drug addiction in severely neglecting families. Many are headed by only the mother, but when the parents live together they tend to be similar in their behavior, thus exacerbating each other's problems. Each blames the other for the problems and misfortunes that have befallen them. This becomes a way of life, providing its own satisfactions for the participants.

These families are conscious that they are outcasts from society, and they respond with an impotent hostility that only alienates them further. If they seek welfare, however, as many of them do, they must at least to some limited extent come to terms with that dominant world that they see as hostile and dangerous. The experience, far from reassuring them, usually alienates them further, and they come to regard social workers as enemies to be evaded, tricked when possible, and mollified. In turn, the children also see the outside world as alien and hostile, but when they turn to their own world, their is no warmth, no security, nobody who cares, nobody who wants them. One little boy who must still have had some hope said to the child welfare worker, "Please lady, could you find me a home?" These are the children without a home.

Neglecting parents too are essentially children, in a pathological sense. Mrs. James is a good example of this. Her husband had deserted, leaving her with seven children. She received welfare, but she had no capacity to manage her meager funds. She was immobilized. She sat in the midst of chaos while the children swirled aimlessly around her. A primarily service-oriented agency tried to help her by relieving her of part of the responsibility, teaching her to budget, providing day care for the younger children, and supplying her with extra food and better facilities. One summer day the social worker took her on a picnic all by herself. Mrs. James had a wonderful time. She had never been on a picnic, and never in her life had she had that kind of attention. On the way home she said shyly, "That was so nice. I wish you'd take the other children sometime." The other children she referred to were the seven she had brought into the world. Mrs. James was a child trying to care for other children—and failing. In the end she found refuge in a mental hospital, but first she asked two things of her social worker: "Take care of my children," and "Please, could you find a home for me?"

Mrs. James could not and did not care for her children, but she stayed with them. Although only rarely do parents in the severe neglect group abandon their children completely, some of them do leave them for days at a time. Mrs. Lane, an alcoholic and a prostitute, left her two children, aged four and six, one Friday at noon. She told them to lock the door and let no one inside. An agency worker came by chance that afternoon and, discovering the situation, called the police. When the police could not locate the mother, they broke down the door. The social worker left a note for the mother and put the children in a shelter. The mother called the agency the following Tuesday: she had just returned.

Situations like this lead to some of the not uncommon reports of children burned to death in fires they have accidentally set. Children of severe neglect sometimes die as a result of the neglect—of starvation, of accidents, of fire. True, most of them live (or, more accurately, survive), but they are often crippled—sometimes physically, more often psychologically. Few of them ever become persons in their own right, with an identity of their own. They are almost inevitably psychologically starved, since severe physical neglect is so often accompanied by emotional indifference that is nearly total.

Moderate Neglect

There is no way of knowing what percentage of all neglecting families falls into the category of severe neglect, but it is certain that they are far outnumbered by situations in which the neglect is more moderate. These less severe situations share many of the same characteristics and behavior patterns with the severely neglecting families, but to a lesser degree. Further, many of them show greater organization in at least one area of their lives. Severely neglecting families are disorganized in every area of life: economic, social, familial, emotional. Moderately neglecting families may have one parent working with some continuity, or may include a happy relationship with a relative or relatives, or may be capable of some responsibility, such as sending children to school regularly.

While moderately neglecting families may fail to feed children properly and meals may be erratic and rarely include the whole family sitting down together, meals are cooked and an effort is made to feed the family. That fact alone marks a major difference, a difference that may be qualitative as well as quantitative. Feeding is so fundamental to life itself, so vital a part of child care, that it represents a definite dividing line. The children of these families may show the results of poor nutrition, but this is often a function not of indifference but of ignorance and poverty; fresh fruits and vegetables tend to be expensive. In these situations the parents do take responsibility for feeding the family, and the children are not searching garbage cans.

Most other areas of the parental behavior will also show degrees of moderation. The house may be very dirty, but there will not be feces in the corner of the living room. Dirty dishes and stale food may litter the kitchen, but the garbage will not be piled in the middle of the floor. Disorder and confusion may be prevalent, but some clean clothes may be stacked on a table or bed. The children may not be clean, but the dirt will not be so encrusted that other children object to sitting next to them in school. The parents or parent may leave the children alone, but for hours, not days. They may ignore a child's chronic cold or defective eyesight, but they will get the child to the emergency room of the nearest hospital if there is a broken bone, a bad cut, or a high fever.

The acute problem will rouse these parents to action, even though the chronic is disregarded. They may not be much concerned about a child's truancy from school, but they will make some effort to send children to school. In short, they do not show the kind and extent of deterioration to be found among the severely neglecting.

(Young, 1981, pp. 1–4)

A thorough understanding of the meaning of neglect should be particularly helpful to the recreation worker, since this is the child who may be the most accessible to intervention. As this child may seek bonding with adults, there may be ample opportunities to not only identify, but to counteract the effects of parental neglect. The chapters discussing the indicator of neglect and the recreator's role in treatment will elaborate on the latter points.

SUMMARY

Recreation and leisure personnel should review not only the definition of abuse and its specific types developed at the national level but also those of respective state and local agencies. Effective intervention and treatment have as their foundation understanding by grass roots or direct service personnel of the definitions of abuse. Such understanding serves as the basis of the recreator's role as an advocate for children.

Chapter Two

HOW SERIOUS IS THE PROBLEM?

INTRODUCTION

Perhaps the most accurate or truthful response to the above question is that no one knows for sure. What is known is that the reported incidences have risen sharply in recent years, particularly since 1976 when reports were first available. Between 1981 and 1985 alone, reports of child abuse rose by 54.9 percent nationwide, according to a 1987 report issued by the U.S. House of Representatives' Select Committee on Children, Youth, and Families. One does not have to be a human services professional to realize that child abuse is a far too common occurrence and a painful reality of life in America and other nations. To understand the scope of child abuse, it needs to be approached from two perspectives: the obstacles to reliable reporting and the available data pertaining to reporting and substantiation. The major obstacles to reliable reportings fall into four major categories: the child, the perpetrator(s), the observer(s) and reporting laws.

THE CHILD

A major obstacle to reliable reporting is the abused child. It is difficult for some to imagine the extremes to which children will go or the amount of pain they will endure to refrain from reporting their abuse. Abused children do not "tell on" their parents for a variety of reasons. One being they do not know they are being abused. What society may consider to be abusive treatment could well be the only type of parental interaction to which the child can relate. The child who has never known tenderness and warmth from a parent may view abuse as being normal.

A young man, who was also a sexually abused child, currently incarcerated for abusing his daughter, was asked by the author why he put up with the behavior of his father so long, responded "I thought it was normal, heck my mom even knew about it. Besides, it was better than being ignored."

17

A second major reason for the child's reluctance to report the parents is the fear of the loss of security. Keeping in mind the above notion of normalcy, it should be noted that the child may have (1) a relatively normal relationship with siblings and the non-abusive parent, (2) his own room, (3) some neighborhood friends, (4) brief periods of calm, and (5) most of the "creature comfort" needs met. This takes on significance when the parent threatens to terminate these positive factors if the child discloses the abuse in the home. As pointed out in the following chapter, many abusive parents do truly love their children, even those that are the primary targets of violent abuse. During the brief periods of calm, the parent may exhibit tenderness and compensate for the abusive behavior by lavishing gifts and affection upon the victim. This only confuses the child and may convince him/her that the abuse is simply a price to be paid for the security of the home.

The third reason is closely related to the second; namely, the fear of rejection and loss of love. As noted, the abused child may have a relatively stable relationship with the siblings and non-abusive parent. The threat of the parent to terminate the relationships and the warning that reporting of abuse could cause a breakup of the home may well cause the abused child to conclude that the siblings and other parent would reject him or stop loving him.

Ironically, the child may also fear rejection by the abusive parent. Often, the child is threatened with the withdrawal of love by the parent. It is regrettably true that many children view abuse as the expression of presence. As one former abused child related, "Getting slapped around a bit is a damn sight better than being totally ignored."

Also, because of parental warnings the child may fear rejection by his peers. The child may well foresee the reaction of some of his friends' parents if they learn of the abuse in his home. Is it probable that some "good" parents would not want their children to associate with "such a sick family"?

In their confused, anxiety-ridden minds some children make the "rationale" decision to play the role of family martyr. This is particularly true in situations where the abused child is the eldest sibling. The victim may perceive his/her role as one of a buffer between an abusive parent and the more defenseless younger brother or sister. They are literally willing to sacrifice their own well-being in order to protect the other children from harm. Such may have been the role assumed by a 16-year-old Long Island girl who was arraigned in the 1986 killing of her father. A newspaper article describing the case stated, " . . . she arranged to have her father killed after he had abused her for four to six years and had planned to begin a similar relationship with her 8-year-old sister."

Finally, the abused child more often than not loves the abusing parent deeply, many times up to the dying breath. As was reported in the Children's Village U.S.A. sponsored T.V. special "A Time for Love," one little girl asked for assurance of her mother's love as they were taking her to the hospital where she would die two hours later. Other children have asked that their parents not be punished. They love their parents and do not want them taken away.

THE PERPETRATOR(S)

The second major obstacle to reliable reporting of child abuse is the perpetrator, most often the parent or responsible adult. Even if the abuser knows what he/she is doing is wrong, there is the problem of social stigma and self-esteem. In our society individual worth and self-concept are frequently determined by social evaluations. Therefore, being publicly stamped a child abuser will likely have a crushing impact on the parent. Therefore, in our attempt to help potential and actual child abusers, we may be asking them to subject themselves to social ridicule. The fear of such ridicule may prevent them from seeking the services they need.

Another type of parent is the rejected-repeater. Simply, some abusive parents are reluctant to resubmit themselves to a system or agency that is cold, condemning, hostile, or non-supportive. Agencies in some communities are staffed by personnel who lack the required sensitivity to the problems of the total family; this usually results from lack of intensive training and academic preparation. Rather than subject themselves to such insensitivity the parents remain out of the mainstream and continue to abuse their children.

A third type of parent is the denier, the one who simply does not see the relationship with the child as being abusive. More often than not they view the violence as normal, acceptable discipline. They may, after all, have been the recipients of such violence in their childhoods. They likely are proponents of the still strong opinion that children are the property of the parents and, consequently, they have the right to exact desired behaviors by any means possible. These individuals may be demonstrating values conveyed to them by their family, the dominant ethnic group, or their religion. In certain elements of Western civilization, such beliefs as "Spare the rod, spoil the child" still prevail and govern the parent-child relationship. These individuals are not psychopaths, they are not psychotic. They have strong opinions as to right and wrong, they take their responsibilities as parents quite seriously, and most love their children deeply.

Then there are parents or care givers who do not report incidences of child abuse because they are, clinically speaking, mentally ill. According to Justice and Justice (1976, p. 48) about 2 percent of all abusers fall into this category. These are individuals who are incapable of distinguishing right from wrong and those who are psychiatrically detached from the realm of reality. There is little in the literature since 1976 to suggest an adjustment of the 2 percent figure.

Finally, a very real barrier to reporting that affects both the victim and the child is shame and embarrassment. The shame and embarrassment may transcend the fear of legal consequence and the fear of societal rejection. The reaction may be based on religious teachings, on family values, or on the personal opinion that disclosure will signify a lack of control and weakness to those who will likely remain loving and supportive. The significant others may even encourage the suspected perpetrator or victim to report with the assurance that they will remain supportive throughout the corrective process. Yet, even all of the assurances cannot overcome the influence individual's self-concept or the need to be perceived as strong, controlled, and mature. The individuals are not mentally ill, though they do exhibit emotional dysfunction. They know right from wrong but delude themselves into believing they can avoid the same and embarrassment by regaining control or ceasing the abusive behaviors void of outside intervention.

THE OBSERVER(S)

Another possible contributor to the difficulty in arriving at accurate reporting relates to the third-party participants in the child abuse drama. Such an individual may be a neighbor, a teacher, or a program specialist in a community leisure services agency. The reasons lay and professional people do not report suspected incidences of abuse are varied, but rarely is one of the reasons that they condone the abuse of children, or that they simply do not care. Most likely, one or more of the following reasons come into play:

- They lack awareness of protections afforded them by the law and are fearful of litigation.
- They fear physical retribution by an individual who has already exhibited a propensity for violence.
- They simply do not realize the consequences of allowing the abuse to continue (it never happens to people we know or care about).
- They reported once before and were rebuked by a constituted authority.
- They do not possess adequate knowledge of the abuse indicators and are fearful of wrongful accusations.
- They did not know the procedures for reporting suspected abuse.
- They, for personal reasons, are so repulsed by the horrors of abuse that they cannot cope emotionally with its realities.
- They assume that once a family is in the child protective network that repeated reports are unnecessary.

A reason voiced repeatedly to child protection workers by individuals suspecting child abuse is, "I didn't want to get involved." Most frequently the reason for not wanting "to get involved" is the fear of being sued by the suspected perpetrator. As will be elaborated upon in a later chapter, each state offers immunity to all individuals reporting abuse, as well as offering protection against criminal and civil litigation. So, the fear of litigation is based upon ignorance of state reporting laws or perhaps upon rumor of litigation that may have occurred before the current protections offered.

A second reason for not reporting or for not wanting "to get involved" may have a sound foundation in reality. The suspecting party may well be fearful of physical reprisal by the individual who has already demonstrated a proclivity for violence or irrational behavior. Unfortunately, it is a matter of police record that individuals reporting domestic conflicts have been in turn victimized by those they reported. Yet, today with the guaranteed immunity of state reporting laws it is unlikely that the reporter's identity will be known unless disclosed voluntarily.

Child abuse is one of the most deplorable or odious behaviors an individual can be accused of by another person. The thought of a friend or family member being guilty of child maltreatment is one with which many individuals cannot cope. Like many other forms of disease and social deviancy, it is one that happens only "to the other guy" or to people in other towns or neighborhoods. The evidence, consequently, may appear circumstantial and the suspicious acquaintance or family member may try to rationalize or make excuses for the behavior, convincing him/herself that it will not happen again. Recreation leaders who often get to know families well because of extended affiliations with family members may discover objectivity easier to profess than practice. In many leisure service agencies program leaders, unlike elementary school teachers, do not pass on their responsibilities for a child to someone at the next grade level. The more intimate the leader becomes with the family, the greater the likelihood he or she will be reluctant to initiate action that may disrupt the family and be deleterious to the worker's relationship with the child and the family. There lies, therefore, the necessity to continuously ask the question of oneself, "Where does my ultimate legal and moral responsibility rest?"

Unfortunately, child protective agencies are not experiencing an equal growth in resources and reported incidences. Once more, the future does not appear to offer much relief, particularly in light of the forecasted austerity that results from the demands to diminish the national debt and to balance the budget. As stated in the Introduction of the 1987 Select Committee Report, "Despite these clear signals that the national tragedy of child abuse and child neglect is deepening, our report documents that States' capacity to address these crises, or to prevent them, has declined significantly and has fallen far behind the need. The commitment of public resources has been far from adequate; the greatest shortfall has come as a result of cuts in federal assistance" (p. IX). Such resource inadequacies may result in poor follow-up on reported incidences or cause staff to appear less than courteous or disinterested. The lack of follow-up may appear to be a rebuke by the reporter. With the pressures of increasing incidence and dwindling resources staff may not have the luxury of what others may consider to be thorough investigation or desirable follow-up.

The estimate that current levels of incidences may be from 20 to 33 percent higher than reported may be, in part, due to the fact that many individuals are not aware of the scope of deviant behaviors that constitute child abuse. This is particularly true in situations of neglect and emotional abuse. Some of these under-informed individuals are aware of their limited knowledge and are, therefore, reluctant to risk wrongful accusations. They are not knowledgeable as to both the physical and behavior indicators that may be exhibited by children and caregivers which may warrant suspicion of abuse. These indicators are discussed at length in Chapters Five through Eight.

Others do not report simply because they are not aware of procedures for reporting suspected abuse. They may not be ignorant of the indicators, but they may well be ignorant of the laws of their respective states governing the reporting of suspected child abuse. As will be demonstrated in Chapter Thirteen, the states have each drafted legislation indicating both who must report and the procedures for reporting. As to the latter, the direction is quite vague. Yet, as indicated in Appendix C, each state has identified an office charged with the responsibility of addressing child abuse issues. Several have also established a toll-free statewide hotline to simplify the reporting process and to respond to inquiries as to resources at the local levels. Likewise, employees of child care agencies, including those responsible for recreational programming, should have specified in agency procedure manuals or policy manuals some instruction as to the reporting of suspected child maltreatment.

Regrettably, some individuals do not report abuse as a consequence of their own emotional weakness. Child abuse suspicion is traumatic and may well cause a person who cannot cope with the potential conflict to simply indulge in denial or other processes of psychological self-preservation. Such individuals may experience guilt over not reporting, but may rationalize that it is a small price to be exacted considering the scope or magnitude of their personal problems. They could well conclude that there are other people with fewer problems who can afford to get involved, that it's the social services job to keep on top of such things, or that it probably was just an isolated event. A concern is that with the current staff deficiencies in child protective services and the increased stress on families, more children will "fall in the cracks." More and more families are struggling to maintain solidarity and to stave off the onslaught by alcohol, drugs, teen pregnancy, divorce, and an economy which is causing more time to be spent out of the home by parents. These families are not abusing their children, but the emotional strain of maintaining the family unit under current pressures may not have enough emotional energy in reserve to get involved in issues outside of the immediate family unit. What is going on in the house next door or across the street cannot, therefore, be addressed.

Finally, the person suspecting abuse may mistakenly assume that once a family is in the child protective network that repeated reports are not necessary. This may be particularly true of individuals working in direct services to children. Once a report is made, child protective agencies will investigate the report in an attempt to determine whether or not a child's welfare and health is endangered. If the evidence affirms the suspicion, the case is referred to as substantiated. However, if the investigation does not produce adequate evidence, the case may be determined to be unsubstantiated. Three factors can result in such a determination. First, in fact there was no abuse—it was an unfortunate accident or the child was seeking revenge. Secondly, the guilty party was successful in misleading the investigation. Third, due to heavy work overloads the investigator overlooked evidence or was unable to extend the inquiry thoroughly. Unless the agency has cause for suspicion or to keep the case on an active status, the resources of the agency will be redirected. The decision of "unsubstantiated" does not mean no abuse occurred, but that the evidence did not warrant the disruption of the family unit. Therefore, those in child or family service agencies must remain alert and report each suspected incidence of abuse—regardless of how frequently the child may "cry wolf." As Table II-7 demonstrates, a child's life may as well be in the balance.

THE LAW

The fourth major problem area related to reliable data on the incidence lies within the law itself. When consulted about a discrepancy in reported data, a state official remarked to the author, "In our state, it is almost impossible to determine what percentage of the reported cases are substantiated. We are required to report all suspected cases to the law enforcement officials, but they are not required to collect data on the cases investigated and report back to us." The problem may be more a matter of what is not mandated than what is required by law. The Select Committee in Children, Youth, and Families 1987 Report addresses the differences in state methods of collecting child abuse information. States may report either duplicated or unduplicated incidences. The latter reports represent more than one report for a family or child during any given year, calendar or fiscal. Unduplicated reports perhaps more accurately depict the number of individual children who are maltreated. The disadvantage with the latter method of reporting are that it (1) does not reflect the true need for protective services, and (2) it does not encourage concentration on troubled families since frequency data is not reported. According to the Select Committee Report only one state, Oregon, reported only substantiated cases while three-fourths of the states indicated the reported figures reflected some degree of screening. This, of course, suggests that a quarter of the states' figures reflect no screening—simply the number of suspected incidences reported. The survey conducted by the Select Committee also disclosed that "Practices vary somewhat from State to State in terms of who receives reports and the types of reports referred. While most statutes and regulations detail the specific steps to be taken in referring cases, some do not" (*Report,* p. 89). In this instance, "referred" relates to law enforcement agencies.

A review of state reporting laws (see Chapter Thirteen) will make some of the barriers to reliable reporting painfully obvious. First, in an attempt to be thorough some statutes have excluded some key categories of personnel in stipulating who must report. In others, the language is confusing as well. A second area of difficulty is that of definition. Some states have broadened their definitions to be more in line with PL93-247 as amended by PL95-266 and PL98-457 (see Appendices E & F). Some states (Georgia, Louisiana, Massachusetts, Montana, Ohio, Texas) have expanded the definition so to exceed the Child Abuse and Prevention Act while others have definitions which are very limited in scope. It is of special interest that few of the state reporting laws specify emotional abuse, even though child health specialists have indicated that it may well be the most deleterious form of abuse and that its effects may take longer to correct. Only 12 percent of the states identified emotional abuse as a specific area of child maltreatment in responding to the Select Committee survey (conducted in May 1986). When asked why his state did not report figures on emotional abuse, one state official replied, "We don't keep such figures since emotional abuse is too difficult to prove and almost impossible to deal with in our state's courts." Yet, he readily admitted that it was a major problem that likely accounted for many of the mental health problems youth in his state face.

Finally, states differ widely on specification of abuse reporting procedures. Some states address the reporting procedures in generalities while others offer detailed instructions as to how reports are to be submitted. A review of State Statute 1986 Reporting Procedure provided by the Clearinghouse on Child Abuse and Neglect Information makes the aforementioned contrasts obvious. For example, the related section of the Idaho code states "shall report or cause to be reported within twenty-four (24) hours such conditions or circumstances . . . " (1987, p. 733). Illinois, however, in contrast provides the potential reporter and the agency administration more thorough direction. Quoting from Illinois' P.A. 84-1318, "Whenever such person is required to report (suspected cases of abused or neglected children) under this Act in his capacity as a member of the staff of a medical or other public or private institution, school, facility or agency, he shall make report immediately to the Department in accordance with the provision of this Act and may also notify the person in charge of such institution, school, facility or agency or his designated agent that such report has been made. Under no circumstances shall persons in charge of such institution, school, facility or agency, or his designated agent to whom such notification has been made, exercise any control, restraint, modification or other change in the report or the forwarding of such report to the Department" (1987, p. 733). Illinois provides additional direction via the Smith-Hard Supplement, stating "All reports . . . shall be made immediately by telephone to the central register . . . or in person or by telephone through the nearest Department office. . . . All reports by persons mandated to report under this Act shall be confirmed in writing to the appropriate Child Protective Service Unit . . . within 48 hours of any initial report. . . . Reports involving known or suspected child abuse or neglect in public or private residential agencies or institutions shall be made and received in the same manner as all other reports made under this Act" (1987, p. 734). The latter leaves little doubt as to how to report suspected abuse, while the first example provides little information as to proper procedures. Additional discussion of the legal implications of abuse on Recreation and Leisure Services personnel is contained in Chapter Thirteen.

Even with the difficulties in obtaining reliable data as to abuse incidence, most concerned agencies share two opinions: (1) the figures are conservative, and (2) that the figures reflect that something is desperately wrong with contemporary society. The data collected over the past twenty years lend credibility to a statement by Fontana in *Somewhere a Child is Crying.* "It is a myth that we, in this nation, love our children" (1976, p. 34). What follows is a collage of estimates or statistical statements as to the incidence of abuse. These figures are distressing, particularly in light of the opinion that they are conservative.

INCIDENCE OF ABUSE

Gil, in his study conducted in the late sixties for the U.S. Children's Bureau, focused primarily on physical abuse. In his results he reported 5,993 cases for 1967 and 6,617 cases for 1968 (Gil, 1970, p. 92). He obtained his figures by reviewing registry reports and responses to questionnaires. Even though he did not view these reported cases as being sufficient enough in number to constitute a significant problem, he did concede, however, that there could be as many as 2,500,000 physically abused children annually. He arrived at the estimate by extrapolating to the total U.S. population the number of cases known personally to a sample he queried during his study.

In *Somewhere a Child is Crying*, Fontana made the following alarming statement. "Conservatively I would estimate that at least 150 children in New York City die each year as a result of maltreatment" (p. 36). He also stated, "I believe that a conservative estimate is that one or two children are being killed at the hands of their own parents in this country every day, at least 700 children are killed every year in the United States by their parents or guardians" (p. 36). He suggests further that thousands (?) of other children are physically and mentally injured permanently by adults (p. 36). An *Associated Press* article appearing in November 1987 indicates that the picture in New York state may have improved somewhat since Fontana's 1976 printing. The article states that the confirmed deaths from child abuse have remained fairly stable the past few years at approximately 100 cases per year. Since this is a statewide estimate, then it must be assumed that the fatality rate in New York City has declined substantially. However, the differing estimates may also reflect the issue of reliable reporting.

Some figures related by O'Brien are even more alarming than those given by Fontana. She states, "In 1978, as a direct result of child abuse, 5,000 children died" (*Child Abuse*, 1981, p. 10). She identified in her 1981 text child battering as the number one cause of death in children, more than automobile accidents and disease (p. 10). O'Brien's estimate for the daily number of deaths resulting from abuse ranges from two to fifteen, or an annual death rate of 728 to 5,460 (p. 10).

O'Brien also relates some figures proffered by Frank Osanka in a 1979 presentation on family violence. Osanka feels that seven children, most of them between birth and three years of age, die each day as a result of abuse. This is a deplorable annual rate of 2,548. He also reported that at least twelve children per day suffered brain damage as a result of some form of abuse, or an annual rate of 4,368. He was fearful that there may be three times as many unreported incidences (pp. 10–11).

A particularly alarming estimate was quoted by Shanas in a 1975 article appearing in the *Phi Delta Kappan.* Shanas quotes a forecast made by Ray Helfer that "unless changes are made in prevention and treatment, there will be millions of reported cases of child abuse in the next 10 years [including] 50,000 deaths and 30,000 permanently injured children—most of whom will be brain damaged" (p. 482).

The American Humane Association in 1980 documented 788,844 cases of officially reported child abuse and neglect. Of this total, 268,000 were substantiated. Of the substantiated cases, 27 percent were categorized as physical abuse. A study released in 1981 by the federal government concluded that annually 10.5 of every 1,000 children younger than 18 are "visibly injured by abusive or neglectful actions of their parents or guardians; 30 percent of these are considered physical child abuse cases." This same report estimates that "for every official report, there are two other cases known to professionals but not reported" (Cohn, 1986, p. 2). It is generally accepted that at least 2,000 children die annually as a direct result of physical abuse alone. This means that one child falls victim to fatal abuse almost every four hours.

Incest is a particularly difficult form of sexual abuse to collect reliable data on due to the secrecy and shame involved. Yet, "A recent effort to compile estimates of incidence and prevalence concludes that there are some 300,000 cases per year involving some form of sexual offense against children. Other studies suggest that as many as 1,000 families per million are involved in sexual abuse of children and youth" (Garbarino and Garbarino, *Maltreatment of Adolescents,* 1986, p. 6). Straus, Gelles, and Steinmetz reported the results of a study conducted in the mid-seventies. Their study revealed the following:

- Approximately 3 parents in 100 kicked, hit, or punched their children in 1975.
- Nearly 8 in 100 stated that they had done these things to the referent child prior to the survey year.
- One child in 1,000 faced a parent who threatened to use a gun or knife on him or her in 1975.

- Three children in 100 have grown up facing a parent who has at least once threatened them with a gun or knife.
- The same proportions hold for children who had guns and knives actually used on them.

The authors extrapolated their findings to the approximately 46 million children between the ages of 3 and 17 who lived with both parents in 1975 and estimated that 3.1 to 4 million children have been hit, kicked or punched sometime in their lives by their parents and that 1 to 1.9 million were recipients of such behavior in 1975 alone (1980, pp. 61–62).

The National Center on Child Abuse and Neglect has reported a significant rise in the number of children reported as abused between 1976 and 1984. The figures reflect an increase of 158 percent, with an increase of 17 percent from 1983 to 1984. The yearly totals are reflected in Table II-1. The figures include all forms of child maltreatment reported.

A major goal of the 1986 study conducted by the U.S. House of Representatives Select Committee on Children, Youth, and Families was to collect data as to reported and substantiated incidences of child abuse.

Table II-1

CHILD ABUSE AND NEGLECT REPORTING BY YEAR

Year	Number of Children Reported
1976	669,000
1977	838,000
1978	836,000
1979	988,000
1980	1,154,000
1981	1,225,000
1982	1,262,000
1983	1,477,000
1984	1,727,000

(Source: Child Abuse and Neglect: An Informed Approach to a Shared Concern, 1986, p. 3)

Tables II-2 through II-7 depict the results of the Select Committee survey. Here, too, the reliability of the reflected data is less than desirable. Such factors as reporting procedures, definition of abuse, and duplicated vs. unduplicated reporting influence the results. Yet, the Select Committee data is the most current available at this writing. It is particularly distressing to have 1,212 substantiated child deaths in two years resulting directly from abuse (Table II-7).

In summary, regardless of the issue of reporting reliability, all substantiated and estimated incidences of abuse reflect one fact; namely, child

Table II-2

1985 TOTAL CHILD PROTECTIVE REPORTS AND PERCENTAGE SUBSTANTIATED[1] (Primary Source - Select Committee on Children, Youth, and Families 1987 Report)

State	Reported Incidences	% Substantiated	State	Reported Incidences	% Substantiated
Alabama	31385	39.0	Montana	6394	50.0
Alaska	7702	13.4 (FY85)	Nebraska	7772	60.6
Arizona	24866	Not available	Nevada	7558	52.0
Arkansas	10305	37.0	New Hampshire	1707	45.0
California	295769	Not available	New Jersey	18058	38.3
Colorado	7987	65.0	New Mexico	16536	57.0
Connecticut	16804	70.0	New York	243321	37.0
Delaware	4651	55.57	North Carolina	10554	39.0
District of			North Dakota	2456	58.7
Columbia	6073	Not available	Ohio	65965	23.18
Florida	5328	57.33	Oklahoma	20275	35.0
Georgia	26511	Not available	Oregon	12765	66.7
Hawaii	2517	57/56[2]	Pennsylvania	10993	36.8
Idaho	7880	46.7	Rhode Island	10457	45.6
Illinois	97199	49.2	South Carolina	25877	30.0
Indiana	33868	48.8/52.3[3]	South Dakota	4563	44.0
Iowa	25238	24.6	Tennessee	47050	80-90[4]
Kansas	23592	28.0	Texas	59863	55.6
Kentucky	34839	44.0	Utah	5569	32.8
Louisiana	42885	37.0	Vermont	1632	52.0
Maine	5730	51.0	Virginia	12213	24.6
Maryland	Not available		Washington	40100	Not Available
Massachusetts	18111	38.0	West Virginia	18000[5]	40.0
Michigan	26376	39.0	Wisconsin	24411	30.32
Minnesota	Not available		Wyoming	2319	64.0
Mississippi	4091	51.0			
Missouri	32120	44.12			

[1]Only nine states include emotional abuse in reporting
[2]L = Family reports, R = child reports
[3]L = Abuse, R = Neglect
[4]Uncertain due to computer tabulation issue estimated
[5]Estimated

Table II-3

1985 REPORTED INCIDENCES OF PHYSICAL ABUSE
(Primary Source - Select Committee on Children, Youth,
and Families 1987 Report)

State	Reported Incidences	State	Reported Incidences
Alabama	8318	Montana	Not available
Alaska	1750	Nebraska	1989
Arizona	Not available	Nevada	826
Arkansas	1935	New Hampshire	478
California	86694	New Jersey	5869
Colorado	Not available	New Mexico	4808
Connecticut	4254	New York	47106
Delaware	974	North Carolina	1509
District of Columbia	Not available	North Dakota	867
		Ohio	1157
Florida	12796	Oklahoma	Not available
Georgia	8553	Oregon	3060
Hawaii	1424	Pennsylvania	4880
Idaho	1877	Rhode Island	3232
Illinois	14716	South Carolina	3638
Indiana	10423	South Dakota	856
Iowa	6355	Tennessee	9071
Kansas	5568	Texas	17013
Kentucky	9081	Utah	1082
Louisiana	8647	Vermont	473
Maine	1924	Virginia	2566
Maryland	Not available	Washington	11733
Massachusetts	5097	West Virginia	Not available
Michigan	5594	Wisconsin	6678
Minnesota	Not available	Wyoming	653
Mississippi	1168		
Missouri	7044		

abuse is a major cause of permanent physical and mental dysfunction and death amongst America's youth. It is painfully clear that the problem will continue to thrive until a comprehensive community approach involving all of those who provide services to children and their families is mounted to prevent, intervene in, and treat those who are abused as well as those that abuse; only in this way can the vicious cycle be broken.

Table II-4

1985 REPORTED INCIDENCES OF SEXUAL ABUSE
(Primary Source - Select Committee on Children, Youth,
and Families 1987 Report)

State	Reported Incidences	State	Reported Incidences
Alabama	2891	Montana	578
Alaska	1192	Nebraska	963
Arizona	Not available	Nevada	438
Arkansas	1692	New Hampshire	359
California	54121	New Jersey	1842
Colorado	Not available	New Mexico	2436
Connecticut	1512	New York	8345
Delaware	513	North Carolina	962
District of Columbia	Not available	North Dakota	351
		Ohio	1609
Florida	5353	Oklahoma	Not available
Georgia	3872	Oregon	4364
Hawaii	277	Pennsylvania	5481
Idaho	1453	Rhode Island	1009
Illinois	10597	South Carolina	1930
Indiana	3318	South Dakota	674
Iowa	3052	Tennessee	8092
Kansas	2808	Texas	9454
Kentucky	3456	Utah	1065
Louisiana	3660	Vermont	607
Maine	1241	Virginia	2012
Maryland	Not available	Washington	9691
Massachusetts	3484	West Virginia	Not available
Michigan	3518	Wisconsin	6609
Minnesota	Not available	Wyoming	461
Mississippi	571		
Missouri	2844		

Table II-5

1985 REPORTED INCIDENCES OF NEGLECT
(Primary Source - Select Committee on Children, Youth,
and Families 1987 Report)

State	Reported Incidences	State	Reported Incidences
Alabama	17652	Montana	1786
Alaska	3701	Nebraska	8314
Arizona	Not available	Nevada	6288
Arkansas	6668	New Hampshire	529
California	143500	New Jersey	7241
Colorado	Not available	New Mexico	9295
Connecticut	6328	New York	68287
Delaware	1755	North Carolina	7293
District of Columbia	Not available	North Dakota	1238
		Ohio	3460
Florida	25072	Oklahoma	Not available
Georgia	16540	Oregon	4476
Hawaii	815	Pennsylvania	516
Idaho	4275	Rhode Island	6010
Illinois	59734	South Carolina	13666
Indiana	20127	South Dakota	3033
Iowa	11584	Tennessee	22172
Kansas	15216	Texas	40638
Kentucky	26327	Utah	3422
Louisiana	30538	Vermont	491
Maine	3248	Virginia	7188
Maryland	Not available	Washington	16414
Massachusetts	3290	West Virginia	Not available
Michigan	17264	Wisconsin	9948
Minnesota	Not available	Wyoming	2084
Mississippi	2032		
Missouri	33537		

Table II-6

PERCENT OF CHANGE IN CHILD ABUSE REPORTING, 1981-85
(Primary Source - Select Committee on Children, Youth,
and Families 1987 Report)

State	% of Change	State	% of Change
Alabama	+68.2	Montana	+5.2
Alaska	+72.1	Nebraska	+96.3
Arizona	+445.4	Nevada	+75.4
Arkansas	+39.5	New Hampshire	+45.5
California	+51.9	New Jersey	+98.4
Colorado	+26.7	New Mexico	+104.3
Connecticut	+65.1	New York	+30.8
Delaware	+69.8	North Carolina	+2.2
District of Columbia	+18.8	North Dakota	+60.3
Florida	+90.5	Ohio	+142.1
Georgia	+99.4	Oklahoma	+65.1
Hawaii	+54.4	Oregon	+367.2
Idaho	+42.4	Pennsylvania	+53.1
Illinois	+43.3	Rhode Island	+195.9
Indiana	+54.4	South Carolina	+49.6
Iowa	+4.9	South Dakota	+82.3
Kansas	+21.0	Tennessee	+6.6
Kentucky	+23.3	Texas	+32.7
Louisiana	+21.8	Utah	+210.2
Maine	+50.7	Vermont	+114.9
Maryland	+65.7	Virginia	+25.4
Massachusetts	+54.2	Washington	+18.5
Michigan	+66.2	West Virginia	+192.1
Minnesota	+67.0	Wisconsin	+186.9
Mississippi	+136.7	Wyoming	-10.4[1]
Missouri	+41.4		

[1]22% decrease in state population from 1981-1985.

Table II-7

29 STATES REPORTING - FATALITIES RESULTING FROM ABUSE, 1984-1985
(Primary Source - Select Committee on Children, Youth,
and Families 1987 Report)

State	1984 Fatalities	1985 Fatalities
Arkansas	19	9
Colorado	20	12
Connecticut	18	7
Florida	7	9
Hawaii	2	1
Idaho	6	1
Illinois	88	115
Indiana	31	29
Iowa	11	9
Kansas	5	9
Kentucky	22	10
Louisiana	33	40
Maine	2	1
Maryland	10	9
Massachusetts	38	27
Missouri	32	24
Nevada	3	6
New Jersey	21	20
New York	136	130
North Carolina	16	8
Oklahoma	16	16
Oregon	3	5
Pennsylvania	42	35
South Carolina	6	21
Utah	5	8
Vermont	0	0
Virginia	16	14
Wisconsin	17	3
Wyoming	0	3
Total	625	587

*Projected 1986 figures exceed 1985 by 23%.

Chapter Three

WHO ARE CHILD ABUSERS?

INTRODUCTION

The following excerpts collected from newspapers over the past several years will, in part, answer the question posed as the title of this chapter.

- November 7, 1987. *Democrat and Chronicle.* "Foster Grandparent Worker, 75, Charged With Sexual Abuse of Girl, 12." A Rochester man who works in the local Foster Grandparents Program has been charged with sexually abusing a 12-year old at School 9.... H., 75, ... was arraigned yesterday in City Court on charges of second-degree sexual abuse and endangering the welfare of a child....
- November 5, 1987. *Associated Press.* "Lawyer Faces Murder Charges in Death of Adopted Daughter." (New York) A Manhattan lawyer is facing murder charges after the death of his adopted 6-year-old daughter from a fierce beating he allegedly inflicted amid the squaller of their apartment, authorities said.... Her father, criminal lawyer Joel S., was to be charged with murder.... Although S. had a good reputation in the legal community and N. (the mother) was a writer and editor of children's books, the couple's apartment was filthy, bloodstained and hadn't been cleaned in months.... Police found S.'s adopted son, 16-month-old M., tied to a chair and wallowing in his own excrement.
- October 16, 1987. *Associated Press.* "Ex-clergyman Accused." A former clergyman was ordered back to a Canadian-counseling program after pleading guilty to several sex-related charges.... L. has been accused of engaging in deviant sex with a 10-year-old boy between Aug. 31 and Sept. 5, 1986, according to city court records.
- August 4, 1987. *Associated Press.* "Ex-Day-Care Provider Charged With Sex Abuse." (Chicago) An indictment accusing a woman who owned two day-care centers of sexually abusing four preschool girls.... The indictment ... accused Sandra F. of molesting the girls at two centers she operated in suburban Palos Hills.
- July 6, 1987. *Newsweek.* "Child-Abuse Charges Rock UNICEF." UNICEF

36

has always stood for the love of children—an image now grotesquely defiled.... Police arrested Josef Verbeeck, director of the Belgium committee for the United Nations Children's Fund, on charges of "indecency and incitement to the debauchery of children."

- June 1, 1987. *Times-Union.* "Teacher Accused in Sex-Abuse Case." School District officials will not decide until later this week to take formal disciplinary action against a teacher accused of sexually abusing a teenager.... Police said the incident allegedly occurred after O. and the youth went to a sporting event.

- March 23, 1987. *Democrat and Chronicle.* "Sex Abuse Alleged." A 54-year-old city man was charged yesterday with raping and sexually abusing his 11 year-old niece.... The girl told a school counselor she had been abused by the uncle and by another person at different times during the last several years....

- February 7, 1987. *Associated Press.* "School Disciplined 3 in 'The Cage.'" A public school official here said yesterday that three children had been isolated in a wire-enclosed area of the school known as "the cage" in past months to discipline them.... The room was adjacent to the supervisor's office and closed off from the middle school's weight lifting area by chicken wire.... She said her son was sent to the room for two days in November because he talked too much in school and disrupted the class. He was not permitted to bring books, she added.

- February 6, 1987. *Times-Union.* "Two Defendants had Sex-Abuse Convictions." Two of four people charged this week with sexually abusing two girls, ages 6 and 7, had been previously convicted of sexual abuse, officials said. The girls' mother, father, 16-year-old brother and a male family friend were charged Wednesday with sodomizing, sexually abusing and endangering the welfare of the children.... The 16 year-old brother ... had been charged March 5, 1986 with first-degree rape in an attack of a 5-year-old girl.... In November, 1984, the father, ... also was convicted of first-degree sexual abuse of one of his daughters, officials said.

- January 25, 1987. *Democrat and Chronicle.* "Scout Camps can be Rugged, Critics Contend." Some Boy Scout leaders seem to think they've recruited a few good men when they trek into the woods with a group of tender-aged boys, critics of the Boy Scouts say.... "Unfortunately, you tend to get people who are attracted to that macho image volunteering as Scout leaders," said Kurman, who has traveled the country publicizing the possible dangers of camping for the past 20 years, ever since his 15-year-old son was killed while camping with a YMCA group.... Kurman cites dozens of what he calls "horror stories" across the nation in which Scouts have been treated improperly or exposed to unnecessary dangers, resulting in physical and mental abuse, sexual abuse, or accidental death.

- December 20, 1986. *Democrat and Chronicle.* "Teacher Admits Sex Counts." . . . Elementary school teacher pleaded guilty to three of 125 counts of first- and second-degree sexual abuse in exchange for a 90-day jail sentence and five year's probation. Robert S. . . . was charged this summer with fondling a girl, who was 10 years old when the incidents began, numerous times during the past three years while the girl lived in his home. . . . S., a fourth grade teacher and a former coach of the . . . School District's girls' soccer team, has been on the school faculty for 16 years.

- June 8, 1986. *Democrat and Chronicle.* "Priest Accused of Sexual Assault." A Roman Catholic priest . . . was arrested and arraigned yesterday . . . on sexual assault charges involving two minors. . . . The Rev. J. . . . was charged with first-degree sodomy, first-degree sexual abuse and unlawfully dealing with a child. . . .

- May 10, 1986. *Democrat and Chronicle.* "Scout Official Charged with Sodomy." State Police yesterday charged a Boy Scout official with multiple counts of sodomy stemming from a series of incidences since 1983 involving a 16-year-old member of his troop. . . . D. has been a committee member of Troop . . . since 1982. . . . D. was in charge of assigning scouts to the tents they would sleep in on camping trips. . . . D. is accused of routinely assigning the 16-year-old to his tent.

- May 8, 1986. *Times-Union.* "Woman Charged with Rape of Boy." A 31-year-old Rochester woman, who police said had sex with a 15-year-old boy, has been charged with rape and endangerment. . . . M. is charged with one count of third-degree rape and two counts each of endangering the welfare of a child and unlawfully dealing with a child.

- March 24, 1986. *Associated Press.* "Pleads Guilty to Sex Abuse." . . . Political figures have expressed sympathy at the plight of state Assemblyman R. . . . . following his guilty plea to a felony sex abuse charge. . . . County prosecutors said it satisfied a three-count grand indictment against the 41-year-old Democrat, which included a first-degree sexual abuse charge and another attempted sexual abuse charge.

- January 14, 1986. *Times-Union.* "Sex Abuse Charged." A 79-year-old . . . man pleaded innocent last night to charges after he was accused of abusing a 13-year-old girl and giving alcohol and pornographic magazines to minors. . . . B. was charged with one count of second-degree sexual abuse and four counts of endangering the welfare of a child. . . .

- April 19, 1985. *Times-Union.* "Minister Held in Abuse Cases." A minister accused of sexually abusing children enrolled in a Virginia religious school was arrested. . . . The indictment accuses J. of a total of 23 counts of statutory rape, aggravated sexual battery and abduction with intent to defile....

These sixteen articles are from more than fifty articles collected from January 1985 to January 1, 1988. One fact should be obvious from reviewing these excerpts and other articles which appear almost daily in newspapers throughout the U.S. and the rest of the Western world; namely, no one is excluded from the list of abusers. Cheryl McCall in her special report on sexual abuse entitled "The Cruelest Crime" (*Life*, December 1984, pp. 35–42) states, "Pedophiles—sexual offenders whose primary victims are children—come from every walk of life, social class, ethnic and religious background. Some are married, some are not. Known offenders range in age from 12 to 94." McCall quotes a noted clinical psychologist from the Seattle area who at the time had evaluated over 1200 sexual offenders for the courts. Doctor Irwin Dreiblatt stated, "Of the last twenty-four I treated, all but two were married. One was a physician, one a psychologist and one a school administrator. What defines a child molester is that they do it." McCall further points out that of the roughly four million child molesters in the U.S. that approximately 5 percent are female (*Life*, December 1984, pp. 35–62).

In the booklet, *It Shouldn't Hurt To Be A Child*, published by the National Committee for Prevention of Child Abuse (NCPCA), there is a section entitled "Who Are the Abusers?" In this section there are two paragraphs that may be helpful in understanding the scope of the issue, particularly in terms of perpetration. The NCPCA states, "Abusers are friends, neighbors, and relatives. It is a sad irony that many abusers genuinely love their children, but they find themselves caught in life situations beyond their control and they do not know how to cope. They are often isolated from friends and family and may have no one to give them emotional support...." It is further stated, "Child abuse does not belong solely in the domain of the poor. Abusers come from all economic, racial, ethnic, and religious groups. Many problems—especially the grinding money problems of the poor—do cause stress, however, and stress contributes to the potential for abuse. Other stresses, such as a shaky, fight-filled marriage, also contribute to abuse" (1983, p. 6). So, it should be obvious that child abusers come from all walks of life. They are all colors; they speak with all accents; they pray to different gods in different ways; they labor at all types of vocations; they live in all communities; they live in one-room apartments and in twenty-room mansions; they represent all levels of the socioeconomic strata; they, for the most part, truly love their children or children in general; they represent all levels of education; and they all share one problem: emotional instability. This latter statement should not be misconstrued as all abusive individuals are psychotic. In fact, fewer than 12 percent of confirmed abusers have been found to be clinically diagnosed as being impaired by psychosis. It is a myth that a person "has to be crazy" to abuse a child. Child abuse is such a complex human and social problem, one that permeates all elements of society, that prediction is far from being an exact science.

FACTORS OF RISK

The most that can be done at this time is to identify those factors that may place a family or individual at risk, or indicate a greater likelihood for the commission of abusive behavior or the neglect of a child. Some understanding of these factors, rather than subscribing to myths of child abuse, may be helpful to the recreation agencies' role in the prevention of abuse. The following factors may be found in or invade all socio-economic, ethnic, and religious elements of society:

- Abusers feel they were not cared about as children. This sensation may result from never having received "things" from an alcoholic, absent father or from being raised by a nanny and being shipped off to camp each summer by parents who seem to go to great expense to avoid having to spend time with them as children. In both instances, the child will likely have had little opportunity to develop positive parenting skills.
- Abusers may have received too much or constant negative criticism from parents. This may result from not keeping the house clean enough by an overly dependent parent to not making good enough grades to warrant acceptance into Harvard by a parent whose social status may be endangered by an underachieving child.
- Abusers may have lived lives of isolation. Isolation may result from poverty that results in a "from the wrong side of the tracks" label, from frequent job moves by an ambitious, upwardly mobile parent that prevents the establishment of "roots" or friendships, or from having a handicapped child within the home that restricts discretionary time by his/her parents and siblings.

- Abusers have no or poor impulse control. They likely had parents or caretakers who had the same shortcoming. Emotionally, they have not matured and respond to any disruption in life-style or life goals with physical and verbal aggressiveness—hitting, shaking, slamming, cursing, screaming, belittling. The reaction may be a response to a poor performance either on the Little League diamond, the tennis or basketball court, in the classroom, or over how the evening meal was prepared for the overworked, frustrated and angry single parent.

Obviously, each of these can result in an adult who is ill-prepared for parenting. A poor self-concept when coupled with unrealistic expectations of children fuel the flames of child abuse, flames that are out of control, burning all of the timbers of society.

An example of emotional neglect in the absence of poverty and other traditional expectations related to child abuse may be found among children coping with anorexia nervosa. These children who are involved in methodical self-starvation often have positive-appearing backgrounds, where all of their needs appear to have been met by attentive and affluent parents. Unfortunately, however, many of the material, social and educational benefits were bestowed without consideration to their desires and needs (Covitz, 1986, p. 11). Such a child may never experience the thrill of creative living, of realizing his/her potential or ever develop a positive self-concept.

SOME MYTHS OF CHILD ABUSE

Perhaps one of the better known investigations related to who abuses children was reported in the Straus, Gelles and Steinmetz text *Behind Closed Doors.* Their study into violence in the American family provides some thought-provoking insights and explodes some myths about who abuse children.

Straus, Gelles and Steinmetz (1981) suggested that every neighborhood has at least one violent household. They estimate that in three out of five homes children are recipients of violence. American children are more likely to be abused in their own homes than in any other setting.

Their research, too, has resulted in the observation that men and women from all economic, educational, social, and ethnic circumstances form the ranks of abusers. The idea that only the poor abuse children resulted in large part from the fact that they could not afford private care and had to rely on low-cost agencies that had to report suspected cases. With the onset of reporting laws which obligated all physicians, the reported incidences among middle- and upper-class families has increased.

Mental Health

Another myth that has been exploded is that only mentally ill adults abuse children. Gelles stated that "in the vast majority of cases of violence in the family, the participants possess none of the symptoms or problems which we normally associate with those who are mentally ill or suffering from personality disorders" (Straus, Gelles and Steinmetz, 1981, p. 125). This does not preclude the reality that most abusers are otherwise impaired.

Education

Many are quick to assume that only the poorly educated abuse their children. In their study Straus, Gelles and Steinmetz (1981, p. 29) found the greatest frequency of abuse among husbands who were high school graduates (18%). The next highest frequency was among subjects with some high school (15%), while the lowest frequency was among those with an eighth grade or less education and those with college educations (11%) each. The results related to wives were not significantly different.

Income

Even though there is a higher percentage of abuse in lower income families, Gelles's research does reveal rather high incidences of physical abuse by parents above the poverty level. For example, it was revealed that 26 percent of the subject families above the $12,000 annual income range were violent enough towards children to place them at risk. Even though there is an inverse relationship between income and physical violence, the figures suggest that a significant number of parents above the poverty level do abuse their children (Straus et al., 1981, p. 129).

Family Size

It is often assumed that the larger the family, the more frequent the abuse. This is true, but only to a point. Parents with two children are 50 percent more likely to physically abuse their children than parents with only one child. Those with five children have the highest rate of abuse, but the lowest rate is among those parents with eight or more children (Gerbner, Ross, and Zigler, 1980, pp. 99–100).

Section of the Country

The myth that poor southerners are more likely to abuse their children has not been upheld by research. Gelles found the highest rate of abuse to be in the Midwest (Gerbner et al., 1980, p. 90).

Race

Blacks are no more likely to abuse their children than whites. No significant difference was found between the two. Cazenave and Straus concluded, "the aid and support in the care of children provided by the black extended family seem to reduce the risk of violent outbursts directed at children" (Gerbner et al., 1980, p. 92).

Community Size

As to community size, Straus, Gelles and Steinmetz's (1981, p. 128) findings did support the notion that large-city residents are more violent. However, they did find that rural parents are more violent towards their children than parents residing in suburban areas and small cities.

SUMMARY

The findings of Straus, Gelles, and Steinmetz have been criticized as to statistical accuracy and overgeneralization. Yet, they have been viewed to provide substantial cause for exploding the aforementioned myths and for staying alert to the potentials for abuse across the entire socio-economic structure of all communities.

Again, all parents are capable of abusing children, and education, social status, and income are not parapets against abuse, even though they do appear to retard its advance. When addressing likely candidates as abusers, Fontana (1976, p. 55) stated, "Some really nice people do it, very ordinary—seemingly people who could be your friends or neighbors and whose values, on the whole, are similar to yours." Finally, redundancy seems appropriate to terminate the discussion of who abuses children, since Recreation and Leisure Services personnel need to repeatedly remind themselves that all children are potential victims, regardless of their status in the community's socioeconomic structure. Perhaps O'Brien says it best:

> Abuse is found in every category we might define. It cuts across every spectrum of American life, regardless of the color of skin, ethnic background, religious heritage, place of residency, or amount of money earned. Abusers are white, black, brown, yellow and red. Abusers are atheistic, agnostic, Protestant, Catholic, and Jewish. They live in the wealthiest areas and in the ghettos. They live in city houses and on rural farms. They are white-collar professionals in high-paying, responsible positions; blue-collar workers in menial jobs; and all collar-colors between.
>
> (*Child Abuse,* 1981, p. 46)

Chapter Four

THE COST OF ABUSE

INTRODUCTION

After searching for seemingly endless hours for a statement that addresses the issue of the cost of abuse to our social structure it was obvious that no one has addressed the issue more poignantly than Peter J. Costigan in his congressional testimony on November 2, 1973. Mr. Costigan was at that time chairperson of New York's Select Committee on Child Abuse and was testifying before the Congress Select Subcommittee on Education of the Committee on Education and Labor. Mr. Costigan during his five pages of testimony stated:

Mr. Chairman, child abuse is a hurt to all communities. It is one small, visible portion of a society in trouble: of a society in which the individual is dehumanized and in which the family is disintegrating. The atrocities committed within the family are both a symptom of our ills and a heritage to generations yet unborn. It is a heritage because those who are abused as children will also abuse their children. The horror inflicted upon the children of one generation becomes the heritage of the next.

We need to mobilize citizen and community support for an effective child protective system. Without one, we consign these children, the victims of deprivation and physical attack, to a life of constant peril. And we consign our community to a future of aggression, drug abuse and violence. As Family Court Judge Vanette Dembitz rightly said: "the root of crime in the streets is neglect of children." From the most practical and most humanitarian points of view, it is less expensive and more humane to protect and rehabilitate these children than it is to endure the social costs of their abuse and maltreatment.

(Hearings, Select Subcommittee on Education, 1974)

This dramatic statement effectively conveys that the cost issue cannot be addressed only in terms of dollars, but that it needs to be viewed from the humanitarian perspective as well. As to the latter, the task is, to say the least, monumental and truthfully impossible to adequately accomplish.

Child abuse affects all of society, each of us who has hopes and dreams for the future of our culture. The child who receives brain damage may have been destined to find the cure for cancer. The same child might have discovered or developed the surgical technique and technology to transplant and make functional central nerve tissues or other vital organs. The child suffering from a severe emotional disorder might have discovered the means by which to bring everlasting peace to the world.

Society's members pay other prices for allowing abuse to flourish. Perhaps the driver of the approaching auto has impaired reflexes due to battering as a child or maybe the teenager driving the approaching car is emotionally distressed as the result of recent abuse by his father. The man lurking in the shadows of the park that teenage girls use for a shortcut may have a deep-seeded hatred towards all women as a result of an abusive mother.

Simply out of desperation the abused child may turn to crime. There is mounting evidence that Karl Menninger was correct when he expressed the opinion that every criminal was unloved and maltreated as a child. Frazier, in a study which focused on murderers from rural areas of Minnesota and Texas, reported that his "study of ninety murderers revealed that as children they had been victims of remorseless brutality" (Fontana, 1976, p. 100). Other studies have found that abused children are likely to become involved in adolescent and adult criminal behavior.

CASE STUDIES

It would be quite easy to discuss the cost of abuse only from the perspective of dollars, but that does not adequately picture the cost in terms of human suffering and lost human resources. Perhaps the most effective means of conveying the cost to the individual victim and to the perpetrator is through case histories. Each of the following individual case histories was either drafted by the individual, dictated to the author, or based upon cases known to the author. In each instance, names and locales are fictitious in order to protect the identity of the abusive family and the abused. Each case study vividly depicts the conditions endured and uses language that could be offensive to some. Yet, no apologies are offered, since any attempts to gloss over the conditions would likely result in a distorted picture of the cost to the parties involved and hamper one of the major goals of this text: to inspire Recreation and Leisure Services personnel to address the issue of abuse. The case studies will likely cause a variety of reactions—disbelief, disgust, shame, sympathy, and anger. The reactions are all desirable, since it is only as a result of such emotional responses that resources and energies seem to be mobilized by our society. As to the necessity for the unmitigated truth, Einstein's advice is well taken. "If you are out to describe the truth, leave elegance to the tailor."

Marge

Marge is a college student who has been in therapy for nine years and who has a history of two years of hospitalization in private psychiatric facilities. She has been married and divorced twice and has a very spotty work history. Since graduating from high school she has been on some sort of public assistance for a total of eleven years. There is also a history of treatment for alcoholism.

"What you're asking me to do isn't going to be easy. I doubt that I would have even agreed to this meeting if I hadn't been through several years of counseling and if I didn't think it was going to do some good. Everybody who works with kids needs to hear stories like mine if this thing can ever be stopped. Oh well, enough preaching and on to my perverted life.

"I've tried to remember exactly when and how the abuse started. As best I can remember I was about three or four when my father started. At first he would always volunteer to bathe all of us kids. Mom was always tired at the end of the day, so I'm sure she appreciated the help and didn't suspect he had other reasons for being so helpful. For some reason, I still don't know why, I was the one he would always wash and dry off last. I have a sister that's a year older, but for some reason he picked me. After awhile, how long I don't really recall, he would also insist on putting us kids to bed. This is when things really started to get sick enough for me to remember better. I can remember that when he tucked me in he would push up my nightgown and pat my genitals— that's all he did at first. At my young age I don't think I felt there was anything too wrong with it; I think I was five or so. As time went on he got more aggressive and finally did something that made me question what he was doing—he did something that hurt. One night he lifted my nightgown and put his finger up inside of me. God, it hurt. When I started to whine he told me that it was okay and that he was doing it because he loved me and that before long it would start to feel good.

Then he told me that it must be our secret, because if mom found out she would get mad and leave all of us and he was sure everyone would hate me for making mom leave. Like a little fool, I believed him for awhile. He did this to me repeatedly and now I find it hard to believe my mother didn't think it was strange that he always tucked me in last and took so long.

"Things really got worse when mom went back to work. She had been a nurse before us kids were born and decided to go back to work when I was about seven. I am the youngest of the four kids. Since she didn't have any seniority at the hospital, she had to take a night shift. She went to work at 3:00 p.m. and didn't get home until about 11:30 or midnight. My father then didn't have to worry about mom catching him. He would get me off alone, sometimes in his and mom's bedroom. He would take out his penis and make me stroke it while he put his finger in me, and one night he made me put my mouth over his penis. I think I was about eight when this happened. I recall getting sick to my stomach and feeling for the first time that something was really wrong. But, he kept telling me it was okay and that he was sure I didn't want to cause mom to leave. It was about this time that I started asking my girl friends about how they got along with their dads and found out that what my father—I still can't call him dad— was doing wasn't normal. I began to feel ashamed and dirty, but I still didn't want mom to leave or see him get in trouble. Things got better for awhile when mom's work schedule was changed to regular days. He would still walk in the bathroom while I was bathing and put his hands all over me when he had a chance. Since the other stuff had stopped I guess I felt lucky and didn't tell anyone about what had happened.

"Then when I was eleven mom came home from work and announced she was up for a promotion as a floor supervisor, but that she would have to go back on nights. Why didn't she suspect something when I begged her not to take the job? She's dead now, but I think she really didn't suspect a thing. After all you don't usually suspect someone you love of such sick behavior. Anyway, my fears were warranted. Mom had been on nights only about a week when it all started again. Finally it happened— one night he made me have intercourse with him. Lord it hurt, and I remember he hit me when I started to scream. I really got scared when he started to cry and beg me not to tell anyone because he would be put in prison and the family would be destroyed. Boy, he was clever the way he put all the responsibility on me. We had intercourse at least once a week until he died when I was 16.

"How did I feel and what did it do to me? I'm still not sure if I fully understand the last part. I felt, as you might expect—dirty, ashamed and fearful. I hated all men, particularly older men. I couldn't stand to even be in a room with a man, even in a classroom with a male teacher. I never dated in school and took a lot of abuse and was accused of being queer. He destroyed my self-confidence and no one could understand why I did so poorly in school and socially since I came from a nice home and had all of the advantages. To this day I can't trust men too much, but I'm getting better. I don't know if I'll ever trust a man enough to get married. I can at least get along well enough to hold a job and go out socially. I'm now 33 years old, and I've been in therapy for nine years. A lot of years have been lost to me, but at least I'm not consumed by anger and shame anymore. One thing still puzzles me though. Why didn't someone—mom, my teachers, my Girl Scout leader—see that something was wrong? If only someone had asked, maybe I would have had a chance at a halfway normal childhood."

Jacob

Jacob is a twenty-nine-year-old male serving a minimum of eight years for the sexual abuse of three young boys in his hometown. He is married (divorce in process) and the father of two daughters, aged one and three years. Jacob was employed as a school teacher and coached the seventh grade basketball team. He is one of seven children, being the only boy. The family could best be described as middle-class. The father owned his own trucking business and was the sole support of the family. The family regularly attended services at a local Protestant church and were viewed, until Jacob's arrest and trial, as an upstanding family in the community.

"It may sound crazy, but I'm glad I'm in prison. Maybe I can get the treatment I need. God, I hate what I did to those boys; I only hope they can get over what I did to them and find some forgiveness in their hearts.

"When did the abuse start? To be honest, I can't remember a time when I wasn't being sexually and physically abused. I remember the physical abuse being first. My father's belief in physical discipline was demonstrated frequently, every time we kids did something he didn't like. The problem was that we never really knew what the rules were or what he wanted of us. He never did any real damage unless he had been drinking or unless things at work hadn't gone well. There were quite a few Mondays that I either missed school or lied to my teachers when they asked about some bruises or an occasional split lip. I was his favorite target because I was such a reckless hell-raiser. I guess I was stupid or something.

"The sex thing started when I was about ten. This is really embarrassing, but it's why I'm in prison. I remember the first time like it happened yesterday. I was asleep when he came in and woke me up. He had been drinking, but I don't think he was what you'd call drunk. All of a sudden he started playing with my penis and then made me play with his. When I resisted, he told me it was okay because grandpa use to do it to him. This happened a couple of times a week, this masturbation thing.

"Another thing he use to do was make fun of me for having such a small penis. He didn't care who he said it in front of—even my sisters and mother.

"I think my whole family was sexually perverted. Nudity was an accepted thing around our house. We got away with it since we lived in the country. As an example, we had a swimming pool in our yard and most of the time we'd all go swimming in the nude. The old man use to swim underwater and play with my privates and then make me do the same. Mom and my sisters must have seen it, but they deny it. On more than one occasion he would push me between my mother's legs. She would just giggle and push me away.

"The only time my father was really gentle with me was when we had sex. Our relationship was one of extremes—I was either beaten or sexually abused. My father, whether his intent or not, took over complete control of my life. I couldn't ever make any decisions on my own. When I was small, if I did make a decision, it was usually wrong and I'd get the crap beaten out of me. It was his decision about where'd I go to school and what I'd study in college. Because what he'd done to my self-concept, I couldn't bear the idea of trying to have a relationship with a woman. Besides, I'd accepted homosexuality as being acceptable. I don't know why I got married. I guess because I was trying to prove to myself and others that I was normal sexually.

"I guess why I molested those boys is that I never grew up, and I was afraid of being rejected by an adult. I thought kids were safer, and I did get away with it for awhile. Lord knows, I should never have been in work that would put me in such close contact with kids, especially boys.

"You know what really pisses me off? That bastard is still on the outside, and I'm in prison for what he did to me. He has cost me my wife and kids, eight years out of my life, my job, and the respect of people I worked and socialized with. I can never go back home, and I'll always be labeled as a sex pervert. People still don't believe what he did to me. He's still in business and living his life like nothing was wrong. He covered his tracks really good. We had all the trappings of a happy, successful family—a big house, a pool, a couple of cars, pillars of the church, and all of us kids were fairly successful in school."

Jacob concluded his statement by saying that he hoped his time in prison would be productive. He hopes he can learn to cope with his problem and establish a new life for himself after his release.

Ronnie

The author met Ronnie in 1972 in a large psychiatric facility where he was sent for evaluation prior to trial for charges of multiple rape. Ronnie was a 32-year-old husband and father of three children—one girl and two boys. Prior to his arrest he had been employed for five years as a shipping supervisor in a large mail-order firm in upstate Illinois. Prior to his arrest he had been perceived as a model father and husband. He had on occasion worked with a community organization that conducted youth-oriented activities.

The community was put in a state of shock when Ronnie was arrested for multiple rapes in four area communities over a period of three years. His family and friends were even more shocked when he admitted to these charges and to fifteen other previously unsolved sexual attacks, a total of 22 attacks. All of the sexual attacks were on middle-aged women. The first attack was committed when Ronnie was 21 years old and prior to his marriage.

During the evaluation by the clinical staff it was discovered that Ronnie would require treatment prior to being returned to court for disposition of his case. The social worker learned from the wife that there were periods when Ronnie "seemed to be out of it" and when he was very depressed and even mentioned suicide; but he always seemed to get better. It was learned that Ronnie had in fact been seeing a psychiatrist recommended by his company's physician. He was being treated principally for depression.

The social worker obtained substantial background information on Ronnie from his wife, siblings, and from Ronnie himself. The interviews and responses to the social work questionnaire disclosed that Ronnie was raised in a matriarchal family, one where the mother demonstrated tyrannical control. The mother seemed to thrive on the berating and humiliation of her only son and frequently told Ronnie that his birth was an accident and if he'd been born dead that the father would not have left home. Throughout his youth Ronnie could never have friends in his home and his mother cared little about his whereabouts. She would never take an interest in his school activities and refused to accompany him to events held after school. When he made the sixth grade basketball team, she refused to attend a game and verbally abused him each evening because he was late for the evening meal due to team practices and games. One sister reported that Ronnie eventually quit the team as a result of the abuse. The same sister related that she could not recall the mother having one kind word for Ronnie.

Upon reaching 18 years of age Ronnie dropped out of school and joined the military. He served for 20 months before receiving a medical discharge after experiencing what he referred to as a "nervous breakdown." It was in his job in supply that he acquired some of the skills he was to use later in his job for the mail-order company.

After leaving the service, he "bounced around for a few years" from job to job. It was during this period that he met his wife-to-be. She reported that he was very shy and fearful over meeting her parents, to which he became quite close over the years. From the time of their meeting up to his arrest, according to his wife, he made no attempt to contact the mother, but became almost uncontrollable when he learned that his sisters' children received Christmas and birthday presents from her while she ignored his children. The wife stated that his reaction upon learning of his mother's death was, "The bitch died before I could kill her." Being aware of the mother's past behavior, the wife said she didn't think the comment to be all that inappropriate.

According to the staff psychiatrist, the rapes were acts of revenge driven by impulses that Ronnie was aware of but could not control.

In this instance the cost of abuse was exceptionally high. The lives of at least 22 women and their families were severely traumatized, the lives of three innocent children and a wife were disrupted, and it cost the state many thousands of dollars to house and treat Ronnie—to say nothing of the cost to Ronnie. As of 1979, Ronnie was still in a state psychiatric facility categorized as an SDP (sexually dangerous person) with no release date under consideration.

Harold

Harold is presently pursuing a degree in a human services discipline at a midwestern state university. He is a single, 33-year-old student who is maintaining a B average while working two student jobs. He is a highly motivated individual who is committed to a career of helping others, particularly those who experienced abuse as children. His is a remarkable story of abuse by a father and by a large, impersonal mental health system, and of an attempt to rise above the quagmire of poverty, loneliness and despair.

"When I was about seven years old my troubles really got started. When I was seven, my mother left home with two of my brothers, leaving me at home with a younger brother and a violent, alcoholic father. Mom left because she could no longer take the beatings. Since I was the oldest, I had to take on a lot of responsibility like fixing meals and taking care of my younger brother. Since my father couldn't any longer beat on his wife, he started on me. The beatings were fairly regular since my father drank almost constantly. I went to school a lot of times with bruises and cuts and I know my teachers and other people had to notice my condition, yet no one ever said anything. I guess they didn't want to get involved, since back in those days they didn't have to. During this time we lived in the worst places you can imagine and barely had enough to eat. We got public assistance, but no one ever checked to see how it was being spent. He spent almost everything on booze. Some of the places we lived didn't even have plumbing or electricity. We did almost everything by candlelight. When I'd go to school, I didn't do very well, especially in English and math, but they'd pass me anyway; I guess they felt sorry for me.

"This all sounds bad enough, but my real trouble started when I was eleven. One really cold night my father came home drunker and madder than usual. I was just settling in on the couch when he started beating and slamming me all over the room. Finally, I was able to crawl out of the house into the snow. The next thing I really remember is waking up in the hospital with bandages on my head and my leg in a cast. I found out later that I had made it to a park and had been picked up by the police. I forgot to mention, I also had a cast on my left arm and had two black eyes and splits in my lips. Apparently I became quite fearful of adults, particularly of adult males. I was afraid they were going to beat me. While in the hospital I was pretty irrational and they told me I became quite delirious. Then I became withdrawn, wouldn't talk to anyone or eat. The doctors and other people then decided that I should be sent to a county psychiatric center. I was twelve at the time. I was locked up by myself and wasn't in school. I spent a year there and was then sent to a state-run psychiatric center; boy, was that some place. There were bars on the windows, you had to walk in lines to meals and activities, they fed you on trays, you had to eat either with your hands or a spoon, and the employees were really something else. They treated us like animals. For example, one afternoon I was just sitting in the dayroom when another patient went off and started attacking me. I took steps to defend myself. I didn't know it, but this guy was a pet of the employees. I was put to the floor, put in restraints, given Thorazine, and stripped of my clothes and then put in the seclusion room. Every hour on the hour for two days they would come and throw a bucket of water on me. The windows were all open and I had a serious asthma attack after the soakings, but luckily an employee came by, found me and took me to the infirmary. It was about this time I made up my mind that no one else was going to help me get stronger, so I'd have to do it myself. My first objective was to get a parole or a grounds pass so I could at least walk around the grounds by myself. This took me a year. I had no contact with my father. I spent all of my Christmases in the hospital. For awhile I cried about those things, but then Christmas and other holidays got to be just other days.

"When I was fifteen I heard of a new unit at the hospital. Mind you, all of this time since leaving home I hadn't been in school at all. One of the goals of the unit was to get patients into the community schools. You had to take a test to get into this unit and into the school program. I took the test and made it. I was only one of three kids on the unit. I started in the ninth grade. I had no friends, because everyone at the school knew I was from the institution and they were afraid of me. I did pretty good in school, except in English and math. No one in the institution even asked me about homework, I just did it on my own. I wasn't allowed to participate in sports, which would have helped me make friends. The doctor at the institution said it would be too strenuous; yet, they didn't think it was too strenuous for me to walk to and from school in all kinds of weather. When I was in the eleventh grade, I was told I was going to be transferred to another hospital. When I asked why, I was told it would allow me to be closer to my family. Mind you, I was eighteen and a voluntary patient and could have signed myself out. But, I wanted to finish school. I had heard that the senior year is so special, so I went to the doctor and he told me I didn't have a choice. So, I was transferred not knowing if I'd be able to finish school. I felt like all my dreams were being swept away. However, a social worker at the new hospital took an interest in my case and helped me enroll in a high school in a neighboring town. It was like a dream, I had so much freedom. I was even able to take driver's education and join the chorus. I did manage to graduate; barely, but I did graduate.

"After my graduation, I was discharged from the hospital as part of a deinstitutionalization program. I was placed in a community residence, but I had no idea what was going on or how to live independently. The social worker unfortunately left me out of all the planning. I got really bored, because there was nothing for me to do. I had no idea what I was going to do with my life. So, I went to talk to my social worker. We decided I should go to an area 4-year college. He set me up in school and had me sign some papers. It was just like in the institution, he did everything; I didn't know how to do anything. The school was quite big, and I didn't know anyone. There were too many demands and I couldn't handle it. My social worker couldn't help, because he was changing jobs. So, I ended up back in the state hospital, but for only about thirty days. After a short while I went back to the same college and did fair for about two years. Yet, I still didn't know what I wanted to do, so I hit the streets. It was awful. I couldn't find a job and I ended up drifting around and living in basements or on the street. I woke up one day and decided I had to do something. I went to a mental health center and got back into counseling and for the first time started to talk about some very personal things. One of the first goals was to get me off of the streets. They forced me to learn all of the ins and outs of social services procedures so I'd know what to do and have some control over my life; this took me about a year. I also had to learn how to shop, cook, act around strangers, dress appropriately—all those things you normally learn from parents. I was about 23 or 24 now. The next thing we decided was that I should try school again, only a community college this time. Since I lacked so many fundamental academic skills, I had to take a lot of remedial courses. It took me five years to get my associate degree. However, I did get involved in a lot of extracurricular activities and was even elected to a student government office.

"After graduation my counselors from the mental health agency and the community college got me to consider what I was going to do with my life. I decided that I wanted to work with people. I decided to apply to some of the state's four-year schools that had programs I would be interested in. Cost was a factor since I had no family. They disowned me since I refused to go to my father's funeral. I was also worried no four-year school would want to take me, since I only had a 2.43 GPA. Thankfully, this school accepted me in its Educational Opportunity Program.

"I have been here for a year now and things have been tough. I know I want to be a social worker, but I don't know if I have what it takes to complete the last year, particularly the biology courses. I'm also worried about the financial part of it. I do work on campus and I have a job at a summer camp which will probably be lost if they ever learn about my past. I have gained a lot of self-confidence here and I've made friends for the first time in my life. I've even been elected as program chairman for my major's club. I just hope that someday I can catch up, graduate from college and have a normal life. I don't know if I'll ever get married and have a family, I'm still afraid of that. It may be enough for me if I can just help in some way to prevent from happening to other kids what happened to me.

I feel I missed several things. First is not having real parents, someone to pat me on the back or just to teach me how to throw a ball. I also missed a lot of key years as far as education goes. The institutions could have provided better programs instead of abusing patients so much. There was a lot of verbal and physical abuse of patients by staff. I missed the normal opportunities to develop a positive self-concept and the coping skills I need for survival. Finally, I still don't trust people the way I know I should. I'm still trying to convince myself that somebody really cares about me."

Kyle

Kyle is a 39-year-old inmate of a medium-security correctional facility in New York. He is approximately one-half of the way through a minimum of eight years of incarceration for the sexual abuse of two young girls, aged 9 and 11 years. His story is one of a nightmarish childhood filled with emotional, physical and sexual abuse by natural and foster parents. Not unlike others imprisoned for sexual offenses, Kyle has expressed the desire to obtain counseling and other forms of therapy for his deviant behavior. He is an active participant in a counseling group for child abuse offenders. Kyle dictated his story, since his writing skills are severely lacking. According to Kyle, "My mind was occupied primarily by survival; little time and energy was left for schoolwork." Kyle's story is particularly explicit and some may find the language offensive, but at least it should help in understanding the impact of abuse on Kyle and innumerable other hapless victims who later become perpetrators.

"Based on what I've been told over the last bunch of years Mom and Dad always fought, I mean beating the hell out of one another. I can remember hearing the shouting and screaming and seeing Mom all screwed up in the face. I couldn't have been but 2 years old when the old man started slapping me around almost every night before I'd go to bed. Some nights the son-of-a-bitch would come home late and come into my bedroom and knock the shit out of me even after I went to bed. He was one mean mother. Well, it got so bad when I was about 5 that Mom decided to divorce the bastard, but she didn't want me or my brother. My grandparents (Dad's folks) decided to take us 'cause Dad didn't want to take the responsibility either. Looking back at it I see now why Dad was the way he was. I can remember laying awake at night listening to my grandparents' arguing and fighting. Boy, they use to get violent—throwing things, slugging, and kicking. One of the things that they fought about the most was my grandmother's boyfriends. Hell, she even had sex with some of them in the house. I caught her once. She told me she'd kill me if I told my grandfather; she would have, too.

"This all went on for about three years until one night around Christmas when my grandfather came home with a buzz on and confronted her about her screwing around. She must have been crazy, because she admitted it and threw this one guy in his face, saying sex with him was a lot better than with my grandfather. Well, to make a long story short, he beat the holy shit out of her. He damn near killed her, it was so bad that she had to go to the hospital for quite awhile and he had to go to jail. The child welfare people jerked my ass out of there and put me in an orphanage in Utica. Even though they never hit me I was exposed to a hell of a lot of violence for three years. They tried to do good by me, but I'd been better off if I'd been put in the orphanage the first thing.

"It may sound crazy, but I look on my two years in the orphanage as the best years as a kid. We were treated pretty good and there were kids there my own age. Just when things seemed to calm down my old man decided he wanted us kids back. He had remarried and convinced the child welfare people that he was reformed. If he was it didn't last long.

"We'd been with him and his new wife about two months when the same old crap started again. This time there was a new twist; he started sexually abusing me, my brother, and my stepsister. We were so scared of him that we let him do anything he wanted. His favorite thing with me was to put his penis between my legs and ejaculate. I don't know for sure what he did to my brother, but I'm sure he had intercourse with my stepsister. Since he and his wife worked different shifts it was real convenient for him. She may have suspected, but she never said anything for a long time. All hell broke loose after about a year and a half when he had apparently gotten a little too rough with M. (the stepsister). She apparently had resisted his advance; he got mad and beat the crap out of her. When her mom got home she asked what had happened and M. told her about everything. Well, all hell broke loose when she confronted him. He started knocking and shoving her around. The fight was over when he pushed her into the wood-burning stove. God, it was awful. She screamed so loud. She was burned horribly on her face, arms, and chest. Same old story; she went to the hospital and he went to jail for a long time.

"Instead of sending me back to the orphanage it was decided that my brother and I would be better off in a foster home. After a few months of a couple of temporary placements we were placed with a family on a farm. It became obvious real quick that the only reason they wanted us was because it meant two more workers for the farm. I didn't mind the work, but what hurt was that he was so easy on his own son. He got to take part in after-school sports and activities and in the Boy Scouts. Also, anytime anything went wrong I always caught hell for it since I was the oldest and not his kid. I remember one time when his son broke all of the windows in the milk barn. The son denied it, so I got blamed. He took the belt to me and then made me pay for the windows through extra work.

"I stayed with this family until I was old enough to quit school and join the service. I wasn't beaten up too much and there was no sex abuse. My foster mother was a good cook and a gentle person, so it was pretty comfortable.

"After the service I went from one job to another. I had real bad nerves and always had trouble getting along with people on the job. I also got in trouble a couple of times and spent some time for a couple of robberies. When in that joint I felt sorry for the real young guys. It reminded me of what my old man did to me. They really got slapped around and used sexually by some of the older guys.

"After my release I met a real nice lady. We went together for awhile before getting married. She'd never been married and didn't have any kids. Things kind of settled for me for awhile, or so it appeared to most people. There were some problems. I drank a little too much, but I never got nasty. Also, our sex life wasn't good. I couldn't seem to be comfortable with sex, but it didn't appear to bother my wife so much as it did me.

"A couple of years ago the plant where I worked had to cut back on the hours for all hourly workers. That hit us pretty hard, because I didn't have that good of a wage to begin with, since I was fairly new and didn't have much seniority. So to make ends meet my wife decided to watch neighborhood kids after school for people she knew. She took in five kids, three girls and two boys. The girls made me feel weird. When they'd play around me I use to get erections and even dream about them. My wife asked me several times to watch the kids when she'd have errands to run. My trouble started, as far as I can remember, the first time the oldest girl sat on my lap and that's the first time I touched her. This happened a few times and then I started putting my hand in her panties and in the younger one's panties. This happened five or six times until the younger one told her mother. She called the cops and here I am. My previous record didn't help.

"I know now why I did what I did and I'm glad I got caught before it got much worse. I feel sorry for what I did to those kids, but I also feel sorry for what I've done to my wife. I'm mad, too. Mad about what happened to me as a kid and about no one having to pay for what they did to me. I'm the one paying for it and I'll have to pay for it the rest of my life. But, compared to my brother I guess I'm getting off easy. He has been in a mental hospital for the past five years and it doesn't look like he'll ever get out. Then again, maybe he's the lucky one."

Additional Case Studies

In the classic text *The Crime of Punishment,* Doctor Karl Menninger makes reference to two case studies used by the late Doctor Adelaide Johnson to illustrate the cycle of violence and its costly effects. Johnson and her coworkers at the Mayo Clinic "were especially impressed with the way in which the violent destructiveness of the criminal is so often a reflection of the cruel and violent way in which he was treated as a child" (Menninger, 1968, p. 212). These case studies, which were first published in 1958, seem to substantiate a comment made to the author in 1970 by Doctor Menninger that (paraphrased) "probably more than 90 percent of the violent offenders are victims of child abuse" (Institute on Law, Psychiatry and the Mentally Disordered Offender: November, 1970).

The comment lends credence to Menninger's published comment that "We all know that in most cases of vicious acts there is a harsh, brutal father or mother in the childhood background" (Menninger, 1968, p. 213). He further states, "Clinical experience has indicated that where a child has been exposed early in his life to episodes of physical violence, whether he himself is the victim or the witness, he will often later demonstrate similar outbursts of uncontrollable rage and violence of his own. Aggression becomes an early outlet through which the child's frustration and tensions flow, not just because of a simple matter of learning that can be just as simply unlearned, not because he is imitating the bad behavior model and can be taught to imitate something more construction, but because these traumatic experiences have overwhelmed him. His own emotional development is too immature to withstand the crippling inner effects of outer violence. Something happens to the child's inner character so his sense of reality to the development of his controls against impulses that may not later be changed easily but which may lend to reactions that in turn provoke more reactions—one or more of which may be 'criminal'" (Menninger, 1968, pp. 214–215). Doctor Menninger with this eloquent and perspicuous statement describes the cost of physical abuse, particularly in terms of three precious human commodities (character, reality, and control). These case studies serve to demonstrate what Menninger, Johnson, Sandford, and some of their present-day colleagues have been telling a far too limited audience for approximately a quarter of a century.

Case 1. In a jealous rage, a 30-year-old man found an ax and, in the presence of neighbors, killed his former sweetheart. Originally, he had seduced her away from his brother when the latter went to Europe on military duty.

This man, the second of six children, had been the target for the most violent uncontrolled brutality on the part of the father, who, although he had a good job as a shop foreman, was a philandering alcoholic and a physical and mental sadist in his relationships with the prisoner's mother. The father's wild beatings of the boy were so frightening that neighbor men often interceded. The mother said she continued to live with the father only "to be sure he did not kill one of the boys," while at the same time her husband doted on the older daughter, of whom the prisoner was violently jealous. The father often beat and choked the mother in the children's presence. He shouted that she was a whore and that he would kill her some day. From the time the boy was 3 years old, the mother said, he recurrently ran away from home because he was so terrified of the father. From the time the boy was 14 years old, his father accused him of vicious sexual practices with girls, a charge which was not true at the time. The mother said that the father constantly "spoke evilly about other people's sex lives" in the presence of the children. At no time did the father ever accept any responsibility for his brutal acts, and he never expressed any remorse. The boy never dared to bring a young friend into the home.

The mother offered no protection to the child against the father's attacks, but she did console him afterward. She never called the police to protect the boy. She and the prisoner leaned on each other emotionally, and apparently he was always tender with her. At no time did the mother express any guilt or responsibility for having kept the boy in such a savage environment, and at the time we saw her the next oldest son was experiencing a similar life with the father. The prisoner said that without her warmth and comfort he would have killed himself long ago. He cried and moaned about his love for her for 15 minutes when she was first mentioned in the interview. He could not recall any conscious hostility toward his mother.

He always felt that his fiancee was better than he and above him socially. He made no protests when she had promiscuous affairs with others and left him. Later, for a time, he tried to win her back, after she had married. However, he began to live with a woman 10 years his senior, an occurrence which prompted his former fiancee to divorce her husband and to attempt to woo him back, promising marriage. As a result of this, he abandoned the woman with whom he had been living, whereupon the former fiancee began to go out with other men. The prisoner found an ax and killed her.

Several facts stand out in this case. First, the patient had seemingly identified with his father. He saw how sadistic his father was toward the mother as well as toward himself. Although consciously he loved his mother, he hated her unconsciously for not protecting him from the years of savage attacks. Similarly, she seduced him with consolations after the assaults and sought his sympathy as years went on and her plight continued. The prisoner stole his brother's girl, felt she was above him, and then for a brief time consoled himself with an older companion. Finally, the savagery he had felt and learned at the hands of his father came out toward the alternately unfaithful and seductive fiancee. She was merely repeating the life-long behavior of his mother, who alternately abandoned him to this father's brutality and then wooed him back with sentimental consolation.

His mother said that the father made no secret of his violent attacks on her sexually, verbally, and physically and that the sons knew all about these attacks. It was only by a stroke of luck that this prisoner actually was not killed by his father. The mother had always feared it and believed the father capable of it. The prisoner had known of his mother's fear for years. This boy, by direct example, learned that frustration and anger were to be handled by violence. He learned that men are brutal to women. The tremendous unconscious hatred for his mother, who submitted to the father and then turned to the prisoner for love, finally overwhelmed him at the expense of his alternately promiscuous and seductive fiancee.

Case 2. This prisoner was 27 years old when he strangled his sweetheart. When we saw him he was unable to account for his killing her. "Those 12 months with her — I wouldn't trade them even to being in this prison for life." He murdered her when she refused to marry him.

He said he wondered if he had not "misidentified" his victim with her interfering mother, of whom he said in all seriousness he would "gladly wring her neck." He also remarked, "If it hadn't been Rosie I killed, it would have been someone else — it was inevitable."

He was exceedingly bitter toward his own mother. "Mom hated me since the day I was conceived. I was an unfortunate burden on her. It wasn't my fault I was born. She has punished me ever since, though, for it. I can remember all the unmerciful beatings she gave me. She is happy now that she has completely destroyed my life."

He said she was vicious; she would choke him and beat him so hard with a barrel stave that he became bruised and bleeding. She used to say to him: "What did I ever do that God thinks I deserved to have you wished on me!"

His mother constantly belittled his father, and, whenever the father protested these humiliations, she threatened him with the "disgrace" of separation. "She destroyed any standing he might have had in my eyes," said the prisoner.

The mother told us of how her father "ran out" on the family when she was 5 years old, and she said he never supported them (a pattern her son repeated in the action of causing two unmarried girls to become pregnant and then abandoning them). Throughout her childhood the mother had been accused by other children of being illegitimate. No mention was allowed of the father by the family, and she had never heard other mention of him until she was 10 years old. It is clear how this hostility toward her father had carried over toward the son.

She reported that "the whole idea of John was a big mistake." She added that she had been angry about the pregnancy, blaming her husband's carelessness. She readily confirmed to us her son's account of her cruel and unusual punishment of him. It was remarkable to the interviewer how devoid she was of any sense of guilt about her rejection and cruelty. She explicitly said of his tantrums and ungovernable rages that "he acted how I felt." Local feeling in the community had been against the boy from the age of 5 years because of his violent temper, and from the age of 7 years he had been wrongly but persistently accused, over many years, of pushing a young companion to his death from a roof.

"His whole childhood was filled with anger," said the mother. She said she always thought he would get into trouble. "He grew up thinking the same way. He felt everyone was against him." At the time we saw her, she said she was glad the son was in prison and she hoped the authorities would never release him.

In this instance we have ample evidence for the prisoner's modeling himself after his vindictive and remorseless mother. She made it clear that the behavior of the son was in accord with her feelings. Satisfactory identification by the boy with his acquiescent, unprotecting father was not possible. The only close friend the boy had was an orphan boy older than himself who had lived with the family for a short while. As a boy, the prisoner often would stay away from school to dig worms for, and to go fishing with, a group of older men, who made much of him. His mother was aware of his truancy with these older men.

In the later life of this prisoner it seems that the mother of his sweetheart was the nominal target for his hostility, but when the girl herself spurned him he had no compunction about turning his vengeance on her. His lack of sense of guilt or restraint was modeled after those defects in his mother.

An interesting note pertaining to these two case studies relates to the criteria for participation in the Johnson, Barron, Frazier, and Littin study. They were to (1) have been convicted of first-degree murder, (2) be white males of normal intelligence, (3) not have denied the offense, and (4) be from middle-class families of good social standing. They were to also be free of drug and alcohol dependency, organic brain disease, and psepliosis prior to the killing. Johnson et al. found that in four of the six prisoners studied there was violence that remorseless physical brutality at the hands of the parents had been a constant..." (Duncan, Frazier, Littin, Johnson and Barron, 1958, p. 1755). Though the offenses took place over thirty years ago, the case studies could well have been written in 1988.

Finally, these case studies were presented to accomplish two goals. First, the studies demonstrate that the relationship of child abuse to adult violent behavior has been suspected for some time. It is not a recent revelation. Secondly, the studies vividly depict the cost of abuse in terms of human resources, let alone the cost to the taxpaying public.

Crime and Abuse

Ann Rule, a former Seattle police officer and recognized authority on serial killers, discussed another potential consequence of child abuse. In the cases she has studied she has discovered that most serial killers had troubles at home as youths. Typically, there was an absent or weak father and a mother who wasn't a good mom. "What I've found is usually when they were young—like 3 to 5 years old—they were either abandoned or humiliated by their mothers. They grow up with this sense of rage that builds and builds." Rule states that many children come from similar horrendous circumstances, but that "The difference seems to be whether they meet up with someone—a teacher, another adult—that makes them feel worthwhile" (McPhillips and Murphy, 1984, p. 8A). In this instance, how does one measure the cost of a Christopher Wilder, a John Wayne Gacy, or a Charles Manson? Could their destiny and the destiny of their numerous victims have been altered by a teacher, a coach, or a recreation leader making them feel worthwhile? It's quite likely.

Also in this vein, Ilene Barth of *Newsday* wrote in 1985, "Disturbed children, left to their sorrow, become disturbed adults. We all recognize the cost of crime: the outlays for private protection devices, the losses due to thefts and arson. Prisons and legions of police bloat tax bills. So do medical costs to patch up victims. Crime increases the cost of insurance and store purchases. These costs pale beside the emotional toll of living in fear. . . . Almost every study of criminal behavior, whether its subjects be serial murders or teenage arsonists, reveals that a significant proportion of perpetrators were seriously mistreated as children" (Barth, 1985, p. 4A).

A final example of the criminal cost of abuse is that of Carroll Edward Cole. On December 6, 1985 Cole was executed by the state of Nevada for the confessed killings of two women. He had also confessed to an additional twelve victims. According to Cole he committed the murders because "he was seeking revenge against his mother, who abused him as a child and forced him not to tell his father about her affairs with other men" (Confessed killer of 13 executed, 1985, p. 5A). Cole apparently never met the "someone" referred to by Ann Rule, and the price paid for Cole's abuse was brutal, heinous, and immeasurable.

It would be difficult to affix a numerical value to the costs reflected in the case histories presented. How can a financial value be tabulated for the losses to the individuals, their families, and their victims? Also, what about the cost to humanity in terms of lost, thwarted, or delayed human resources? The costs surely transcend all creative and mathematical potential.

WHAT ABOUT $$?

Unfortunately, programs are often initiated primarily because of their potential to make or save money. However, to establish a rationale for recreation's involvement in abuse prevention, intervention, and treatment on the basis of dollars earned and saved would be difficult due to the myriad ways the consequences of abuse are exhibited. Also, where child abuse exists so do a multitude of other problems. Often, the abuse is only one symptom of a sick, maladjusted and dysfunctional family. Therefore, it is difficult to isolate what portion of the overall dollar cost should be affixed or contributed to the abuse itself.

The attempt to obtain exact figures related to the expenditures of funds for specific types of abuse as related to debilitating conditions was both exhausting and fruitless. The attempts were complicated by state agency inability to provide the data. For example, none of the agencies consulted could provide the expenditures for abuse-related substance abuse rehabilitation or for the rehabilitation of abuse-related developmental disability. Consequently, a small number of state and private agencies were consulted to obtain data related to abuse-related expenditures. Each agency cautioned that the estimates on the precentage of clients receiving treatment due to the results of child abuse were conservative. The figures which follow reflect the estimated average of per diem and/or per annum cost per client or resident. To gain some insight into the potential cost to the public coffers the figures can be extrapolated to the general population. The potentials are mind-boggling, particularly with the recognition that the figures provided are, in all probability, conservative.

In all fairness to the states, there are some major obstacles to obtaining such specific data. First, abuse awareness is still a major issue. Few agencies, for example, even inquire as to the abuse relatedness of the dysfunction on intake. Secondly, the coordination effort between the various state agencies addressing abuse is a major issue. As one state official in the Northwest stated, "It is almost impossible to track an individual reported case once it passes from our protective agency to law enforcement, and then to the courts or to mental health. To tell you the financial expenditure for an individual case is impossible. Our systems simply aren't that sophisticated as of yet. We hope to be, because we know we should be. Not only are we likely squandering dollars, but we are also loosing people in the current system." Third, the state agencies are often grossly understaffed and inadequately funded. Such a specific, sophisticated system of accountability is extremely time consuming, both to design and maintain. Until such a system is devised, if it is in fact necessary, it will remain difficult to impossible to determine how costly physical abuse is to criminal justice or mental health systems, for example.

Substance Abuse

One of the major issues facing contemporary society is substance abuse. Concomitant with the technological advances is the ever-increasing use of illicit drugs and alcohol. It is not uncommon to find in the substance abuser's background some form of child abuse. Some of the figures related to substance abuse rehabilitation are alarming. Gary Metz, who is Assistant Professor of Health Science, Coordinator of the Alcohol and Chemical Dependency Studies Program at SUNY College at Brockport and Director of the federally funded Sheriff's Against Substance Abuse Project, has (based on his experience and research) estimated the average per-day cost of in-hospital treatment to be approximately $300. Therefore, a treatment regimen of 30 days' duration may well cost in excess of $9000. At approximately $75 per session of counseling, the same amount could be expended in just 120 days. That could be personally costly, as well, since most insurance companies providing coverage for such programs cover only 30 days per year. According to Metz, of the hundreds of cases he has reviewed and been clinically and administratively involved, an estimated 70 percent of substance abuse cases among youth are related to abusive homes. If this is true of a hundred cases, $630,000 of the total expended could well be attributed to abuse.

Head Trauma

The victims of child abuse often suffer from head trauma as the result of violent shaking and severe blows to the head. Often, the damage is of such severity to require constant care and supervision in community- or institutional-based programs for developmentally disabled. An example of the potential cost to the taxpayer is the case of Salley. Salley was born a perfectly healthy baby and developed normally for the first two years of her life. When 2 years old her father, who had a history of violent outbursts, picked her up and slammed her head into a wall. Since shortly after the incident Salley has been a resident of first a state-operated developmental center and now of an Intermediate Care Facility (ICF) group home. She is now 26 years old and in excellent physical health. The fiscal officer for the agency that is currently providing care for Salley estimates that the amount spent on her care prior to transfer to the agency Intermediate Care Facility was conservatively $900,000. Estimated cost in the six years since transfer to the ICF is $250,000. At the current per diem cost of $115 the cost for the next forty years of care is the monumental sum of $1,674,400. So, without costing-in the inflationary factor and assuming Salley will live to be at least 66 years old, the conservative estimate of the one incidence of physical abuse is $2,824,400.

Another agency consulted provides care totally through CRs (Community Residences) for developmentally disabled. One of its residents, Ken, is multiply disabled as the result of head trauma received from a number of abusive incidences. Ken, who is moderately mentally retarded, is also hearing and sight impaired and has periodic seizures. Ken is now 22 years old and in robust physical condition. He works in a sheltered workshop and requires little supervision. Yet, it is unlikely that he will ever be able to live independently. The fiscal officer estimates that cost of his care up to his placement in the agency's CR group home amounted to approximately $750,000, a large part due to some surgical attempts to improve sight and hearing. The measures to control the seizure activity has also been costly. Assuming that Ken may well live an additional 50 years, the cost of his care at the current rate of $30 per diem may well amount to $546,000. This does, again, not include the inflation factor, nor does it include the likelihood of additional medical expenditures. The total cost of Ken's abuse is, in all probability, going to exceed $1,300,000.

Criminal Activity

As the case studies in the earlier part of this chapter reflect, an all-too-frequent consequence of child abuse is criminal activities, of violent consequences resulting in the loss of human life. At an average expenditure of $20,000 per year of incarceration, the total cost for the abuse of Kyle and Jacob, for example, is approximately $320,000, not including law enforcement and court costs. At today's per annum costs of incarceration, the individual beginning his life sentence at 25 years of age may cost the taxpayer in excess of $1 million. If each state was to have only 20 inmates each serving for an offense resulting from abuse victimization or perpetration, the annual expenditure to taxpayers at the aforementioned per annum is a staggering $1 billion. If recreation programs could prevent even 10 percent of those incarcerations by providing opportunities for social bonding, appropriate stress alleviation and expression of aggressive impulses, the savings to taxpayers could approach $100 million.

Emotionally Disturbed

An agency in upstate New York provides services exclusively to emotionally disturbed youth. Currently, the ages range from seven to 21 years. The youth are housed in one of two primary care units if felt in need of in-house care. The first is an RTF (Residential Treatment Facility). The child housed in RTF is assessed as being in need of structured, goal-oriented treatment for a serious to severe emotional disorder. Such children are often characterized by suicide threats, self-abusive behaviors, violent and aggressive outbursts and severe depression. Approximately 40 children are housed in this unit in three cottages. The average length of residence is 18 months for all residents of the main campus. At a per diem of $171, the cost for the forty children for the eighteen-month period approaches $3,800,000.

The agency houses approximately another 100 youth in the RCF (Residential Care Facility). These children require, primarily, only a structured, caring living environment. Their emotional disturbances are not assessed as being severe enough to require a structured, goal-oriented treatment format. At a per diem of $98 the expenditure for care for the eighteen-month period approaches $5,400,000. The approximate cost for the care of the 140 children at this one agency's main campus alone approaches $9,200,000. The agency also provides day treatment programs to another sixty children. The cost per client for the eighteen-month period is $27,504 or a total of $12,650,240. These three major programs (there are others) cost approximately $10,850,240. According to the agency's clinical director, approximately 60 percent of the children need care as a direct result of abusive homes. Consequently, $6,510,144. is expended as a direct result of child abuse. Remember, this is just one agency and reflects only eighteen months of care.

SUMMARY

These examples vividly demonstrate only a portion of the monetary cost of child abuse, in that the costs to their victims, other family members and the costs of intervention and ajudication are not inferred. Often, such expenditures are absorbed in agencies other than child protective services. It is not difficult, however, to estimate even with the most conservative extrapolation that child abuse is a multi-billion-dollar enterprise of intergenerational decimation.

The Congressional Select Committee on Child, Youth, and Families provides some helpful data that depicts some costs in a forthright manner. Table IV-1 depicts for reporting states the total funding to confront child abuse, comparing levels of reporting and levels of total funding (state and federal) for FY's 1981 and 1985. The table depicts a total funding of $2,271,680,957 for 1985 and a net gain of 5.9 percent, while reported incidences rose by 79.3 percent between 1981 and 1985.

Table IV-2 depicts the levels of financial commitment by reporting states for FY 1985. The total is comprised of monies from state general funds ($961,529,916), children's trust funds ($1,673,809), local funds ($139,711,364) and from other sources of state revenue ($104,584,008). The level of state and local initiatives rose by 16.3 percent between 1981 and 1985. Again, however, the reported incidences rose by 79.3 percent. The picture is made even more dismal by the 3.9 percent cutback in the level of federal funds for the same period. As mind boggling as the level of funding may be, it is obvious that the financial resources are not keeping pace with the need.

To summarize, this chapter has attempted to elucidate the cost of child abuse from the perspectives of human and monetary resources. Child abuse is, without a doubt, a major consumer of both and its appetite appears to be growing. Recreation programs could play a major role in curtailing the wasting of the most precious of these resources.

Confronting Child Abuse Through Recreation

Table IV-1

TRENDS IN CHILD ABUSE REPORTING COMPARED TO TRENDS IN TOTAL
FUNDING TO ADDRESS CHILD ABUSE 1981-1985 BY STATE

	Percent Change in Child Abuse Reports			Percent Change in Total Funding(Constant Dollars)		
State	Percent 1981	1985	Percent Change	1981	1985	Percent Change
Alabama	18,654	31,385	68.2%	47,192,707	49,469,963	+4.8%
Alaska	7,748	13,382	72.1%	.	.	.
Arizona	7,892	43,043	445.4%	31,108,673	30,420,142	-2.2%
Arkansas	14,393	20,081	39.5%	3,271,365	5,482,849	+67.6%
California	179,735	272,953	51.9%	385,147,404	480,603,448	+24.8%
Colorado	10,908	13,825	26.7%	.	.	.
Connecticut	10,180	16,804	65.1%	.	.	.
Delaware	4,741	8,051	69.8%	.	.	.
Dist.of Col.	5,113	6,073	18.8%	.	.	.
Florida	68,446	130,393	90.5%	102,551,889	129,952,127	+26.7%
Georgia	22,763	45,489	99.4%	11,324,069	40,217,404	+255.2%
Hawaii	2,635	4,069	54.4%	20,576,844	18,592,175	-9.6%
Idaho	9,578	13,640	42.4%	11,905,195	10,293,964	-13.5%
Illinois	47,586	68,203	43.3%	186,599,854	198,047,688	+6.1%
Indiana	21,929	33,868	54.4%	45,465,077	46,288,642	+1.8%
Iowa	24,349	25,534	4.9%	50,222,135	46,695,877	-7.0%
Kansas	19,492	23,592	21.0%	.	.	.
Kentucky	28,266	34,839	23.3%	28,597,431	34,880,171	+21.9%
Louisiana	29,406	35,802	21.8%	68,458,767	70,644,109	+3.2%
Maine	6,714	10,121	50.7%	23,446,467	27,624,999	+17.8%
Maryland	11,698	19,934	65.7%	89,122,266	59.577,428	-33.2%
Massachusts	30,525	47,060	54.2%	.	.	.
Michigan	57,235	95,114	66.2%	126,264,136	143,273,017	+13.5%
Minnesota	13,205	22,046	67.0%	109,148,143	99,025,850	-9.3%
Mississippi	5,881	13,921	136.7%	28,057,952	23,593,667	-15.9%
Missouri	53,772	75,953	41.4%	100,437,497	62,073,991	-38.2%
Montana	5,243	5,516	5.2%	8,591,328	9,383,104	+9.2%

Table IV-1 continued

TRENDS IN CHILD ABUSE REPORTING COMPARED TO TRENDS IN TOTAL
FUNDING TO ADDRESS CHILD ABUSE 1981-1985 BY STATE

	Percent Change in Child Abuse Reports			Percent Change in Total Funding(Constant Dollars)		
State	1981	1985	Percent Change	1981	1985	Percent Change
Nebraska	7,013	13,765	96.3%	.	.	.
Nevada	6,354	11,144	75.4%	10,209,400	9,618,703	-5.8%
New Hampshire	4,478	6,517	45.5%	.	.	.
New Jersey	23,758	47,126	98.4%	121,495,718	125,857,758	+3.6%
New Mexico	5,904	12,061	104.3%	16,883,508	18,493,118	+9.5%
New York	106,295	139,032	30.8%	.	.	.
N Carolina	27,017	27,625	2.2%	.	.	.
N Dakota	2,944	4,719	60.3%	11,413,224	8,726,035	-23.5%
Ohio	27,248	65,965	142.1%	.	.	.
Oklahoma	12,283	20,275	65.1%	.	.	.
Oregon	2,732	12,765	367.2%	.	.	.
Pennsylvania	13,703	20,980	53.1%	238,686,296	245,431,035	+2.8%
Rhode Island	3,784	11,196	195.9%	.	.	.
S Carolina	19,289	28,861	49.6%	35,199,143	32,940,517	-6.4%
S Dakota	4,890	8,913	82.3%	3,787,917	2,380,441	-37.2%
Tennessee	44,146	47,050	6.6%	69,422,070	70,592,044	+1.7%
Texas	81,819	108,561	32.7%	100,914,220	116,120,935	+15.1%
Utah	5,832	18,089	210.2%	.	.	.
Vermont	2,072	4,452	114.9%	.	.	.
Virginia	39,685	49,765	25.4%	37,057,163	26,309,239	-29.0%
Washington	33,832	40,100	18.5%	.	.	.
W Virginia	7,111	20,772	192.1%	22,692,720	29,090,517	+28.2%
Wisconsin	8,508	24,411	186.9%	.	.	.
Wyoming	2,589	2,319	-10.4%	.	.	.

Source: <u>Select</u> <u>Committee</u>.... pp. 64-65)

Table IV-2

CHILD ABUSE FUNDING, FY 1985--STATE AND LOCAL SOURCES ONLY

State	Total State & Local Funding
Alabama	$ 10,031,380
Arizona	23,834,483
Arkansas	596,987
California	367,155,172
Florida	64,147,347
Georgia	16,002,743
Hawaii	5,275,737
Idaho	3,392,241
Illinois	55,435,159
Indiana	25,011,801
Iowa	28,023,935
Kentucky	15,927,586
Louisiana	14,806,320
Maine	14,938,793
Maryland	35,095,395
Michigan	75,193,450
Minnesota	47,423,707
Mississippi	5,528,448
Missouri	18,863,852
Montana	4,979,569
Nevada	2,866,339
New Jersey	89,135,344
New Mexico	7,719,880
North Dakota	671,290
Pennsylvania	188,836,207
South Carolina	10,161,207
South Dakota	288,968
Tennessee	15,685,793
Texas	41,357,657
Virginia	6,431,273
West Virginia	12,681,034
Total	$1,207,499,097

(Source: <u>Select Committee</u>.... pp. 66-77)

Chapter Five

INDICATORS OF SEXUAL ABUSE

INTRODUCTION

As discussed earlier, the syndrome referred to as sexual abuse is quite broad in scope and involves numerous forms of deviant behaviors perpetrated upon the child. Also, since sexual abuse is not an individual affair, a knowledge of the behavioral and physical indicators as they relate to the victim and the immediate care unit, namely, the family, is essential for a comprehensive program of intervention by Recreation and Leisure Services personnel.

The purpose of this and the following chapters relating to indicators is to make the recreation specialist aware of those physical and behavioral characteristics which may indicate a child is being abused. The indicators relate both to the child and the family and must be applied with care and judgment. A knowledge of indicators is necessary for the recreation specialist to be able to make a rational decision to whether or not initiate intervention measures. Yet, the recreation specialist must use caution and not jump to unwarranted conclusions that a child is being sexually abused solely on the basis of the existence of a single indicator. Persistence is the key. If one or more of the indicators are persistently evidenced, or if the child freely admits to being abused, then intervention must be initiated.

BEHAVIORAL INDICATORS

The sexual abuse of a child may be indicated through her or his behavior, particularly how she or he relates to adults and to peers. First of all, the child may be wary of adults. Physical contact with adults may be particularly threatening or anxiety-producing for the child. In a recreation program, most children are accepting of closeness with the adult leader and may even compete with peers for physical stroking such as hugs, pats, or other appropriate forms of physical recognition. The sexually abused child, on the other hand, will likely seek to avoid any type of physical contact with the adult leader, as well as with group members of the opposite gender. Avoidance may be demonstrated through refusal to participate in activities where physical contact is inherent, by cowering at the approach of an adult or peer of opposite gender, by shrinking at the touch of the adult or peer, or by verbally instructing the adult or peer to not touch them. The child may also become visibly agitated or even approach hysteria when touched.

The sexually abused child may also demonstrate extremes in behaviors. Frequently, the sexually abused child may exhibit swings from extreme withdrawal to extreme anger or aggressiveness. The child may appear to be depressed or to be preoccupied with fantasy inappropriate to the age level. The sexually abused child may likewise appear to regress to a lower age level, or to be retarded when their intelligence is known to be within normal range.

Sexually abused children are frequently angry and resentful of being abused. In addition to demonstrating aggressive or withdrawal behaviors, they may express the desire to live with a friend, the recreation specialist, another family member, a foster family or to live alone. The child may also threaten to become a runaway or, in fact, have a history of being a runaway or of being unaccounted for for lengthy periods of time between departure from recreation areas and arrival at home. Avoidance of the home environment is a common indication of sexual abuse or other forms of abuse and domestic strife.

Recreation personnel should be alert to the deterioration of the child's peer relationships. The child's anger over being abused may be displaced upon the peers or the fear of the abuse being discovered may lead to the development of insulatory behavior patterns. The withdrawal of the child from peer groups may also be a direct result of the abuser's attempt to keep the victim isolated in order to prevent detection. The child may well be under duress to discontinue after-school and weekend activities in order to prevent the perpetrator's deviant behavior from being disclosed.

As a result of firsthand exposure to deviant sexual activity, the victim may appear to be well advanced of his or her peers in terms of sexual knowledge. Frequently, the victim's sexual behavior may appear to be bizarre or sophisticated to peers and may result in fear of the victimized child. Behavior such as sexual aggressiveness towards peers could well be indicative of the aggressor's sexual abuse at home.

Another behavior indicative of possible sexual abuse is the unwillingness to change clothing or to shower in the presence of peers of like gender.

Such behavior may reflect the child's fear of having bruised or otherwise injured genital areas observed by peers or adult supervisors. It may also be the result of the abuser's instructions to the child in order to prevent disclosure of the deviant behavior.

Sexual abuse frequently results in painful injury to the child's body, particularly the genitalia. Consequently, sustained movement and physical activity may be uncomfortable. The sexually abused child may, therefore, be unwilling to participate in physical activities or appear to be in pain during participation in such activities. The trauma may be severe enough to cause even walking and sitting to be difficult or discomforting.

Children may choose from a variety of means of escaping the realities of sexual abuse. Substance abuse—alcohol and drugs—may be the means the abused child selects for coping with his or her feelings of anger, shame, resentment, or poor self-concept. The sudden onset of or the chronic use of alcohol and drugs may be cause for the recreation leader to be alerted to the possibility of sexual abuse.

An incestuous relationship of a long-term nature may result in something beyond sexual sophistication and aggression towards peers. Young males and females who have been raised in family situations where it is considered normal for adult care givers to have overt sexual relationships with children may be sexually aggressive with recreation leaders or be perceived as being seductive.

Recreation workers are frequently privy to conversations between their youthful participants. The children will frequently share their concerns about others' performance in school, for example. The recreation worker should stay attuned to information concerning sharp changes in academic performance of children. One form of sexual abuse, incest, often begins as children approach or enter the adolescent years. A dramatic drop-off in school performance could be indicative of a family crisis, including incest and sexual abuse. Likewise, the recreation worker should be alert to similar performance changes in the recreation setting—diminished interest, shortened attention span, sudden inability to follow activity or game instructions, and declining performance level.

All professionals working directly with children need to be cognizant of the fact that sexual abuse can be perpetrated by a family member other than a parent or another adult. Though less frequent in occurrence, sibling sexual abuse also occurs. Mayhall and Norgard (1983, pp. 180–181) identify some indicators that may alert the recreation worker to possible deviant sexual liaison between siblings. These may include:

1. A brother and sister who behave like a girlfriend and boyfriend.
2. A child who fears being left alone with a sibling.
3. A brother and sister who appear to be embarrassed when found alone.
4. A situation in which a child antagonizes the sibling but the sibling does not retaliate (for fear of exposing secret).

Another clue to a sibling sexual relationship that may be observed in the recreational setting is jealousy of attention a sibling may receive from another child, particularly if the child receives such attention from a member of the opposite sex.

Finally, with respect to the child's behavioral indicators, the recreation worker must not discount a child's reports of being sexually abused. Since the child may have agonized for an extensive period of time to gather the courage to report incidences of abuse, he or she will very likely only do so once unless the worker responds favorably. A worker response that reflects disinterest or disbelief may result in the child's continued withdrawal and in reinforcement of the notions that abuse is acceptable, children are chattel of the parents, or that society does in fact not care for the welfare of children.

As alluded to previously, there are also behavioral indicators of sexual abuse that are familial in nature. Since many structured recreational activities are designed for family participation, the recreation worker in public, private, and commercial leisure service agencies is in a unique position to observe how the family functions as a unit. Again, it is Mayhall and Norgard who offer some possible indicators that sexual abuse may be a problem within a family. These are (1983, p. 181):

1. A dysfunctional family system characterized by blurring of generational lives within the family—father and/or mother becomes the child and daughter and/or son take on the role of wife/mother or husband/father.
2. Strained marital relationships.
3. Parent often alone with one child.
4. Favoritism by parent toward one child over other children.
5. Overly protective parent. The parent who is involved in incest may become overly protective and jealous of the youth and try to isolate the youth from other contacts within and outside the family. The parent is not only afraid that the child will tell, but also afraid that the child may find another sexual partner.

The responsible recreation worker must not allow responsible action to be prevented by a distorted commitment to the notion that "A family that plays together stays together." Rather, the supervisor of the recreational activity should remain attuned to the type of family interaction or the family play process.

O'Brien, in her highly praised work *Child Abuse: A Crying Shame,* has identified some characteristics of abusive parents which may assist recreation and leisure services personnel in the identification of abusive parents, including those sexually abusing their children. One such characteristic is "the preference for privacy that leads to isolation. Abusing parents are isolated from supportive groups such as friends, relatives or kin, neighbors, and community groups. They also consistently fail to keep appointments, discourage social contact, and seldom or never participate in "back-to-school" nights, parent-teacher conferences, or community gatherings" (O'Brien, 1981, p. 46). The key term is "consistently." The recreation worker should be alerted to the parent or guardian that refuses to return calls or to meet concerning the child's behavior or physical appearance or that consistently refuses to participate with the child in agency-sponsored activities.

Another characteristic O'Brien discusses that may readily be observed by Recreation and Leisure Services personnel is "unrealistic expectations of their children. They expect and demand behavior that is beyond the child's years or abilities" (1981, p. 47). The reasons for such may relate to a lack of knowledge and understanding of human development or to a need to live vicariously, through the child. It may also relate to a conscious strategy to cover-up abuse. How can a parent who wants so much for his child be anything other than a good, loving parent? O'Brien also contributes such parental behavior to the possibility that "The child may be seen as a source of love or support for the parent, instead of a developing personality that needs love and support from the parent" (1981, p. 47).

A third characteristic O'Brien discusses is the abusive parent's "belief in harsh punishment for children" (1981, p. 48). The sexually abusive parent may react harshly and encourage or administer corporal punishment for reported sexual behavior by the child. This may reflect jealousy on the part of the parent or it may also reflect a concern over being disclosed as a sex abuser. Yet, it may also be reflective of a belief in the appropriateness of harsh punishment for any socially inappropriate behavior.

Recreation personnel should also be alerted to the fact that "Abusive parents usually go to great lengths to hide their child's injuries" (O'Brien, 1981, p. 49). Parents who also insist their child not be required or even allowed to change clothing or shower in view of other children or adult supervisors may be motivated by something other than a concern for the child's modesty. The concern may be the disclosure of trauma to the child's body, particularly the genitalia. Likewise, the parent wishing to cover-up evidence of sexual abuse may send the child to activities pre-changed in order to prevent the change of clothing at the activity center; i.e. the child wears the bathing suit to the pool and home rather than changing with other children in the available locker room.

A fifth characteristic of a sexually abusive parent is poor self-esteem. "They see themselves as failures, worthless, unable to fulfill the expectations others have had for them" (O'Brien, 1981, p. 48). For the sexually abusive parent, this may be a demonstration of feelings of sexual inadequacy. The parent who consistently responds in a self-degrading manner when requested to assume leadership in an aspect of the recreation program may be reflecting feelings consequential of abusive behavior. This poor self-concept may be so consuming that the parent overcompensates by never touching the child or maintaining even eye contact with the child during agency functions or activities. Consumed by self-pity the parent may abuse as a result of a total lack of understanding or appreciation of the child's needs.

A behavior indicator which may be indicative of a sexually abusive home environment is the parent who frequently or "often initiates sexual contact with the child by hugging and kissing ... " (Heindl et al., 1979, p. 21). Such behavior was described by a colleague to the author when discussing a confirmed incidence of sexual abuse, "The father never seemed to be able to keep his hands off of his daughter, that's what made us suspicious."

PHYSICAL INDICATORS

In addition to the aforementioned behavioral indicators of possible sexual abuse, Recreation and Leisure Services personnel should also be aware that there are physical indicators which may provide visual evidence of sexual abuse. Only those indicators that may be noted by casual observation during the normal course of program routine will be identified—identified, but not discussed, since no explanation is warranted. As with the behavioral indicators, the physical indicators are not proof of abuse but cause for suspicion of abuse and further investigation.

1. Bruises in the area of external genitalia, vagina, or anal regions.
2. Bleeding from external genitalia, vagina, or anal regions.

(Mayhall & Norgard, 1983, p. 179)

1. Difficulty in walking or sitting.
2. Torn, stained, or bloody underclothing.
3. Complaints of pain or itching in the genital area.

(Broadhurst, 1984, p. 18)

In addition to those mentioned by Mayhall, Norgard and Broadhurst, two other physical indicators which may be observed by recreation personnel are blood in urine and lower abdominal distress. These, as well as the aforementioned, may be indicators of something other than sexual abuse; nonetheless, they warrant noting and further observation. Finally, bruises on and bleeding from areas of the body other than the genital area may be incurred during sexual assault and should not be overlooked or arbitrarily contributed to youthful proclivity. As with all indicators, the recreation worker must take note of pattern or consistency of indicator presence.

SUMMARY

In summary, the possible listing of indicators is almost endless. Such is the result of the incredibly creative and devious methods derived by perpetrators to sexually abuse their youthful victims. The recreation worker should constantly remind him/herself of the possible indicators and be aware that the indicators rarely appear alone but usually in the company of one or more others.

Chapter Six

INDICATORS OF PHYSICAL ABUSE

INTRODUCTION

The syndrome known as physical abuse is broad in scope and involves numerous and ingenious means of pain infliction. As with sexual abuse, there are both behavioral and physical indications that a child is being beaten, tortured, or otherwise physically maltreated. Here, too, when discussing behavioral indicators, focus should be upon the behavior of the family unit as well as upon the child. An awareness of these and of the physical indicators is particularly critical, since of all the forms of child abuse, it is physical abuse that is the most likely to result in either death or permanent physical disabling of the child. The ignoring of the evidence or a lack of awareness of the indicators could well result in the recreation worker's passive participation in the death of a child. Early intervention is absolutely critical, for physical abuse tends to "take place over a period of time, and its effects add up. The longer physical abuse continues, the more serious it becomes, the more serious is the injury to the child, and the more difficult is the abuse to stop" (Cohn, 1983, p. 1).

As with sexual abuse, the presence of one or more indicators of physical abuse does not necessarily mean a child is being victimized. Children, particularly in the pre-teen and early teen stages of development, are active and awkward. This, when coupled with a propensity towards recklessness and little thought given to consequence of risk-taking behavior, results in numerous injuries of varying degrees of seriousness. Again, it is persistence that is the key. For example, if the child returns to the community center two consecutive Mondays with a cut lip, there is reason to suspect violence in his home and that intervention procedures need to be initiated, particularly if other indicators are noted upon closer review and investigation.

BEHAVIORAL INDICATORS

Physically abused children frequently demonstrate certain behaviors that are characteristic of victims. As the child gets older, it may be behavior that will provide the strongest clues to abuse. Older children tend to be much more creative in covering-up the physical or medical evidence of their abuse.

The following are behavior indicators provided by Broadhurst. The child:

- is wary of physical contact with adults. In the classroom, most children accept physical closeness to a teacher. The abused child will often avoid it, sometimes even shrinking at the touch or approach of an adult.
- becomes apprehensive when other children cry.
- demonstrates extremes in behavior — extreme aggressiveness or extreme withdrawal, for example — behavior which lies outside the range expected for the child's age group.
- seems frightened of the parents.
- states he/she is afraid to go home, or cries when it is time to leave.
- reports injury by a parent.

(Broadhurst, 1979, p. 16)

These indicators, though addressed to educators, apply as well to a variety of recreational settings, i.e. the community center, an after-school latchkey program, etc. Again, the recreation worker should not reach premature conclusions; perhaps the child is crying because he's having such an enjoyable time he doesn't want to leave, or perhaps the parent has deferred punishment until the evening for truly inappropriate behavior by the child — if so, it is likely the child may seem unhappy to see the parents.

There are other, numerous behavioral indicators of physical abuse. First, and related to one of those mentioned by Broadhurst, is the fear of the home environment. Not only may the child attempt to postpone going home, but he or she may very well be waiting for the agency's front door to open each morning. The child may volunteer to arrive early and leave late each day to assist the agency's recreation staff with cleaning or setting up for activities. The abused child may also remain on the grounds even after activities are terminated and the facilities locked. The child will also likely refuse staff offers to transport him or her home and may be observed walking home by an indirect route. If the child does accept a ride with a staff member, he will likely consistently request he be taken to a friend's house or that he be "dropped off" at the shopping mall, the library, the teen hangout, or any place other than home.

Older children, particularly those in their teens, are quite innovative in the means they devise to cover-up evidence of their physical abuse. Today, because of the lack of a dress code or criteria as to what constitutes appropriate dress, recreation personnel need to pay careful attention as to what is the current mode of dress for special social and age groupings represented in their programs. The change of seasons is no longer the major determinant of clothing appropriateness. The miracles of science have produced new, lightweight and attractive fabrics which make it no longer inappropriate to wear long sleeves in July in Carbondale, Illinois or Memphis, Tennessee. The new fabrics and the individualized modes of dress make it much easier to cover-up bruised and burned arms and legs. However, if in a specific age and social group one member is wearing long pants consistently when the others are wearing shorts, and the recreation leader knows the family can financially afford the variety of clothing, then suspicion of abuse cover-up may be warranted. Also, if the child wears a long-sleeve, wool shirt when it is 95 degrees and other children are all wearing short-sleeve shirts, there is cause for suspicion of an abuse cover-up. Common ways of covering up injuries to the facial area are the wearing of dark sunglasses and the heavy application of cosmetics. The child who wears sunglasses in an artificially lighted or darkened room and does so with regularity may be masking injury to the eyes. Likewise, the girl who wears cosmetics unevenly or unusually heavy consistently or at regular intervals may be attempting to cover facial bruises. In both of these examples, however, the recreation worker needs to be aware of youthful fashion trends when assessing the appropriateness of behaviors.

It is not uncommon for children who are victims of physical abuse to aggressively seek the affection of other adults, either other parents or program personnel. These children are in search of a non-violent, supportive adult relationship. The child who is always volunteering to assist the leader, who is constantly "under foot," or who is continuously seeking the leader's attention may be seeking relief from an abusive environment.

The bruised, burned or otherwise physically maltreated child will, as related previously, go to great measures to keep the injuries from being discovered. One measure may be to refuse to change clothing or shower in the presence of other children or program staff. Physically abused children may arrive at the center already attired in their sweats and then refuse to shower after rigorous activity, giving as an excuse that they have no clothes to change into. Another strategy to prevent disclosure may be to refuse to participate in such activities such as swimming, particularly at regular intervals. For example, the child refusing to participate in pool activities each Monday evening may be covering-up evidence of a violent weekend. Physically abused children may also become agitated when such an activity as camping is mentioned. Camping does not afford many opportunities for physical privacy.

The physically abused child, as the one who is sexually abused, may be reluctant or even refuse to participate in physical activities, particularly those requiring excessive gross motor movement, the explanation being that traumatized muscles hurt when exercised. If a child who has a history of enjoying physical activity refuses participation each Saturday morning, the activity supervisor may well have cause to suspect the child is experiencing abusive Friday evenings.

The child who is being abused by a parent or guardian who lives vicariously through the child's performance may refuse to participate in activities where success is not guaranteed. The price for failure may well be painful. It is a shameful commentary on contemporary American society, but many children are physically punished for poor performance on the sports fields and courts of our nation. A frustrated father who sees his last opportunity for success and recognition being thwarted by reckless or inadequate performance may be lacking in coping skills and displace his feelings on the one he sees as responsible: his son in the Little League uniform!

Another indicator relates to one mentioned by Broadhurst but warrants its own identity. Broadhurst alerts the professional to extremes in behavior. Extremes are readily observable, but not so observable are the subtle changes in behavior. A child who has a history of being outgoing, assertive and successful in agency programs may gradually become taciturn. Or, a child who has even been bumptious may gradually become passive and apologetic. Likewise, a passive and cooperative child may gradually evolve into a truculent individual whose behavior may also be characterized by temerity. The extreme may not be immediately obvious, so it is important that any changes in behavior be noted.

Physically abused children tend to be defensive, particularly when asked about an injury. The defensiveness may be the result of a parental threat to cause additional pain and injury if the child discusses the circumstances of the injury. Also, the child may be concerned about other consequences of disclosure. Perhaps he or she does not want to be viewed as responsible for further disruption of the family. Finally, disclosure of physical abuse can be detrimental to social position and can result in unfavorable labeling by peers. Consequently, Recreation and Leisure Services personnel should be alerted to defensive reactions to inquiries about physical injuries and not arbitrarily report such to parents or guardians. Such action could have deleterious consequences for the child, namely, additional and more severe abuse.

Families, particularly parents and guardians, also may exhibit behaviors that could alert the recreation worker to the possibility of a physically abusive home environment. As mentioned when discussing sexual abuse, Recreation and Leisure Services personnel are in unique positions to observe the family as a unit and to relate to adult members. Recreation and Leisures personnel and adult family members should share one common concern: the growth and development of the child.

The 1984 edition of the New York State Child Protective Services' *Mandated Reporter Manual* lists numerous parent behavioral indicators, some of which the recreation worker may have opportunity to observe. These are as follows:

- Seems unconcerned about the child
- Misuses alcohol or drugs
- Takes an unusual amounts of time to obtain medical care for the child
- Offers an inadequate or inappropriate explanation for the child's injury
- Gives different explanation for the same injury
- Has poor impulse control
- Attempts to conceal the child's injury

(p. 30)

Broadhurst (1986, p. 5), when discussing how to recognize abuse, alerts the teacher to signs that the parent or guardian may be abusive. Since the role of the recreation and leisure services professional in some settings parallels that of the teacher, an awareness of these signs may be helpful. According to Broadhurst, the parent:

- shows little concern for the child, rarely responding to the school's request for information, conferences, or for home visits;
- asks the classroom teacher to use harsh physical discipline if the child misbehaves;
- sees the child as entirely bad, worthless or burdensome;
- demands perfection or a level of physical or academic performance the child cannot achieve; or

• looks primarily to the child for care, attention, and satisfaction of emotional needs.

Parents who are physically abusive frequently live isolated or insulated life-styles that provide them no or few outlets for their emotions (Mayhall and Norgard, 1983, p. 113). The traditional extended family is rapidly becoming a vanishing institution. Gone with it are the opportunities for respite from the trials of parenthood. Often in the pursuit of economic opportunity, families will relocate in areas that are void of supportive services or so large that access to services is perceived as difficult or impossible. Recreation workers, particularly those in inner-city agencies, are likely exposed to children from such potentially explosive home environments and should, consequently, be alerted to the potential for family violence, including child abuse.

PHYSICAL INDICATORS

The physical or medical indicators of physical abuse may be more readily detectable than in other forms of abuse. Table VI-1 depicts physical indicators of physical abuse identified by Heindl et al. and Broadhurst.

Mayhall and Norgard, summarizing the indicators, state "Primary indicators of physical child abuse are injuries to the skin, injuries to the face or head, burns, eye injuries, brain injuries, abdominal visceral injuries, or bone injuries" (1983, p. 111).

Finally, Recreation and Leisure Services personnel should keep all of the indicators reviewed in mind but should also remain cognizant of the probability that the list is not all-inclusive. Due to man's ingenuity, new and creative means of inflicting pain upon children are being contrived almost daily. The instruments of abuse are numerous and include coat hangers, rulers, knives, teeth, hot gas and electric burners, cigars, cigarettes, boiling water and grease, ball bats, shoes and boots, mop and broom handles, belts, cleaning chemicals, hairbrushes, razor blades, lead or iron pipes, chains, guns, cigarette lighters and matches, bricks, rolled magazines and newspapers, electrical cords, and any other item that can be held by the human hand. With these instruments parents, guardians, aunts, uncles or other adults beat, stab, burn, slice, strangle and poison children. To intervene in such barbarism, the recreation worker must remain diligent and remind him/herself that, as with all forms of abuse,

Table VI-1

PHYSICAL INDICATORS OF PHYSICAL ABUSE

·Unexplained Bruises and Welts:
- on face, lips, mouth
- on torso, back, buttocks, thighs
- in various stages of healing
- clustered, forming, regular patterns
- reflecting shape of article used to inflict (electrical cord, belt buckle)
- on several different surface areas
- regularly appear after absence, weekend or vacation
·Unexplained Burns:
- cigar-cigarette burns, especially on soles, palms, back or buttocks
- immersion burns (sock-like, glove-like, doughnut shaped on buttocks or genitalia)
- patterned like electric burner, iron, etc.
- rope burns on arms, legs, neck or torso
- infected burns, indicating delay in seeking treatment
·Unexplained Fractures:
- to the skull, nose or facial structure
- in various stages of healing (indicating they occur at different times)
- multiple or spiral fracture
- swollen or tender limbs
- any fracture in a child under the age of two
·Unexplained Lacerations and Abrasions:
- to the mouth, lips, gums or eyes
- to the external genitalia
- on the backs of the arms, legs, or torso
·Unexplained Abdominal Injuries:
- swelling of the abdomen
- localized tenderness
- constant vomiting
·Bald Patches on the Scalp
·Human Bite Marks:
- adult size or recurrent

(Heindl, et. al. 1979, p. 10)
(Broadhurst, 1979, p. 15)

the indicators will not likely appear alone but usually in conjunction with one or more others. A lack of diligence may well result in a child's death or permanent disability.

Chapter Seven

INDICATORS OF EMOTIONAL ABUSE

INTRODUCTION

Perhaps the greatest barrier to the intervention of emotional abuse is its identification. Harrison and Edwards state, "While physical abuse can be identified by the marks left on the child, emotional abuse leaves few physical signs. It can be hidden in a tone of voice or an attitude toward a child. There are no sharp lines where emotional abuse begins, no easy, reliable, or standard measurement of its effects on the battered mind. Yet, emotional abuse is potentially the most harmful form of all the abuses" (1983, p. 15). The problem with the indicators of emotional abuse is that unlike those of physical and sexual abuse they do not call immediate attention to a problem. A child with a black eye, a split lip, bite marks, cigarette burns, bruised genitalia causes alert signs to flash and instantly cause the adult supervisor to think, "We might have a serious problem here." Yet, though the indicators are usually much more subtle in nature, the need for indicator awareness and intervention measures is just as important as for the more violent forms of abuse. Perhaps this need was most eloquently related by Rebecca Harrison and Jean Edwards: "The scars from emotional battering are much greater than those received from physical or sexual abuse. While physical bruises heal, emotional scars run deep, leaving their marks for years in feelings of depression, inadequacy, low self-esteem, or in other less obvious personality traits" (1983, p. 15). An alarming statistics in today's contemporary society may suggest that emotional abuse is as deadly as physical abuse. Namely, suicide is now at alarming proportions, particularly among American teens and young adults.

BEHAVIORAL INDICATORS

Mayhall and Norgard come to our assistance in the attempt to identify children suffering from emotional abuse. Today's family faces numerous stressful situations which could result in a child becoming the target of emotional abuse. Some of these "emotional issues" are:

- Continuous friction in the home
- Mentally ill parents
- Marital discord
- Immature parents
- Excessive drinking by the parents or other family members
- Alcoholism within the family
- Drug addiction within the family
- Criminal involvement on the part of one or more of the family members
- Illicit sexual relations within the family
- Overly severe control and discipline by the parents
- Encouragement of delinquency
- Mentally retarded parents
- Harsh and improper language
- Nonsupport of the child's interests and pursuits
- Parental values that conflict with society's values
- Divorces and frequent re-marriages
- Failure to offer motivation and stimulation toward learning
- Failure to provide wholesome recreation for the family and the children
- Failure to individualize children and their needs
- Failure to give the child constructive limit-setting or discipline
- Promiscuity and prostitution

(1983, pp. 155–156)

To this listing should be added:

- Rejecting parents who withhold love.
- Discriminatory treatment among children.

(Harrison and Edwards, 1983, p. 59)

And the parent:

- Blames or belittles the child.
- Doesn't seem to care much about the child's problems.
- Is cold and rejecting.

Recreation and Leisure Services personnel, like school teachers, are often in positions to observe or learn of such family or environmental indicators of potential emotional abuse. We may learn of their existence through conversations with our young participants, by overhearing conversations between the children, through our attempts to involve the family unit in our programs, or through a dialogue with child care workers.

Recreation personnel also need to be alerted to the child's behavior. There are some behavioral indicators a child may demonstrate to suggest the possibility of emotional abuse at home or elsewhere (the baby-sitter's, for example).

First, after years of constant rejection, berating, and being emotionally terrorized, a child may become quite apathetic and uncaring about almost everything and everyone. Garbarino and Garbarino report that "victims have a deeply ingrained lack of empathy: they have trouble recognizing and appreciating the needs and feelings of others" (*Emotional Maltreatment of Children*, 1986, p. 16).

In our culture, people who are physically ill receive a lot of attention, often in the form of extra support and sympathy. Children are very astute observers of society and quickly learn how to manipulate the environment to meet their conscious or unconscious needs. Emotionally, maltreated children may, consequently, seek the attention they are not receiving at home by reporting illnesses or complaining of not feeling well for numerous reasons. The child who is constantly complaining of having a headache, a cold, the flu, or of having a sore arm, twisted knee, a sprained ankle or of having some exotic-sounding diseases that likely could have been learned of only out of a physician's reference is likely searching for attention and it may be because he or she is emotionally abused at home. It may also be a demonstration of the way attention is successfully obtained in the home environment.

Children who are constantly berated, threatened, rejected, or ignored tend to build walls around themselves. The interaction with their families and significant others has a history of being so anxiety-producing or tumultuous that psychological barriers are constructed. This may often be displayed by patterns of depressed or withdrawn behaviors. Such children are frequently labeled as being apathetic. Their vocabularies are characterized almost constantly by such responses as "Who cares? Who gives a damn? What do you really care? I don't give a shit. Why ask me? Why should I care? I don't care about anything. Anything you want is okay. or My opinion doesn't mean a thing." There are, of course, many other such responses, but they all convey, if consistently elicited, a problem with self-concept or a fear of not responding in the desired fashion. These children may be so fearful of failure and the resulting belittling they may have to endure on the home front that they will simply refuse to participate in any activity where there is the slightest opportunity for failure. They will likely express any interest in doing something new or challenging, unless it is something of extremely low visibility or non-competitive in nature.

"Often, as teenagers, the victims find it difficult to trust, to participate fully and happily in enduring interpersonal relationships . . ." (Garbarino and Garbarino, *Emotional Maltreatment of Children,* pp. 16–17). These children likely want to be able to trust others, particularly adults. But why should they trust? They have repeatedly been humiliated and terrorized by those they should be able to trust the most and have again and again had their trust violated by the most significant adults in their lives: their parents, their teachers and their recreation leaders. The child may appear to be reluctant to let another adult "get close" by sharing personal feelings. They will likely appear very guarded with respect to conversations—casual or otherwise.

Emotionally abused children frequently develop psychoneurotic reactions as a means of insulating themselves from a maladjusted home environment or from additional degradation. In addition to some of the psychosomatic complaints mentioned previously, the child may often express or demonstrate certain phobias. The child, to prevent failure in aquatic activities, may develop a morbid fear of water, or hydrophobia. Likewise, a child that is fearful of failing in a group setting may express fear of being in a confined space with others, or appear to be claustrophobic. Finally, a child may voice acrophobic fears to prevent failures related to activities involving high elements. Any all-consuming or morbid fear may well be a defensive measure against further failure and subsequent humiliation by parents or other adults.

The question of possible emotional abuse should also be addressed when "The child is very concerned about conforming to the instructions of the adult, that is, teacher, doctor or others in authority, and their conformity seems to be disproportionate to other children of the same age group" (Mayhall and Norgard, 1983, p. 158). All recreation leaders are used to spending time answering questions to clarify rules and responding to "Did I do it right? Did you see me do . . . ? or What did I do wrong?" That is part of the recreation territory and we allot time for such questions, particularly when our charges are elementary school age or younger. However, as our participants progress through their adolescence we expect the questions to become less frequent and for the individual child to be more self-assured. Not so with many emotionally abused youngsters. They may want constant reassurance and the elimination of most of the margin for error. But, would not most of us if all we have heard from our parents is "You're stupid! Nothing you do turns out right! Why can't you be successful like your sister?" or "You're too dumb to decide anything." This over-concern for compliance with rules or guidelines may also be motivated by the need for adult recognition that is positive, reassuring and controlled.

Berating, humiliating, rejecting responses to failure or anything less than perfection may well seem "normal" to the emotionally abused child. Consequently, that may be exactly the way he or she will react to peers that fail. Peer failure may be followed by outbursts of loud, degrading remarks blaming them for group failure. The child who appears on the surface to be grossly intolerant of imperfection in others may in fact be demonstrating what he has been conditioned to perceive as an acceptable response to failure or less-than-perfect performance.

Strong indications of emotional abuse are such comments as "My dad says I'll never amount to anything." "My mother says I am worthless," or "My folks say I'll never be as good as my brother." Such comments are indicative of a non-supportive and elusive home environment. Regrettably, these children are often convinced that their parents' assessment of them is accurate. Just as regrettable is the fact that such children often hear such comments from other adults—coaches, teachers and recreation leaders.

Browbeaten youngsters may also be perceived as being over-submissive, ones who will not defend themselves under any circumstances. They appear to be easily intimidated and manipulated by others, peers and adults. Due to the terror in the home environment, they opt to not "make waves" or to keep peace, regardless of the cost. This over-submissiveness may also be motivated by the need to be accepted by someone, anyone. Consequently, they refrain from doing or saying anything that may result in rejection. This is, of course, not a rational strategy, but these children are desperate for acceptance.

Emotionally abused children may also appear to be developmentally lagging, or they cannot perform or react to the environment in an age-appropriate fashion. A child that has been ignored and has been deprived of normal stimulation will likely exhibit stifled emotional, physical and intellectual development. The same is true of the child that has been rejected. Children grow when nurtured, whether physically, emotionally or intellectually. If children are not positively reinforced by parents for appropriate responses to environmental stimuli, responses tend to become less mature in terms of context.

Conduct disorders are frequently exhibited by abused children, including those emotionally abused. "The child acts up and is considered by teachers and other adults to be a behavior problem in the classroom or in other situations where children need to follow rules or have set standards of behavior" (Mayhall and Norgard, 1983, p. 158). First of all, these children are not accustomed, for the most part, to peace and quiet. Their responses have been conditioned by disordered, hostile experiences. Rules are something they could understandably have little appreciation of or trust in, since they likely changed from day to day. Also, emotionally abused children may well have no perception of what constitutes the "set standards of behavior." The home experiences of these children may demonstrate to them that standards of behavior are inconsistent and are whimsically adapted to meet the needs of the parents.

Another observation by numerous child care specialists relates directly to the mission of recreation and leisure programs: play. Children who are emotionally abused do not know how to play; that and most spontaneous expression has been thwarted or suppressed. Often, playtime has never been provided or encouraged. Some victims reported (to the author) that as soon as they were old enough to walk they had to spend all of their free time either "being quiet" or "doing chores." On some occasions the attitudes against play and fun were contributed to a religious doctrine. Regardless of the reasons, some children do not know the meaning of fun nor have they experienced an enjoyable activity. This inability to enjoy or to play may be demonstrated in the school environment or later in life when the child experiments with various recreative opportunities. The author in 1981 spoke to a 12-year-old boy who had never been on a piece of playground equipment. His mother convinced him that he was too awkward and that such play was too dangerous. Consequently, his play opportunities were sharply curtailed and his circle of friends was extremely limited, as were his play skills. A major treatment goal for this young man was to teach him how to play. Additionally, the mother was undergoing counseling in an attempt to intervene in her abusive interaction with her son and other children.

Eventually the abuse scars so deeply that the child may contemplate putting an end to the abuse in his own way. A frequent avenue for escape from the rejecting, terrorizing, and otherwise emotionally deviant home environment is to strike out. Since the child has likely been convinced he or she is worthless or a cause of shame to the family, the striking out will likely be directed inward. Threats of suicide or even casual remarks or questions about suicide should always be taken seriously. If not related to an abusive home environment, such behavior does reflect emotional problems precipitated by other factors. Regardless, immediate intervention is required.

PHYSICAL INDICATORS

Though not as numerous as for the other types of abuse already discussed, there are some physical indicators of emotional abuse. These are as follows:

- enuresis
- encopresis*
- lags in physical development*
- skin rashes
- speech disorders
- nervous twitching

SUMMARY

Emotional abuse continues to be a problem long after the abrasions and bruises of more violent forms of child maltreatment heal. The scars and the end results can be as deadly as those of physical abuse. The indicators of emotional abuse are not as blatant as those of other forms of abuse, and discovery of their existence require close observation and a stronger commitment to child welfare. As with all indicators, however, none of those discussed are absolute proof that emotional abuse has occurred or is occurring. They are, nonetheless, signs to watch for and reason to remain alert to the possibility of emotional abuse.

---

*From Harrison and Edwards, 1983, p. 114.

Chapter Eight

INDICATORS OF NEGLECT

INTRODUCTION

There has been a substantial amount of debate by authorities in the field of child abuse and maltreatment if neglect is in fact abuse. The key or pivotal issue seems to be that of intent on the part of parents or guardians. However, as pointed out by Fontana, "Neglect may not be abuse, but it is maltreatment. Similarly, neglect may not always be deliberate, but it is damaging" (1976, p. 21). As members of the child care team, Recreation and Leisure Services professionals ought to remain uninvolved in the neglect-abuse debate and accept Doctor Fontana's assessment of the deleterious effects of abuse. The results of ignoring the neglected child can be as equally detrimental to the child as ignoring the other more violent and blatant forms of child abuse. Whether the child sustains brain damage via physical battering or by nutritional neglect the results are the same: the child will never attain inherent potential. Pernicious anemia can be as deadly as a ruptured spleen. Once a child expires, it is of little consequence to the child how he died; dead is dead.

Like those indicators of emotional abuse, the indicators of neglect may be more difficult to spot than those of sexual and physical abuse. Yet, Recreation and Leisure Services personnel may be, likely will be, exposed to more neglected children than children otherwise abused. Polansky points out that "Whereas allusive parents typically restrict the child's social experiences outside the home, neglectful parents do not actively forbid such attachments. Nor is the neglectful parent so prone to derogatory remarks about his child" (Polansky, DeSaix, and Sharlino, 1973, p. 3). Furthermore, "The fact that neglecting parents do not forbid outside connections and relationships for their child may actually shield the child from some of the emotional side-effects of neglect" (Mayhall and Norgard, 1983, p. 137). It is this lack of interest in what happens to the child that permits the child to connect emotionally with others—frequently his teacher, community center staff, playground supervisor, church youth leader, or scouting leader. Due to this potential for emotional bonding, the Recreation and Leisure Services worker may have a unique opportunity to interrupt the pattern of neglectful abuse behavior. To do so, an awareness of the indicators is critical.

BEHAVIORAL INDICATORS

As with the other forms of child maltreatment, there are behavioral patterns demonstrated by the family and the child which may be signaling neglect. Erickson, McEvoy and Colucci identify some behavioral characteristics of neglectful parents which may be cause for suspecting abuse. These psychological traits are as follows:

- Inability to tolerate stress or frustration;
- Inability to express anger directly and deal with anger by sulking;
- Have a desire to be rid of the demands of their children;
- Show an indifference toward being a parent; and/or
- Display little in the ways of parental planning.

(1984, pp. 35–36)

These traits, as with other signals which are categorized as family behavioral indicators, the Recreation and Leisure Services personnel may have limited opportunity to observe firsthand. It is not likely that most neglectful parents will be active participants with their children in agency programs, particularly those parents guilty of severe neglect (see Chapter One). However, as previously noted, often neglected children will emotionally bond with adult leaders. Consequently, the children may share with the leaders their experiences with their parents and this sharing may disclose the aforementioned psychological or behavioral traits. This disclosure, when coupled with direct or firsthand observations of parental behavior or with the physical signals of child neglect, should spur the recreation leader to action.

Other familial signals could be characterized as environmental indicators of possible neglect. Harrison and Edwards have identified the following:

- a large family with marital disruption
- long-term parental illness
- poverty
- indifferent parental attitude
- situational stress, such as unemployment

- lack of material resources
- parental characteristics stemming from neglect

(1983, p. 57)

With respect to the latter characteristic, Harrison and Edwards define these parental or personal characteristics further. These characteristics are as follows:

- apathetic
- craving for excitement, change
- desire to be rid of the demands of the child
- lack of interest in child's activities
- low acceptance of child's dependency needs
- unskilled as parents
- little planning or organization
- frequently unkempt

(1983, p. 58)

The recreation leader need not be reminded that apathy can be a temporary condition. A response of "I don't care what she does" when an inquiry is made about a child's possible participation in a special event does not mean the child is neglected. It may mean that there was a bad day at the home or office, that there were other or more serious issues that day with other children, or that the parent was physically ill and wished not to talk on the phone. However, if the parent consistently or repeatedly responds in such a manner or refuses to return permission or waiver forms, it could be a strong indication of possible neglect.

A parent may be the participant in the recreation program. The adult who is known to have children who consistently avoids family oriented activities, perhaps giving such excuses as "I can be around the kids any time" or "My kids will never do that," may be conveying that he is trying to distance himself from his children and that he lacks interest in their activities, desires freedom from their demands, or that he does not understand the dependency needs of his children.

Likewise, the adult participant who is known to have a family that frequently changes employment and that is constantly changing his emphasis in the recreation program may be demonstrating the craving for excitement and change. Such behavior may be signaling total consumption with self and the neglecting of parental responsibilities to his children. Recreation and Leisure Services personnel should, once this pattern is noted, attempt to observe whether or not this behavioral pattern is totally exclusive of family. Neglectful parents will not permit family members to be involved in the quest for the new life.

Most of us, whether we are employed by or volunteer with the Scouts, Y's, or community-sponsored recreation programs, have been confronted with the issue of getting parents involved. Occasionally, we are faced with excuses of "Gee, I don't know if I'll be able to come," "I don't know what's going on then," or "There's always too much to do." All three excuses may in fact be legitimate for parents at a given time; but here again the key signal is consistency. If this becomes the established pattern of response or if the responses are incongruous with what is known of the parent's commitments (i.e. number of children, social and service activities, employment, etc.), then the responses may be indicative of a life out of control or one lacking the ability to organize or prioritize. A parent who is incapable of identifying and prioritizing his or her own needs is likely ill-prepared to nurture the child or to fulfill the role as a parent.

Few people are immaculately or well-groomed at all times. At the same time, just as few people are at all times slovenly in appearance. Recreation leaders may be in the position to observe the hygiene and dress habits of the parents or to hear children discuss the parent's appearance. Caution, here too, is advised. A parent may pick up the child after working a long, hot grueling day at construction or in a mining industry. Perhaps the parent is a diesel mechanic that has just completed his day's employment. Though they are a rapidly disappearing breed, there are still some steel workers employed in the U.S. That too is an occupation that results in the worker appearing unkempt. Recreation personnel should, however, remain alert to the parent or guardian who appears unkempt consistently and at varying times of the day. The neglectful parent is more likely to appear slovenly and slothful with respect to dress and hygiene. Hair may not be groomed, skin may be dirty and blemished, clothing may be soiled and disheveled, clothing may be dated and not color-coordinated, urine and fecal odor may be present, clothing weight or layering may be seasonally inappropriate, and teeth may be discolored and otherwise indicate the need of care. Again, the consistent presence of one or more of these indicators constitutes probably cause to suspect a neglectful home environment.

Finally, with respect to characteristics of neglectful parents, Heindl et al. specify the following indicators that the child care specialist may have occasion to observe or become aware of:

- may have a chaotic home life
- may live in unsafe conditions (no food; garbage and excrement in living areas; exposed wiring; drugs and poisons kept within the reach of children)
- may abuse drugs or alcohol
- lack understanding of well-child needs
- may be mentally retarded, have low I.Q., or have a flat personality
- may be impulsive individuals who seek immediate gratification without regard to long-term consequences
- may be motivated and employed but unable to find or afford child care
- generally have not experienced success
- had emotional needs which were not met by their parents
- have low self-esteem
- have little motivation or skill to effect changes in their lives
- are socially isolated, have no support system
- tend to be passive
- experienced inappropriate parenting

(1979, pp. 19–20)

Again, all of the aforementioned indicators are related to alert the recreation worker to a condition that may exist in the child's home.

A personal experience of the author may be helpful in understanding the need for caution. In 1977 my oldest son played in a community youth baseball league. I attended as many games as possible. At each game, I noticed a gentleman who would sit by himself to watch the games. On one occasion, I sat close to the man and immediately became suspicious of possible child neglect (his son was on my son's team). The man was quite unkempt—his clothes were very soiled, his skin was filthy, and his body odor was very strong. I asked my son about this individual's son and learned that the boy often came to school "dressed funny" and "smelling bad." The next game I observed some behavior that lessened my concern about neglect. The father hugged his son and offered to contribute to the post-game ritual of taking all the team members for ice cream at the local Dairy Queen. I also learned after additional inquiry that the man was highly motivated to provide for his family to the best of his ability by working two jobs—one as a garbage collector and the other in the local junkyard. What I had observed was not neglect but a family that did care for its children. The children were loved and happy, but the resources were limited and the family chose to struggle rather than accept welfare. I later learned that the family had previously been investigated formally for child neglect and exonerated. I also learned that the parents were emotionally devastated by the charges. I was grateful I had not added to the family's difficulties. The lesson here is, obviously, that poor and dirty do not equal neglect. I did not have the "total picture." I had only limited knowledge of the parents and even less of the children.

The other element of the "total picture" is the child. Children also will provide Recreation and Leisure Services personnel with behavioral and physical indicators of neglect. Mayhall and Norgard specify behavioral indicators of physical and emotional neglect. They are as follows:

- Begging for and/or stealing food
- Withdrawal from the peer groups
- Extended stay at school, in public places, or at a neighbor's house
- Undue fatigue, listlessness, falling asleep at times that are inappropriate, or other obvious medical signs
- Alcohol or drug abuse
- Delinquency
- Child tells you that there is no caretaker.

(1983, p. 135)

Harrison and Edwards add the following indicators:

- Dull, apathetic appearance
- Engaging in vandalism
- Engaging in sexual misconduct
- Squinting
- Poor learning.

(1983, p. 57)

Another possible indication that the child's home environment is neglectful is the child's consistent reliance upon others to get home from the recreation program or center. The neglected child may have no pre-arranged means of getting home and may frequently ask the program staff or other participants for "a lift home."

Consistent risk-taking behavior or participation in dangerous activity may also warrant the suspicion of a neglectful home environment. Such children may have been given "carte blanche" by the parents who have neglected to set limits for the children or to assist in the perception of their own immortality. Children often believe themselves to be imperishable or indestructible. Part of an attentive parent's role is to help the child to understand concepts such as safe, dangerous, pain, death and to establish boundaries for behavior that are appropriate for age, physical development and to the values of the prevalent culture. Left to their own volition children are apt to seek these limits by experimentation; such may appear to be risky or dangerous to the observer. Also, if such behavior results in the lavishing of concern by others, the behavior may well continue. It has accomplished something the child is not getting at home—attention and affirmation of their importance to others. Therefore, children may not walk the edge because they like danger but because they thrive on the attention. The same may be said for other inappropriate behaviors.

PHYSICAL INDICATORS

Children may also display physical signals of parental neglect. Some of these are as follows:

- unattended injuries or illness
- inadequate clothing for climatic conditions
- constant fatigue
- poor vision, uncorrected
- persistent hunger
- poor dental care
- poor hygiene: soiled skin and clothing, body odor, matted and unkempt hair, etc.

Again, Recreation and Leisure Services personnel should consider such factors as parental resources, cultural values, and existence and persistence of both physical indicators and behavioral patterns.

SUMMARY

Child neglect is as potentially harmful and fatal as other more obvious and aggressive forms of child maltreatment. Also, it is a form of abuse in which personnel may have the best opportunity to intervene. The neglected child may well be in search of emotional bonding and not have the obstacle of parental interference. Neglectful parents may, in fact, be pleased that their child finds someone else to "latch on to." The neglected child typically is not berated or threatened by his parents and may, consequently, be quite open about the home conditions. Finally, whether the child's dental care or vision is being neglected for reasons of cultural or ethnic values, poverty, or parental inadequacy, the results will be the same if recreation personnel do not remain cognizant of the indicators of neglect and remain committed to responsible intervention and child advocacy.

Chapter Nine

CHILDREN UNDER STRESS

Joseph E. Balog and Linda F. Balog

Recently, Doctor Linda F. Balog, Executive Director of the Child and Adolescent Stress Management Institute of the State University of New York at Brockport, New York, asked an elementary-school class, "Did anything happen over Christmas to make you feel stressed?"

"When my grandpa died," said one child.

"When my mom got married," said another.

"When I moved from England," said a third.

Johnny, an eight-year-old boy, was asked to read out loud in front of his class. While observing him as he waited for his turn, it was noted that he was squirming at his desk. His face was tense, flushed, and contained a look of fright.

Sara, an 11-year-old, said "I don't ever want to get married." She explained her parents are so angry at each other that she never wants to go through the same kind of experience.

Bobbie's dad stated his ten-year-old son is having unexplained headaches for the past month. When asked, "When does Bobbie get his headaches?" his father pointed out they seem to always come on Friday and Saturday nights. "What does Bobbie usually do on Saturdays and Sundays?"

"He plays hockey," said Bobbie's dad, "for the town's youth hockey team."

Sasha lies awake in her room for much of the night. She worries about her alcoholic father, her parents arguing, and one of them coming into her room to yell at her.

Finally, Elizabeth Stroebel, who with her husband, Charles F. Stroebel, runs the Institute for the Advanced Studies in Behavioral Medicine in Hartford, Connecticut, tells about a not so unusual twelve-year-old girl who says, "I worry most about getting a mortgage on a house" (Stroebel, 1984).

What do these children all have in common? The answer is stress.

Children, like adults, experience stress. They may be smaller than adults, but this does not mean they have less stress or that they are more immune to the harmful effects of stress.

Often, in fact, childhood stress may be much greater than the stress experienced by adults. Consider, for example, that many times children: (1) have fewer socially learned coping skills like time management or relaxation activities to deal with stress; (2) have less overt ways of channelling their stress like going on shopping sprees or visiting neighborhood bars; (3) have lower levels of self-awareness and cognition which can help them understand and solve their problems of stress; and (4) have less control of their environment to reduce their stress as they are more a product in, than a producer of, their society. As a result, children are many times more susceptible and vulnerable to internalizing the physical and emotional reactions of stress. This stress, unfortunately, can cause unhealthy psychological, physiological, sociological, and behavioral changes in their lives.

These changes, which can be viewed as warning signs and symptoms of stress, range from minor problems of bed-wetting, stomachaches, temper tantrums, or nervous feelings to critical problems of depression, drug use, anorexia, and suicide. More and more, health and behavioral problems are being linked to stress, and documents such as *Healthy People — The Surgeon General's Report on Health Promotion and Disease Prevention,* (U.S. DHEW, 1979; U.S. DHEW, 1979), the American Public Health Association's report, *Monitoring Children's Health: Key Indicators* (Miller, 1986), and other research (Coddington, 1972, Elkind, 1981, 1984; Humphrey, 1984; Humphrey & Humphrey, 1985; Kliman, 1986; Miller, 1982; Newberry, 1987; Phillips, 1978; Ramos, 1975; Rutter, 1983; Wolff, 1981) implicate stress as a key factor leading to numerous health problems in our children. In fact, stress has been identified as a major contributing factor to the overall declining health status of American youngsters.

These research reports support what parents, educators, and clinicians have been observing in society over the past several years. Children are experiencing more stress than ever before. As Elizabeth Stroebel concludes from her many years of working with children in the classroom and now in a clinical setting, "There's no doubt in my mind that stress in kids is increasing" (Stroebel, 1984).

In addition to children having more stress, there is also mounting evidence indicating today's children face more severe types of stress. Doctor Elliot Gershon of the National Institute of Mental Health highlighted this claim as he points out that the percentage of teenagers attempting suicide, the incidence of drug abuse, and anorexia and bulimia has increased more than fivefold over the past forty years. These serious problems in youngsters may be in part, or in total, explained as negative responses to stress (Gershon, 1986).

Another alarming trend about stress is that it is affecting younger and younger children. Doctor Barbara S. Kuczen, researcher and author of *Childhood Stress — Don't Let Your Child Be A Victim* (Kuczen, 1982), points out children as young as five years old are developing ulcers or even attempting suicide in response to harmful levels of stress. Doctor David Elkind, who also extensively studies and writes on this problem, makes similar observations. For instance, Doctor Elkind notes the incredible fact that "We are seeing depression in school-aged children which we never saw before, low-mood, apathy, actual thoughts of self-destruction . . ." (ABC World News Tonight, 1983).

In summary, stress is not a problem confined to adults. Each year millions of children suffer from stress, and there is an ever-growing body of knowledge which links stress to a wide variety of health and behavioral problems. Sometimes they are emotional in nature, such as frequent crying or feelings of anger. Sometimes they are physical in nature, such as chronic fatigue or nausea. And sometimes they are behavioral in nature, such as nail-biting or drug use. Regardless of how stress is expressed in children, we must never lose sight of the fact that children are people, and like big people, they are affected by the same psychological, sociological, and biological pressures and forces which affect all of us.

Thus, children are victims of stress just as are adults, and according to Doctor Kuczen, "Rushing about as we all do means our children live with more stress than we ever did" (Kuczen, 1984, p. 23). When today's children must cope with a world in which both parents work, high divorce rates, increasing poverty, and where sex, drugs, and violence are now in grade school, why should adults be surprised about the fact that their children are under stress? But if not surprised, adults should be alarmed, because as the above research informs us, this stress is having a serious toll on our children. This negative stress is resulting in poor health and an increasing tendency among youngsters to use negative coping behaviors such as drug use to escape from their stress.

These signs, symptoms, and negative coping behaviors are indicators that something is seriously wrong in our society, something that is negatively impacting on our children's health and welfare, something which must not continue to go unchecked, or this form of neglect may perhaps someday be looked back upon as child abuse.

IDENTIFYING, UNDERSTANDING, AND DIRECTING THE FORCES OF STRESS

In order to help children deal with their stress we must first understand what is stress and what factors cause stress in children. Perhaps a good way to begin is with a story about the famous arctic explorer, Sir Edward W. Parry. Parry once found himself and his North Pole expedition travelling straight toward the North Pole at a rate of 10 miles a day. Days later, however, Parry and his men were puzzled by the fact they were not getting any closer to their destination. The reason for this, as they were to discover, is the ice they were travelling over was drifting straight toward the equator at a rate of 12 miles a day. Parry's expedition never reached its destination, because they made the vital mistake of not taking into consideration all other forces and factors that affected their journey. As a consequence, these explorers found themselves being directed as opposed to directing their own destiny.

When it comes to deciding how to help our children in dealing with stress, we must avoid making a similar error. We must become familiar with what is stress and the factors which cause stress in children. Then, as adults, we must learn how to direct the forces which will help children in controlling their stress. If not, our children may never reach the destination which we wish for them: a life full of health and happiness.

Defining Stress

The first step in helping to direct and control childhood stress is to increase our understanding of stress. This is by no means an easy task, because contrary to popular belief, there is no one agreed upon way of viewing stress (Monat and Lazarus, 1985). This disagreement is due to the fact that stress is both an intricate phenomenon and a culturally defined concept. As a result, there exists many different interpretations of stress. However, for our purposes we will define stress from a well-accepted and popular psychosomatic and biological perspective.

To begin, let us realize that stress is ever-present. It is an inevitable part of living. In fact, stress is essential to a normal and healthy existence, for quite simply it is the way we physically and emotionally respond to any changes or demands in life, whether they are big, small, good, or bad. In its positive form, stress can help us adapt to life changes, achieve new goals, and make life more interesting. In its negative form, however, stress can have a harmful effect on physical, mental, and social well-being. Thus, children, as well as adults, need stress but need moderate levels of it. Too little or too much stress interferes with the body's internal balance. When this happens, health can suffer.

To better understand how stress can both enrich and harm life, think of life as a harp string. Pull it too tight and it goes out of tune or the string breaks. If, on the other hand, the string is too loose, it makes no music at all. Thus, the major challenge facing adults in this stress-filled world is one of discovering and helping to create a level of tension which is right for our children, a level which keeps them in tune and in balance.

The Stress Response

Going off to school for the first time, having to read out loud in front of classmates, or adjusting to the divorce of one's parents, can all cause a child to experience a chain reaction of increased physical and mental activity called the *stress response* (Selye, 1976). Another common name for the stress response is the "fight-or-flight" response. This fight-or-flight response is believed to be a primitive and natural instinct, which, when confronted with a stressor, prepares the body to fight or flee. The whole body goes on alert, ready to do battle or to escape to safety.

This physical and emotional stress response was a real life-saver for primitive human beings when facing life-threatening stressors, like wild animals, natural disasters, and territorial conflicts. Today, however, children are not usually confronted with such life events. Rather, their stressors are more likely to be their siblings, fights with parents, divorce of parents, school problems, or fears about nuclear war. Instead of running from bears, children are running to catch an after-school program. Instead of fighting enemies, children are fighting anxieties. Instead of fearing avalanches, children are worrying about staying home alone.

The physical and emotional changes which take place during this stress response are completely natural and instinctive. However, when stress becomes prolonged, intense, or particularly frustrating, it can become harmful. One way to determine whether children are experiencing harmful levels of stress is to become more aware of their signs and symptoms of negative stress. Identifying these early warning signs is one of the most important steps in helping children who suffer from stress.

Review the following warning signs which Doctor Kuczen (Kuczen, 1982) offers in her book, *Childhood Stress—Don't Let Your Child Be A Victim*, to help in identifying stress in young children. As Doctor Kuczen notes, it is normal for children to demonstrate a few of the behaviors from the below list—depending on their stage of development; but a number of signs existing over an extended period of time can signal that stress is taking a toll:

- Bed-wetting
- Boasts of superiority
- Complaints of feeling afraid or upset without being able to identify the source
- Complaints of neck or back pain
- Complaints of pounding heart
- Complaints of stomach upset, queasiness, or vomiting
- Compulsive cleanliness
- Compulsive ear tugging, hair pulling, or eyebrow plucking
- Cruel behavior toward people or pets
- Decline in school achievement
- Defiance
- Depression
- Dirtying pants
- Dislike of school
- Downgrading of self
- Easily startled by unexpected sounds
- Explosive crying
- Extreme nervousness
- Frequent daydreaming and retreats from reality
- Frequent urination or diarrhea
- Extreme worry
- Headaches
- Irritability
- Listlessness or lack of enthusiasm
- Loss of interest in activities usually approached with vigor
- Lying
- Nightmares or night terrors
- Nervous laughter
- Nervous tics, twitches, or muscle spasms
- Obvious attention-seeking
- Overeating
- Poor concentration
- Poor eating
- Poor sleep
- Psychosomatic illnesses
- Stealing
- Stuttering
- Teeth grinding (sometimes during sleep)
- Thumb-sucking
- Uncontrollable urge to run and hide
- Unusual difficulty in getting along with friends
- Unusual jealousy of close friends and siblings
- Unusual sexual behavior such as spying or exhibitionism
- Withdrawal from usual social activities

Symptoms of Stress and the Stress Response

The aforementioned symptoms of stress are early warning signals. They indicate that our children's stress response is stuck in the "on" position and they cannot quite turn it off. Typically, a child's stress response is a short-term state of increased physical and mental activity. When they are stressed, their bodies rev up their internal engines in preparation of meeting an immediate and recognizable challenge. Faced with this challenge, a child's body and mind undergoes a chain reaction of physical and mental activity which includes increases in muscle tension, blood pressure, respiratory rate, and heart rate. The child may also perspire more and even feel more mentally alert and focused. This increasing level of physical and mental arousal is, as noted above, the stress response.

Once the challenge is met, the child's body and mind relaxes and returns to a normal level of activity or homeostasis.

However, if the child is experiencing too much stress, there is no true relaxation between one stress "crisis" and the next. The child's body and mind remains geared up. The child's stress response is more intense, and his or her short-term reaction develops into a continuous and chronic condition. As a result of this ongoing stress, the child experiences physical and emotional strain, and this is when the child's symptoms of stress begin to appear. If left unattended, these symptoms of stress may evolve into illness.

Causes of Stress

As the saying goes, "The one thing in life that is constant is change." To be alive is to change, and a child's reaction to change is the essence of stress. Change causes stress, or, more accurately, a child's evaluation of a life event (or perception of the life event) along with the child's mental and physical reaction to the life event is the essence of stress.

People in general, and certainly children too, do not always react to change or life events in the same degree or intensity. For instance, some children appear to have stress-resistant personalities. Researchers refer to this trait as a hardiness personality or describe these children as resilient children (Kobasa, 1985; Werner, 1988; Werner and Smith, 1982). Some of the characteristics of these children are: (1) a positive belief about controlling or influencing their sources of stress; (2) a tendency to positively view change, even it causes pain or suffering; (3) an ability to feel deeply involved or committed to activities in their life; (4) an ability from infancy on to gain other people's positive attention; and (5) a strong ability to use faith in order to maintain a positive vision of a meaningful life.

The point of introducing these types of children is to recognize that life events are major sources of stress, but all children do not necessarily experience negative stress in reaction to all of life's changes. Keep in mind that factors like a child's personality, coping ability, perception of change, and the use of stress-reducing activities can all play a major role in determining the level of stress experienced by that child. On the other hand, however, some important research shows us that certain common life events in children's lives consistently place demands on them. If these changes are frequent or intense enough, this negative stress can lead to many of the warning signs noted or even evolve into health and behavioral problems.

Doctor David Elkind (1981) in his book, *The Hurried Child,* provides one version of a life event scale which gives an estimate of the impact of various changes in a child's life that stresses them. Review the following scale, add up the total points for all of the items a child experiences in the past year, and determine whether the child you are evaluating is undergoing too many changes and too much stress:

LIFE EVENT SCALE FOR CHILDREN

Stress	*Points*	*Child's Score*
Parent dies	100	
Parents divorce	73	
Parents separate	65	
Parent travels as part of job	63	
Close family member dies	63	
Personal illness or injury	53	
Parent remarries	50	
Parent fired from work	47	
Parents reconcile	45	
Mother goes to work	45	
Change in health of a family member	44	
Mother becomes pregnant	40	
School difficulties	39	
Birth of a sibling	39	
School readjustment (new teacher or class)	39	
Change in family's financial condition	38	
Injury or illness of a close friend	37	
Starts a new (or changes) extra-curricular activity (music lessons, Brownies, and so forth)	36	
Change in number of fights with siblings	35	
Threatened by violence at school	31	
Theft of personal possessions	30	
Changes responsibilities at home	29	

Older brother or sister leaves home	29
Trouble with grandparents	29
Outstanding personal achievement	28
Move to another city	26
Move to another part of town	26
Receives or loses a pet	25
Changes personal habits	24
Trouble with teacher	24
Change in hours with baby-sitter or at day-care center	20
Move to a new house	20
Changes to a new school	20
Changes play habits	19
Vacations with family	19
Changes friends	18
Attends summer camp	17
Changes sleeping habits	16
Change in number of family get-togethers	15
Changes eating habits	15
Changes amount of TV viewing	13
Birthday party	12
Punished for not "telling the truth"	11

A high score on this scale is the result of experiencing several life changes or key stressors in a child's life within a relatively short period of time. A high score, above 300 points, indicates that a child is probably having a lot of stress and more likely to be at risk of having a stress-related problem. A low score, below 150 points, reflects that a child is experiencing a small number of changes or key stressors and is less likely to have a stress-related problem. A score between 150 and 300 points indicates that a child has a moderate to high level of stress and has a better than average chance of showing some symptoms of stress. Remember, though, a high score does not mean a child will have health problems. As mentioned above, there are other factors which can influence whether life events will develop into negative or positive stress. Thus, the strength of using this scale is to: (1) give us another barometer which we can use in making us more aware of children's sources of stress; (2) help us determine if children are being exposed to too many life changes; and (3) assist us in linking up children's symptoms of stress with their sources of stress.

The above list of life events is not all-inclusive. Rather, it is a list of common life events which are present in today's children and which can cause stress. There are obviously many more sources of stress in children.

To help in identifying and understanding the impact of these stressors on children, let us briefly take an historical and comprehensive look at some major social, health, and life changes which have taken place in the last two centuries.

Historical Lessons and Modern-Day Stressors of Children

The Danish philosopher, Soren Kierkegaad, once said "Life must be lived forwards, but can only be understood backwards." With this thought in mind, let us try to increase our understanding of the problem of stress in children by briefly examining past events which have significantly impacted on this modern-day dilemma.

To begin our brief historical review, let us first note that in the past 100 years, our American society has: (1) entered into the atomic age, the space age, and the computer age; (2) experienced an increase in life expectancy at birth of over 57 percent since 1900, from 47 years to over 74 years today; (3) been a part of a global population which has more than doubled in the past 50 years; and (4) lived in a time period where 75 percent of all the information that has ever been known in history of the world has been developed and introduced only in the last 25 years. In sum, like no other time in human history are children exposed to so much change and so many stressors. As Doctor Hans Selye, the father of the study of stress, pointed out, Americans today are having to cope with more than 50,000 new stressors which were not present at the beginning of the twentieth century (Selye, 1978).

Some romanticists suggest the solution to a stress-filled life is to go back in time and re-create a simpler life-style like our forefathers and foremothers. This is not a new idea. Rousseau, during the period of Enlightenment, believed civilization and luxury spoiled people physically and corrupted them mentally. He suggested men and women go back to a simpler and more natural style of life to improve their health. In regard to this idea, Rousseau wrote in *Discours sur les sciences et les art*, "Beneath the rustic garb of the plowman and not beneath the gildings of the courtier will strength and vigor of the body be found" (Rousseau, 1946, p. 46). The problem with this view, of course, is that we cannot go back in time, nor would we want to. A good reason for why we shouldn't turn back the clock can be seen by the following example on increased life expectancy and decreased death rates of young children.

During the last two centuries, as indicated above in point two, Americans have experienced an unprecedented increase in life expectancy. In general, the major reason for this dramatic increase is because infant mortality rates have equally, in the opposite direction, also undergone a dramatic change. For instance, Thomas McKeown, professor emeritus at the University of Birmingham, England, points out that:

> It is no exaggeration to say that health, especially the health of infants and young children, has been transformed since the eighteenth century. For the first time in history, a mother knows it is likely that all her children will live to maturity. Before the nineteenth century, only about three out of every 10 newborn infants lived beyond the age of 25. Of the seven who died, two or three never reached their first birthday, and five or six died before they were six. Today, in developed countries fewer than one in 20 children die before they reach adulthood (McKeown, 1984).

There are several factors which have been responsible for this decrease in death rates of young children and, consequently, the increase in life expectancy of the general population. The predominant reason is a reduction of deaths in children from infectious disease. There is some disagreement as to which factors were most responsible for a reduction of death from infectious disease. However, most experts believe that increased food supplies, better nutrition, improved hygiene, purification of water, efficient sewage, the pasteurization of milk, and improved working and living conditions were the major factors which increased our resistance to, and reduced our contact with, infectious diseases. To a lesser extent, immunizations and medical interventions also played a role. And finally, a major role was played by the changes in reproductive behaviors which caused the birth rate to decline and allowed the above advances not to be overtaken by a too rapidly increasing population.

Given this example, it is easier for us to understand why we would not want to trade today's life-styles for yesterday's. What parent would want to see the majority of their children die before reaching the age of 25? Relatively speaking, the exposure to negative stress seems preferable.

Another lesson contained in this example of life expectancy and death rates of children is that there has been a significant changing pattern of disease in the twentieth century. Microorganisms no longer pose the greatest threat to Americans and our children. Rather, health problems related to behavioral and environmental causes are now our major concern. As a result, the leading causes of death in our children are no longer tuberculosis, gastroenteritis, flu, or pneumonia. Our youngsters today now die from motor vehicle accidents, other accidents, substance abuse, suicide, and homicide, and to a lesser degree, biological and environmentally related deaths such as heart disease and congenital anomalies.

In other words, the reduction in infectious disease and the increase in life expectancy certainly provides us with health benefits, but this shifting pattern of disease, at the same time, presents us with many new health burdens. Stress appears to be a major contributing factor to these new burdens. Furthermore, when we consider the dramatic changes which have taken place in recent history, the fact that stress-related health and social problems in children are increasing can now be better understood as, perhaps, a very natural response to an evolution of change in the lives of children.

In addition to the above health and social changes which have taken place in the last two centuries, we should also take into account some of the more recent changes which children are living with in contemporary society. Major institutions like family and school are undergoing great alterations, and children are being asked to cope with such major pressures as sex and drugs even in grade school. For instance, consider the fact that in America children live in a society where:

- three in five children born today will be raised in a single-parent household;
- two of four children age 13 and under live in a dual-career family unit;
- one in six has tried marijuana and one in three have tried drinking before ninth grade;
- the share of girls under 15 who have had sex has tripled in two decades;
- the rate of suicide for youths under 15 has tripled since 1960;
- rates of child abuse are increasing;
- over seven million children are cared for in family day-care homes or in child-care centers;
- second-grade curriculum is now in first grade, and the first-grade curriculum is being taught in kindergarten;
- quality time spent with parents is decreasing to about an average of 8 minutes a day;
- the numbers of latchkey children are growing;
- television has become a substitute for family interaction; and
- one out of five children are raised in poverty.

When all these changes and factors are totalled, we can see how the magic and innocence of childhood is being altered by the real pressures of a changing and stress-filled style of life.

Children aren't children anymore. They are, as David Elkind points out, "hurried children" who are growing up too fast and too soon (Elkind, 1981). Children are facing a host of physical, psychological, and social changes which create enormous pressure on them. They are no longer dying from flu, but they are being asked to cope with more major stressors than any other previous generation of children. As a result, it is no wonder why health experts report seeing an alarming increase in stress-induced health problems in today's children.

HELPING CHILDREN TO COPE

The rising and alarming rate of stress in children represents the failures of our successes in improving the health of children. Tuberculosis, pneumonia, polio, and ear abscesses are no longer major threats to our children's health. The infant mortality rate is much lower than it has been in the past, and today, our children's life expectancy is at an all-time high. However, the paradox of life and health teaches us that as one major health problem is bumped off the top of the list, there is always another health problem to take its place. In this sense, our past successes in greatly reducing the threat of infectious disease in children has presented us with new problems to overcome. These new problems are the failures of our success, and the new health nemesis for today's children is stress.

Stress, as Hans Selye taught us, is a natural part of life which cannot be avoided, but harmful levels of stress must be reduced and controlled for today's children to achieve and maintain a healthy style of life. Thus, the challenge now facing parents education, health and leisure services professionals is one of helping children to coexist with the ever presence of stress. This is a formidable task, for many of the changes mentioned above which contribute to our hurried and stress-filled lives are difficult to alter. As a result, we must be creative in developing stress management programs and act like the great musical artist, Duke Ellington, when he composed music. Duke Ellington explained, "Since many of his musicians could reach and play certain notes beautifully, but not all notes, he had to write his music within limits." So too, do we need to compose stress management plans within society's and our own limitations. The task is difficult, but if we want our children to "sing" we must try.

The Need for Comprehensive Stress Management

In the Platonic dialogue, *Charmides,* Socrates criticized the Greek physicians for foolishly neglecting the whole when attempting to heal a part. Socrates (Plato [translated by Spraguel], 1973) argued that: "Just as one must not attempt to cure the eyes without the head or the head without the body, so neither the body without the soul."

So too must we take a holistic and comprehensive approach to managing stress for our children. We must focus on the whole child, but we must not limit our interventions to only the child. That is, comprehensive and effective stress management needs to include parental, life-style, and societal changes.

Intervening in Childhood Stress

Intervention methods for managing stress in children are numerous. These methods can include, as Doctor Louis A. Chandler, Clinic Director of the Psychoeducational Clinic at the University of Pittsburgh, points out: (1) environmental manipulation, (2) child behavior management techniques, (3) parent counseling, (4) parent education and training, and (5) individual and group psychotherapy (Chandler, 1985).

In many cases, depending upon the source of stress in children, any or a combination of all of these approaches could be appropriate. Without further information, it would be impossible for the readers of this chapter to diagnose and decide which method is best for the child they are concerned about. However, this chapter should make the reader more aware of the causes and problems of stress in children, and the following information should provide some approaches for helping children to coexist with stress.

In general, a comprehensive intervention strategy should attend to: (1) helping children develop stress-reducing skills; (2) providing opportunities for children to channel and dissipate their stress; (3) nurturing a stress-resilient child; and (4) manipulating the physical, psychological, and social environment of children to reduce and control the number of harmful stressors in a child's life.

Stress-Reducing Skill Development

When a child is under negative stress, no matter whether it is small or large stress, it is a very unpleasant state. It is a state which you immediately want the child to get out of, because left unattended, the stress response can lead to physical and emotional strain and serious health problems. Thus, a fast and good way to start managing stress is to give children effective "first aid" for immediate relief from distress.

This first aid for negative stress is helping children to develop and use techniques for relaxation. Relaxation, however, is not automatically achieved by just saying "I need to relax more." Relaxation is achieved only after children establish and practice relaxation and stress-reduction techniques on a regular basis.

There are many techniques for relaxing and reducing stress which can be adapted for children. Try several of these techniques with children and help them choose the one that they find most comfortable and agreeable to their taste and life-style. Some of these stress-reducing activities are: (1) programs on deep breathing, or a particular variation of deep breathing called the Quieting Reflex for children, better known as Kiddie QR; (2) programs for calming the mind like the Relaxation Response and meditation; (3) visualization exercise which aim at producing feelings of relaxation by using a child's imagination to think about and create relaxing scenes in their mind; (4) autogenic training where the basic idea is to have children learn how to tell their bodies to relax; and (5) physical exercises like progressive muscle relaxation, or just some good physical activity like walking, running, or playing a game which uses a lot of physical movement and energy.

Stress Breakers for Dissipating Stress

Relaxation and stress-reducing techniques are good activities for children to use in controlling stress and reducing the stress response. However, there are many times and situations when children, or the adults who are working with children, just do not want to use these methods for controlling stress. In these cases, a second strategy for managing stress involves using stress breakers. They are simple and comfortable to use and very helpful in channelling, dissipating, and breaking-up stress. A list of some stress breakers are provided below which should be used to supplement, but not put in place of, some good old-fashioned play time. Children need to be children, and play is very important for helping children to be healthy and less stressed. So one of the best ways to help children deal with their stress is to allow for leisure-time activities and recreational fun.

When children are experiencing negative stress and their stress response tips their physical and emotional levels of activity out of balance, let the children have some playtime, with friends if possible, and select one or more of the following stress breakers suggested by Doctor Kuczen (1982, 1984) and others to bring them back into balance. These activities give children a break away from stress and a chance to unwind. Stress breakers and leisure-time activities aren't the ultimate solution, but they can help children to regain control of their stress. Have children try one or two of the following stress breakers a day:

STRESS BREAKERS FOR CHILDREN

- Enjoy a good laugh, watch a silly TV show, tell a joke, be a little silly yourself
- Find images in the clouds
- Hunt for a four-leaf clover
- Go fishing
- Go to a movie
- Play a game with parents or friends, like hide-and-seek
- Take a camera and go find an interesting picture
- Color, paint, doodle
- Read a favorite story
- Plan a pretend vacation
- Get a backrub
- Give someone a big hug
- Wrestle or tickle Mom or Dad
- Shake it all out vigorously— shake arms, hands, body, legs, and head for a few seconds and then suddenly relax
- Call a special friend on the telephone
- Observe fish swimming in a tank
- Listen to the rain fall
- Have a picnic
- Take a nice walk
- Sing, dance
- Talk to a friend
- Keep a diary, write a journal
- Get lost in a nice positive daydream
- Play with a family pet
- Be alone for a few minutes
- Have a good cry
- Make up fairy tales
- Make some popcorn
- Plan and rehearse how to handle stress the next time

Developing Stress-Resilient Children

The above two strategies are good for helping children to deal with their immediate stress. They are good coping activities which help children to physically and emotionally reduce negative stress when it occurs. However, we cannot afford to stop here. Adults must also use strategies which help insulate and protect children from stress throughout their lives. The way to do this, says Doctor Emmy E. Werner (1988), is by creating a balance between the stressful life events which a child faces and the protective factors which enhance a child's resiliency to stress. As Doctor Werner (1988, p. 95) found in her research on resilient children, "As long as the balance between stressful life events and protective factors is manageable for children they can cope."

The major advice which Doctor Werner (1982, 1988) gives to help tilt the balance of stress in favor of the child includes the willingness to:

- accept children's temperamental idiosyncracies and allow them some experiences that challenge, but do not overwhelm, their coping abilities;
- convey to children a sense of responsibility and caring and, in turn, reward them for helpfulness and cooperation;
- encourage a child to develop a special interest, hobby, or activity that can serve as a source of gratification and self-esteem;
- model, by example, a conviction that life makes sense despite the inevitable adversities that each of us encounters; and
- encourage children to reach out beyond their nuclear family to a beloved relative or friend.

Finally, Doctor Werner's (1982) research on resilient children teaches us that adults can help children, even when they are experiencing high levels of stress, if children encounter people who give meaning to their lives and a reason of commitment and caring. "Each of us can impart this gift to a child," said Doctor Werner (1988, p. 97), "in the classroom, on the playground, in the neighborhood, and in the family—if we care enough." This stress-protecting strategy helps to insulate the child from negative stress. They become less vulnerable and more resilient to stress as a sense of purpose in their life acts like glue which can hold them together when experiencing high levels of stress.

Manipulating the Environment

It is not always effective, nor is it always right or fair, to ask the child to constantly adjust to a stress-inducing situation. Thus, helping children to coexist with stress and restore balance many times requires adults to alter the child's environment. This can be accomplished by having adults take on the responsibility to either remove a child from a stress-filled environment or change the environment in a positive way.

Sometimes environmental manipulation can be accomplished with a reasonable amount of effort. For instance, parents can have a great deal of influence on helping to encourage certain friendships, making sure children have time to play, reinforcing certain healthy behaviors, cutting down of chores, reducing expectations, or in choosing proper food, shelter, and clothing. Parents can also work with teachers and the school environment to help reduce stress. For example, sometimes it is quite appropriate for teachers and parents to agree to transfer a child to another classroom if the change appears beneficial.

On the other hand, environmental manipulation can be very helpful but also very difficult to procure. For instance, there is a great need in society for more accessible and affordable child care. However, implementing environmental changes, such as this, come from well-organized efforts which understand how to influence community, organizational, and political processes. As one can imagine, this is not an easy task, as manipulating the environment in this manner requires much more than just individual effort.

Social change is possible and it should not be overlooked. For instance, in regard to the need for child care, we have seen adults who have children and attend college, organize and initiate evening child care for their children while they go to classes. Similarly, we have known individuals such as Lyn Coffery-Edelman, a mother of four and a secretary from Rochester, New York, who helped in organizing a local contingent of concerned parents to travel to Washington, D.C. to lobby for legislation on child-care matters. Efforts like these are certainly demanding, time consuming, and perhaps the most difficult to implement. Nonetheless, this strategy must not be overlooked, for environmental manipulation and social change many times contains the most potential for reducing childhood stress.

ONE LAST WORD

A single acorn can grow and develop into a massive oak tree by means of natural growth; no commitment is necessary. Likewise, a young colt matures into a strong and powerful horse by instinct. But childhood development is not just natural and instinctive. It is greatly shaped by the decisions and commitments made by the adults in the lives of children. Thus, use the information provided in this chapter to become more aware of childhood stress and make the commitment to develop a sound strategy for managing stress in children. Yes, stress will always be a fact of life for our children, but it should not have to be a way of life for our children.

Chapter Ten

BECOMING A MEMBER OF THE TEAM

INTRODUCTION:
WHY A COMPREHENSIVE COMMUNITY APPROACH?

This question was perhaps best answered by Jenkins, MacDicken, and Ormsby when they stated, "No single individual, agency, or professional discipline has the necessary knowledge, skills or resources to provide all of the services needed by families where abuse or neglect occurs. Only through the development of a comprehensive, community-wide approach to the total problem of child maltreatment can any community expect to resolve these problems" (1979, p. 1). They continue by stating "Effective service delivery must involve the combined skills of various disciplines" (1979, p. 1).

Cohn, when discussing prevention of child abuse and community organization activities, responds to the question posed by stating, "To increase the availability of social service, health, and education resources and of the other supports that reduce family stress, community organization activities will be necessary. A community-based planning or coordinating body is certainly required, one that represents the views of different community groups and agencies. This body will have the important role of determining priorities from proposed prevention programs" (1983, p. 29). She states further, "To be effective, prevention programs must be developed at the local level and must be tailored to local needs, values, and norms. This can only happen if local groups are actively involved in the development of such programs" (1983, p. 30).

Kempe, when discussing the "basic ingredients" of a community-wide approach to child abuse intervention and treatment, states, "First, there must be recognition that putting the whole burden of responsibility on the social worker will no longer work and that a broadly based team effort—using experts from many disciplines—should take the place of that system" (1978, pp. 114–115).

Summit, in *Dealing with Sexual Child Abuse,* offers additional rationale for a comprehensive community approach to child abuse. When discussing the process of resocialization of the abusive family he addresses the ability of the primary therapist to meet all of the needs of all members of the family and to keep up with the ever-increasing work load. He counsels, "Therapists who deal with abusive families should learn to be receptive to many diverse therapeutic adjuncts if they are to avoid being overwhelmed with more demands than they can meet" (Bulkley et al., 1982, p. 26).

Finally, Mayhall and Norgard discuss the need for a shared responsibility in the battle against child abuse and neglect. According to them the positive change in the alarming rate of incidence will occur only when abusive families have a wide range of needs addressed. These include:

- belief that change is desirable
- belief that change is possible
- economic resources to survive and change
- supportive interpersonal relationships
- long-range supportive services
- competence in basic social skills
- competence in basic work skills
- competence in appropriate parenting skills

(1983, p. 353)

They close their discussion by emphasizing the obvious when they state, "There is no one to whom the responsibility for valuing children and families and preventing child abuse and neglect can be delegated. Responsibility for change belongs to everyone. It begins in assessing where we are and acting on our best knowledge in order to achieve and maintain change" (p. 354).

The challenge, then, is for all disciplines and professionals who champion the rights of children or who contend their mission includes the fostering of social, emotional and physical growth and development of children to join forces.

OUTSIDE SUPPORT FOR RECREATION JOINING THE TEAM

Recreation and Leisure Services professionals may be surprised to learn that there is significant support for their team membership in the comprehensive community attack on child abuse and neglect. There may be some individual exceptions by uninformed or out-of-touch "professionals," but, overall, the climate is quite favorable for Recreation and Leisure Services professionals to contribute to the struggle against abuse in all three of the major phases: prevention, intervention and treatment. Several authors and authorities in child maltreatment have placed significant emphasis on the important role recreation can and should assume in the confrontation of abuse.

Isolation from the mainstream of the community mainstream has been identified repeatedly as a contributing factor in the apparent rise in abuse. People may be isolated in terms of geographical proximity or due to the fact that they are new to the community and simply unaware of its resources. This type of isolation may exist even when the family resides in the geographical center of the city or in one of its established neighborhoods. This type of social isolation may well be more difficult to overcome than that which is primarily geographical in nature. Having an automobile or other mode of transportation available may be all that is necessary to resolve the latter. Imagine, however, the frustration and anxiety that must result from realizing that simply securing transportation will not alleviate the isolation or suppress loneliness. Such overwhelming anxiety and frustration frequently displays itself as hostile, aggressive activity against those even more helpless who are "trapped" along with the parent or guardian. Straus, Gelles and Steinmetz when addressing ways to reduce domestic violence suggest we "integrate families into a network of kin and community" (1981, p. 240). They seem to be suggesting more of an effort than simply providing transportation as necessary. "Kin and community" challenges those who are concerned about coping with child abuse to:

- make a personal commitment
- make a professional commitment
- combine and unify resources with others who are equally concerned

Straus and his coauthors are calling for a community approach in combating a major contributor to family violence: social isolation. What better way to combat social isolation than through recreation participation?

The aforementioned authors confirm the role of recreation in preventing and treating family violence when they relate to the work done by James Prescott of the National Institute of Child Health and Development. They refer to one of Prescott's proposals as one of the "innovative methods for treating violent families" (1981, p. 236). What Prescott contends is something that many Recreation and Leisure Service professionals have been suggesting for years; namely, "experiencing pleasure and inflicting pain are incompatible in human beings" (1981, p. 236). It seems that the results of Prescott's research disclosed that "many violent individuals did not, and had not, experienced physical pleasure" (1981, p. 236). Prescott suggests that the experiencing of physical pleasure will make violent family members less violent. Prescott has offered an alternative to the traditional and sometimes sterile and dull counseling sessions that are held in the confines of the counselor's office or the conference room. "He has proposed that, instead of the numbing counseling session held in an office, counselors should take families skiing or swimming or camping. He believes that families need to learn to have fun with one another, and that if they do, there might be less violence" (Straus et al., p. 236).

Further support for the role of recreation is proffered by Mayhall and Norgard. They too address recreation's potential for combating the contributing factor of social isolation. They state, "Since families in which abuse and neglect takes place are usually isolated from the community, they may not even be aware of the recreational option available to them at no or minimal charges or have the energy to seek them out" (1983, p. 302). They point out that recreational opportunities are available through a variety of agencies for both adults and youth. Both private and public agencies such as churches, community park and recreation departments, and sports leagues are mentioned by Mayhall and Norgard. As to the value of recreation in combating abuse they state, "Recreation, in addition to structuring time, can be a healthy means of relieving stress, meeting people, developing skills, and having fun as a family" (1983, p. 302). They go on to point out, however, that, "Families in which abuse and/or neglect is common are not likely to seek out these possibilities on their own. Help in taking the first step and in developing enough connection with other people to get involved in the activities may be necessary" (1983, p. 302).

Later, in *Child Abuse and Neglect* Mayhall and Norgard address the role of recreation in the treatment process of child abuse confrontation. They point out that often the consequences of the abusive act or acts are so traumatic that perpetrators and victims alike cannot verbalize their problems or their feelings about their lives or the abuse. "Recreation or occupational therapy can be utilized as a method of encouraging these youths to work through their feelings and actually reach resolution to problems. Sports, games, and projects such as leather work, ceramics, etc. are used as the medium to conduct recreational and occupational therapy" (1983, p. 345). Such strong support should be cherished by recreation professionals, even though it is shared by our colleagues in Occupational Therapy.

In Chapter Nine, Doctors Linda and Joseph Balog address stress and children. In their chapter they discuss the negative stress that is heaped upon children by the hurrying of contemporary society. Society is paying a heavy and painful cost for this abusive tendency to hurry young people through childhood. Divorce, single-parent homes, an uncertain economy, dual-employed parents, and other social pressures are forcing children to take on adult roles before they are either physically and emotionally prepared. Schools often only exacerbate the stress and social abuse children are experiencing by applying pressure for academic excellence. Many children simply are not equipped to cope with the competition, test regulated schools that place heavy emphasis on the need to excel. This pressure is frequently increased on the child who has displayed a unique skill in sports, the arts, or in a particular academic area. The school often becomes an unwitting partner with parents in the "premature structuring" of the child. This stress may be damaging enough, but it may be further abusive, in that "What often happens is that the child becomes so specialized so early that other parts of his or her personality are somewhat underdeveloped" (Elkind: *The Hurried Child,* 1981, p. 177).

Elkind (1981, pp. 192–198) suggests that what is the business of recreation, play, may be the best "antidote to hurrying." In this respect, Elkind expresses the opinion that perhaps the best evidence of the degree to which our youth are hurried is the shortage of play opportunities available to them. Furthermore, he suggests that the abuse of hurrying can be defined as the social pressure on children to accommodate society rather than play. We can combat the abuse of hurrying our children by providing opportunities for children to play for the sake of play or to simply have fun. Elkind appears to be of the opinion that play is the most effective way to deal with childhood stress caused by the abusive hurrying of parents and the various social entities.

Wayne and Avery discuss the application of recreationally oriented activities in the important termination phase of the group therapy process for a group of mothers involved in a program of the Boston District Office of Children's Protection Services. The group members were saddened to see the group end, because it had also become a social focus of their lives. The group leader agreed to extend the group for three months and to concentrate on the social emphasis. The chosen activities were to enhance the social skills, self-concepts, self-confidence, community integration, and emotional independence of the group members (Wayne and Avery, 1980).

When discussing the results of the recreationally oriented group termination Wayne and Avery state, "All members sustained the positive personal and social gains they had made in the group. They continued to seek out new pleasant experiences, including family outings and vacations. During the stressful periods many were able to ask for therapeutic intervention before reverting back to old behaviors. Appropriate reaching out replaced destructive striking out" (1980, pp. 64–65). They relate further, "By encouraging the social and creative development of the group members, the termination phase was used as a time of transition instead of only as a time of ending. It was the important phase between being in treatment and being an independent, functioning, contributing adult. Though these women originally needed the greater intensity of the insight oriented discussion group, they made other important gains from the recreational and social aspects of this kind of termination phase" (1980, p. 65). The authors end their assessment of this group termination experience by stating, "The fact that members did not drop out of the group during the last few meetings, as frequently happens in group termination, attests to the positive contribution to individual members that this approach did make. The results were gratifying for everyone involved" (1980, p. 65).

What about other phases of the group treatment process? Wayne and Avery also discuss the use of recreational activities as a means of group initiation. In this particular instance the emphasis of the group was the prevention of abuse. The group leader requested referrals of young women in their twenties who were living isolated life-styles with young children. The contact in this instance was the Visiting Nurses who had knowledge of such women. The Visiting Nurses discussed group participation with women approved by the social workers. At the initial gathering of the women eventually selected for group participation it was explained that the group could be used to just talk over a cup of coffee or for activities. The young mothers quickly responded favorably to the activities suggestion. The leader intended the activities to act as a means to make women comfortable with each other and with the atmosphere. "Thus, the activities would not be presented as the group's aim, but rather as a means of reaching that goal" (1980, p. 52).

The activities had the additional benefits of:

- development of trust in the leader,
- provision of opportunities to discuss feelings about a variety of emotions, and
- providing the leader opportunities to observe the group member's ability to make decisions, cope with frustrations, and follow through on commitments.

When assessing the success of the recreation-oriented group Wayne and Avery state, "The group experience had broken through their isolation and had helped them to move into the world around them, a world with people who could provide the emotional support to help them not hurt their children" (1980, p. 59).

Frequently, victims of child abuse, particularly teenage victims, are placed in group homes. The National Advisory Committee for Juvenile Justice and Delinquency Prevention has noted the importance of leisure-time activity in its official definition of a group home. This definition suggests that recreation professionals have a key role to play in this particular aspect of abuse intervention and treatment. The 1980 standards define a group home as:

an open community-based residential facility which provides care for juveniles who can reasonably be expected to succeed in a nonrestrictive environment in which a substantial part of their time will ordinarily be spent in the surrounding community, attending school or working, pursuing leisure time activities, participating in community service programs recommended by the court or the treatment staff.

(*Standards,* 1980, p. 436)

As with their education, these children will likely require some professional guidance in their leisure-time choices. Leisure and recreation education may well be a primary need.

In summary, support for recreation's active participation in a comprehensive community approach to combat child abuse is substantial. Respected authorities in child maltreatment have either indirectly suggested its involvement by encouraging a multidisciplinary approach by all concerned with child welfare, or have defined its specific benefits in the prevention and treatment of abuse. Recreation (as a profession) has done little to engender such support, yet it does exist among some respected leaders (emphasis on "some"). The cornerstone for the building of recreation's respect and contribution to the team effort have been laid by those outside of our profession. The challenge now is for recreators to benefit the youth of contemporary society and the future by expanding the scope of support and by devising innovative ways to apply their craft.

SUPPORT FROM WITHIN

A review of contemporary Recreation and Leisure Service's professional literature reveals an abundance of support for active participation in the war against child abuse. This is not, or should not be, a revelation to the practitioner who is a graduate of a "legitimate" academic program. However, the eclectic nature of many comprehensive leisure services agencies has resulted in the employment of graduates of related academic programs. These individuals, though they make significant and valuable contributions, frequently are lacking in the foundations of Recreation and Leisure Services. Physical Education, Art, Industrial Arts and Dance students rarely (if ever) are required, or even encouraged, to enroll in courses addressing the foundations—goals, purpose or benefits—of participation in recreation programs. What follows is a brief review of the benefits identified by some Recreation and Leisure Studies scholars. Such evidence of "internal" support will hopefully further convince all personnel of the obligation to become committed to the struggle against child abuse.

The late, eminent scholar Charles K. Brightbill was of the opinion that leisure has a considerable influence on the development of personality. In *The Challenge of Leisure* he asks, "What would life be like for the child without the moments for play? What would it be like for all humans without leisure and the chance for its recreative use?" (1960, p. 70). Brightbill was also of the opinion that if through leisure people (including children) can create a world apart from the tensions and frustrations of daily living that the effects can be both preventative and therapeutic in terms of physical, psychological and social dysfunction (1960, pp. 86–88).

Meyer and Brightbill (1964, pp. 353–355) address the role of recreation in combating delinquency. They point out that juvenile delinquency results from one or more of several conditions, among which are family breakdown, lack of family emphasis or positive social values, adult exploitation, abuse, and neglect. When addressing the role of recreation in preventing delinquency, they point out that the community recreation staff member has a unique opportunity to identify children who may be in crisis—those who appear antagonistic, hostile, or apathetic (also indicators of possible abuse). Community recreation can also play a role in delinquency prevention by providing for opportunities for the satisfaction of needs not being met in the neglectful or abusive family. They cautioned that recreation is not likely to be the solution in and of itself; however, they did express the opinion that recreation does have a definite role in addressing the negative influences that lead to delinquency (abuse being one such influence).

Carlson, Deppe and MacLean (1963, pp. 18–19) contend that recreation is beneficial in numerous areas which have previously been identified as problem areas for abused children. Recreation may well be the least threatening or stressful setting to address development lags in the personal areas of physical development, mental and emotional health, ability to assume responsibility, character development, intellectual development, social adjustment, and aesthetic and spiritual values.

Richard Kraus, one of the more prolific Recreation and Leisure Studies scholars, addresses recreation's potential to address the isolation the abused child and family may be experiencing. He states, "At every age level, recreation contributes to healthy socialization. It provides an outstanding opportunity for children, youth, and adults to share enjoyable group pastimes with each other. In social clubs, sports teams, informal playground or community center groups, and similar settings, young people gain a sense of acceptance and close friendship with others" (1985, p. 11).

It is also Kraus (1984, pp. 122–123) who discusses the need for the human service focus by public recreation and park agencies. He states, "The conviction is widely shared that recreation professionals must return to the strong social-activism orientation that characterized the early decades of this movement. Proponents of this view argue that recreation must serve the disadvantaged, handicapped, and other populations, and must strive to achieve significant goals by reducing social pathology, contributing to neighborhood strengths, and building family unity and intergroup understanding." It appears that Kraus has struck at the very heart of the child abuse issue in this passage.

In perhaps one of the most significant articles ever published by the National Recreation and Park Association's *Parks and Recreation,* Gray and Greben (July 1974, p. 53) recommend that recreation and parks professionals initiate actions that will lead to the attainment of the following goals:

- Adapt a humanistic ethic as the central value system of the recreation movement.

- Develop and act on a social conscious that focuses park and recreation services on the great social problem of our time and develop programs designed to contribute to the amelioration of those problems.
- Develop a set of guidelines for programs that emphasize human welfare, human development, and social action.
- Foster integration, coherence, and growth in the recreation and park movement because our movement represents a major potential in the worldwide thrust for positive life experience.
- Reorganize and reorient our agencies in a way that will renew their energies, improve their sense of mission, and make them more responsive to human needs and social change.

The goals and others mentioned by Gray and Greben may well be served by the active confrontation of child abuse. Who would disagree that child abuse is a major social issue, or that it is deleterious to human welfare and development?

In summary, contemporary professional literature abounds with support for Recreation and Leisure Service's active role in the confrontation of child abuse. The scholars remind all of us, academics and practitioners alike, that we have a responsibility, even a mandate, to contribute to the amelioration of some of society's greatest ills. Our mission must be responsive to the needs of human welfare, human development, and to the need for a healthy society. The abuse of our children is perceived by many to be at the heart of a large number of our contemporary society's ills. From both within the Recreation and Leisure Services professional circles and from without another message is being conveyed. That is, recreation has a role to play and it is time to proceed.

RECREATION'S FOUNDATIONS AND ABUSE CONFRONTATION

It should come as no startling revelation to most Recreation and Leisure Service professionals to learn that their chosen career has some of its roots firmly planted in a concern over the abuse of children. An historical review of four pioneers of the modern recreation movement which began in the last half of the nineteenth century reveals that this concept of recreation as an intervention in the maltreatment of children is indeed not contemporary. Innovators such as Frederick Law Olmsted,

Jane Addams, Walter Vroom, and Joseph Lee chose to act against the effects of rampant urbanization on children during the industrialization of the United States. The "Rapid unplanned growth of the world's great commercial centers had begun to make urban life intolerable by the 1850's" (Fabos, Milde and Weinmayr, 1970, p. 17).

Children were the most obvious victims of urban explosion. They often had no place to play other than in dangerous, crowded streets or on narrow stoops. Children were frequently maimed or fatally injured under the wheels of wagons or from falls from stoops or the tops of the increasingly towering buildings.

Other forms of abuse were also inflicted upon the youthful victims of industrial expansion. It was common for children to be arrested and jailed for public disorder (playing) in the streets. While incarcerated, children were frequently physically abused and even killed for the odious crime of recreating in the streets or under the window of a cantankerous neighbor.

The conditions of inadequate play space, inadequate schools, poor sanitation, cramped living quarters, and the economic exploitation of children and their parents created the stage for adult violence against children. Vroom, when writing of the conditions facing children of the era, stated that the children

> are driven from their crowded homes in the morning . . . are chased from the streets by police when they attempt to play, and beaten with the broom handle of the janitor's wife when found in the hallway, or on the stairs. No wonder they learn to chew and smoke tobacco before they can read, and take a fiendish delight in breaking windows, in petty thievery, and in gambling their pennies.
>
> (Vroom, 1894, p. 286)

The uncontrolled, helter-skeltered urban development negatively affected family structure. Families that had worked together on the small farms and had hunted, fished, and roamed the woods and plains together in search of food or just to occupy their limited leisure were now faced with the stresses of urban living. Parents, initially attracted by the promised riches or wealth of the cities, had to take more and more time away from the family in order to pay the grossly inflated costs of food and housing. Mother was, for the first time, forced to seek work outside of the home. Often the only work opportunities were in crowded, unsanitary, and dangerous factories that paid ridiculously low salaries. Some luckier mothers were able to secure positions as domestics with wealthy families. The salaries were as low or lower than those in the factories, but at least the working conditions were less crowded, more sanitary, and not as dangerous.

The economic crisis frequently meant that the children of these disillusioned families were forced to drop out of school (if they were fortunate enough to even begin) in order to secure employment. Daughters often worked alongside their mothers in the urban sweatshops or as domestics. The boys were likely to be subjected to back-breaking labor in factories, steel mills, mines or on the docks of port cities. The children, as their parents, had few opportunities for relief from the soot, concrete, unbearable heat or cold, noise, crime, crowding and the other stresses related to the urban conditions. But help was on the way.

Frederick Law Olmsted

In New York City there had been a long-recognized need for open spaces. In 1857, as a result of public demand, construction was begun on Central Park. The park construction was in response to such public sentiment as was demonstrated by an article in a city newspaper addressed to elected officials. It read in part:

> It is a very general complaint that there is not in this great city, nor in its environs, any one proper spot, where its numerous inhabitants can enjoy, with convenience, that exercise that is necessary for health and amusement.

> (Doell and Fitzgerald, 1954, p. 25)

Selected as the primary architects for the project were Calvert Vaux and Frederick Law Olmsted, the latter being the principal force in the park's design. It was Olmsted's belief that parks should provide opportunities for "neighborly" recreation that can be counteractive to the "degeneration and demoralization" of urban areas. He held that parks should by their design foster close relationships for families as association between children and their parents (Stevenson, 1977, p. 300).

Olmsted was deeply concerned about the welfare of children and reflected this concern via his park design and his correspondence to his longtime friend, Charles Loring Brace. Brace made his lifetime work the Children's Aid Society. In 1853 Olmsted urged him to "Go ahead with the Children's Aid and get up parks, gardens, music, dancing schools, reunions which will be so attractive as to force into contact the good and bad, the gentlemanly and the rowdy. And the state ought to assist these sort of things as it does Schools and Agricultural Societies" (Roper, 1973, p. 94). Thirty-one years later, reflecting on the accomplishments of the years, he again displayed his concern for children. He wrote to Brace, "You decidedly have the best and most worthily successful life of all I have known. The C.A. is the most satisfactory of all the benevolent works of our time" (Roper, 1973, p. 401).

Olmsted then can be accurately described as more than a landscape architect. He was a man of compassion who saw the value of recreation and parks in combating the abuses being heaped upon the nation's youth by a society out of control. His works are more than 100 years later fulfilling his mission.

Jane Addams

A key player in the drama that unfolded in the late 1800s was the founder of Chicago's Hull House, Jane Addams. The conditions in Chicago during the 1880s were as deplorable as those in New York City. Settlement houses (now referred to as neighborhood centers) such as Hull House were founded in the slum neighborhoods of the nation's large cities. The founders sought to help poor people—particularly immigrants—"adjust to American life by providing services concerned with education, religious activities, family life, and community improvement" (Kraus, 1971, p. 182).

One of the strongest advocates for the role of recreation in the mission of settlement houses was Miss Addams. She and her able assistant and longtime friend, Ellen Starr, saw recreation as a means of controlling crime and other forms of asocial behavior. She expressed her support when she stated, "It is as if our cities had not yet developed a sense of responsibility in regard to the life of the streets, and continually forget that recreation is stronger than vice and that recreation alone stifle the best for vice" (Kraus, 1971, p. 182).

Addams was truly a driven woman in her quest to improve the quality of life for Chicago's immigrant inner-city dwellers. Davis describes her commitment and energy:

Jane went from the Women's Club to the anarchist Sunday school, from elegant receptions in the palatial townhouses of Chicago's Gold Coast to safaris through the worst slums, from lecturing to some of the wealthiest women in the city to teaching poor and dirty children how to model clay and cut out Greek vases from colored paper.

(Davis, 1973, p. 58)

Addams' concern for the welfare of the children of Chicago's slums was demonstrated in her aggressive negotiations with property owner William Kent in 1892. Kent was the owner of a ramshackled building near Hull House. Addams wanted the property for a playground. She was affected deeply by the plight of the children and the fact that they had no safe places to play and develop. Her skill as a negotiator was demonstrated not only by Kent's donation of the property but by the additional fact that she convinced him to pay for the demolition of the old building and for the taxes on the property (Linn, 1968, p. 127). This action led to the development of the first public playground in Chicago, one that would become the model for others in Chicago and throughout the country. Due to the efforts of Miss Addams, an obscure Chicago property owner became one of the unsung heros of the recreation movement and of one of the earliest efforts to combat the societal abuse of children.

Addams and Starr were to some extent guided in their quest of creative play opportunities by the familiarity with the work of Friedrick Froebel. Froebel argued that children should be treated as human beings and helped to learn through opportunities for creative play. It was this quest that led to the establishment of the kindergarten at Hull House (Davis, 1973, pp. 66–67).

In addition to the playground and the kindergarten Addams and Starr offered a wide variety of activities to the children and their parents. Some of these activities included a boy's club, a club for employed girls, lectures by college faculty and clergy, Italian Evenings, German Klatches, games for kids, singing, dancing, and discussion groups for women (Davis, 1973, p. 67).

In summary, Jane Addams' life was devoted to enhancing the lives of others, particularly children. She was a strong advocate for the role of recreation in combating society's abuse of children. She not only was one of the original founders of the Playground Association of America, but she also contended early in her illustrious career that social work, recreation, and education were similar functions. It may be good for professionals in these three services to remind themselves occasionally of this last point that the Hull House experience demonstrated so successfully.

Walter Vroom

Another early advocate of recreation as a means of counteracting abuse, Walter Vroom, was quoted earlier. He described the conditions facing the inner-city children of the time. Vroom, who was the founder of the New York Society for Parks and Playgrounds, in 1890 pointed out to the citizens of New York City that in their city there were "350,000 children without a single public playground they could call their own" (Kraus, 1971, p. 183). Vroom led the fight in New York City to make some of the 6000-plus acres of parklands available for children and to locate playgrounds in areas where the greatest number of children in need would have access. He rallied educators, social workers, reformers, church leaders, business leaders, newspaper publishers, and civic leaders and officials to address the issue discussed by a prominent physician: "The varied opportunities of a park would educate him and his family in the enjoyment of open-air pleasures. Deprived of these, he and his are educated into the ways of disease and vice by the character of their surroundings" (Kraus, 1971, p. 184). Vroom is simply another example of one who dedicated his time and resources to addressing the plight of disadvantaged and maltreated children through the provision of recreational opportunities. He was a vehement or passionate proponent of the importance of play or recreation to the favorable growth and development of children and ultimately to the preservation of a civilized life-style in America's urban areas.

Joseph Lee

Born in 1862 to a wealthy New England family, Joseph Lee was to become one of "the most influential of the pioneers of the recreation movement" (Kraus, 1971, p. 245). He was to become known as the father of the American playground. At the age of 20 he participated in a survey done by Boston's Family Welfare Society. The survey was of play opportunities available to Boston's youth. He was dismayed and shocked into taking action when he saw boys arrested and detained for simply playing in the streets. His reactions resulted in the establishment of a playground that he both organized and supervised. Not satisfied with this action he went on to create a model playground for Boston's children that was located on Columbus Avenue.

Lee, who was the president of the Playground Association of American from 1910 until his 1937 death, felt play was too important to children to leave it purely to chance. He felt it required responsible leadership. He also professed the child's need to be exposed to a wide variety of recreational activities. Lee saw, according to Kraus, children's "play as an important factor in combating social pathology, not in the specific sense of its preventing or reducing juvenile delinquency, but because of its positive contributions to physical fitness, opportunities for group involvements, sense of joy, and appreciation of beauty" (1971, p. 247).

SUMMARY

The founders of modern recreation demonstrated with dramatic commitment their convictions that children are the business of recreation. Olmsted, Addams, Vroom, Lee and others dedicated their lives and resources to provide recreational opportunities to combat the abuse of this nation's children by a society consumed by the concerns of economic growth and industrial expansion. Perhaps in their own ways they knew what today's experts on the needs of children tell us today; namely, children have:

- the need to achieve
- the need for economic security
- the need to belong
- the need for love and affection
- the need for self-respect through participation
- the need for variety as relief from boredom and ignorance
- the need to feel free from intense feelings of guilt
- the need to be free from fear

They obviously felt that recreation offered significant opportunities for children to realize their potentials.

Finally, a review of recreation's foundations and the contemporary literature in child abuse reveals that recreation has significant support for participation in a comprehensive community approach to abuse prevention, intervention, and treatment.

Yet, recreation professionals may find that their individual communities view the issue of child abuse from the traditional point of view; namely, it is only a social work concern. Consequently, recreators choosing to become active team members may have to educate preventive services leaders as to the foundations of recreation; its benefits; its potential contributions to prevention, intervention and treatment; the scope of services available; and even the type of academic preparation staff, particularly those with training in therapeutic recreation. It, also, may be helpful to convey a familiarity with the child abuse literature — particularly that related to indicators, needs of victims and perpetrators, and the dynamics of abusive families. It is regrettable, but recreation professionals frequently are not perceived by social workers, physicians, and educators as human service colleagues. If this is the case, the recreation agency may have to initiate the dialogue to ensure that the welfare of the community's children is truly being guarded by a comprehensive community child abuse team.

WHAT IF A TEAM DOESN'T EXIST?

The research conducted in preparation of the chapter related to frequency of abuse disclosed a regrettable truth: in many locales the battle against child abuse is poorly manned and even more poorly organized. As one state official remarked, "It pains me to admit this, but quite frankly there are communities in our state where one agency literally has no idea what the other one is doing. Consequently, not only do we have duplicity of reports, but a lot of kids fall between the cracks." Similar comments were made by four other state-level child protective services officials. Apparently, then, some recreation professionals will yet today be situated in communities lacking a well-organized team effort. If this is the unfortunate situation, why not make an effort to rectify the problem? Perhaps our courses relating to organization and leadership could be of some benefit. Do you have an obligation to the community's children?

What To Do

If the recreation administrator or one of his/her staff decide to initiate a comprehensive community approach (and why not?), there are some suggestions that may be useful. Erickson et al. (1984, p. 61) advise the following:

- contact governmental, private, and volunteer agencies
  - a) child protective services
  - b) police
  - c) schools
  - d) social services
  - e) medical facilities
  - f) medical associations
  - g) Parents Anonymous, etc.
  - h) mental health agencies
  - i) visiting nurse organizations
  - j) fellow recreation professionals
  - k) clergy, ecumenical counsel, etc.
- keep the eventual task force to a workable size (5–8 people)

It may also be advisable to:

- get supervisor approval. The community recreation director should obtain approval of mayor, city counsel, etc.
- familiarize yourself with legal mandates and,
- keep the local media advised

The task force will be responsible for drafting the "plan of attack," which will include defining responsibilities and lines of communication. The intent is to develop a unified and comprehensive application of community resources. This will require a candid assessment of the strengths and weaknesses in the community, particularly any weak links in the network.

The task force must remain cognizant of the need to educate the entire community. Therefore, a well-designed program of community workshops, hearings, etc. should be developed. Quite simply, abuse cannot be confronted if it is not reported.

FINAL NOTE

Child abuse can most effectively be combated through a comprehensive community approach. Authorities in the prevention and treatment of abuse have testified to the fact that the scope of the problem dictates a multidisciplinary approach. Some authorities have identified recreation as a key component in both the prevention and treatment of abuse. Likewise, the founders of the recreation and playground movements were strong advocates for the rights of children and the role of recreation in combating what they perceived as societal abuse of America's youth.

The support of recreation's participation in a comprehensive approach to abuse exists, both within its own historical foundations and from other related services. The challenge, then, is for recreation professionals to pursue a place on the team, to serve when drafted, or to initiate the team.

Chapter Eleven

DEVELOPING ABUSE POLICIES

INTRODUCTION

C hapters Fourteen and Fifteen address measures Recreation and Leisure Service agencies can take to combat abuse. Programs are key to the agency's role in abuse intervention and treatment, as is a plan for the recruitment, screening, and hiring of personnel. These measures, however, may have little consequence if the agency does not formulate, implement, disseminate and enforce policies on child abuse, particularly ones related to the reporting of suspected abuse. Failure to establish such policies may inadvertently commit the Recreation and Leisure Services agency to inaction and the projection of the impression of abuse tolerance. The results of such inaction and distorted public image could result in numerous less-than-positive consequences to the agency, the community and the youthful participants.

First, in a abuse-sensitive community the Recreation and Leisure Services agency (as all youth-serving agencies) will likely be under close scrutiny by parents and child protective bodies. "Lag time" between incidence of suspected abuse and reporting may not be an available luxury to the agency administration. Indecisiveness that results in "outsiders" taking the initiative to disclose and report the suspected abuse will, in all likelihood, result in a crippling loss of faith or trust in the agency's leadership and mission. Unfortunately, in today's media climate hesitancy to act is often distorted and portrayed by innuendo or direct accusation as a cover-up, a condoning of criminal behavior or gross mismanagement. The lack of a clearly defined child abuse policy will likely, unfortunately, only lend credence to these fabricated accusations.

As to be discussed in Chapter Twelve caution in the recruitment, screening and hiring of personnel and volunteers is key in the prevention of abuse and its intervention and treatment. As many experienced administrators can attest, foolproof personnel policies do not exist, except perhaps in Utopia. The reality is that people who simply should not be in direct contact with children do "slip through" even the most elaborately structured screening procedures. Recreation agencies that do not possess explicit child abuse policies run the risk of attracting such deviant personalities. Policies which portray the agency's intolerance of abuse, however, will likely deter pedophiles and other potential child abusers from pursuing employment beyond the interview phase of the employment process.

Good parks and recreation programs are a source of pride in communities, regardless of their sizes. Individual citizens and professional and business leaders frequently focus on the community's public and private recreational opportunities in promotional campaigns designed to attract family and friends, new professionals (doctors, dentists, etc.), and employees. Rarely will a chamber of commerce exclude a mention or emphasis on its community's park lands and recreational facilities. Both are major factors reflecting the community's quality of life. Consequently, when a source of such pride is scandalized the entire community may be demoralized and feel betrayed by an agency to whom they have entrusted their children. Most citizens are not naive enough to not know that abuse may occur occasionally in the best-designed, lighted and supervised park or during a well-planned and appropriately staffed program; yet, these same citizens may become the most adversarial upon learning that the agency allowed it to occur or appear to be insensitive to the potential as evidenced by the absence of appropriate policies.

Another potential negative consequence to the community of the absence of enforced policies relates to litigation and subsequent reduction of services which may result from monetary restitution to the injured party. Whether the settlement is provided by municipal general funds or by an insurance carrier the result will be the same: less discretionary monies. Damages are likely to be awarded if the lack of enforced policies contributed to (1) the actual abuse or (2) the severity of the abusive activity. As discussed in the next chapter, the current trend of the courts is to decide in favor of municipal liability, particularly if evidence exists that appropriate risk management policies and procedures do not exist or are poorly managed. Whether the decrease in discretionary funds results from a depleted general fund or from a sharp increase in insurance premiums the result is the same: less money for necessary staffing, commodities and equipment, or less service to the citizenry.

Children will obviously benefit the most from explicit and enforced abuse policies. The mere existence of policies pertaining to child abuse will serve as a reminder to staff of their responsibility to report suspected abuse and of the importance of appropriate physical and verbal interaction with youthful participants.

Absence of such policies may result in a lack of staff intervention as a consequence of:

(a) a lack of understanding of what constitutes abuse
(b) a lack of awareness of legal obligation to report
(c) a lack of guidelines relating to reporting procedures
(d) a lack of awareness of protection afforded to staff reporting
(e) a lack of awareness of consequences to the child, the agency and self for not reporting—beyond legal consequences.

As a result of the absence of policies the child is consequently exposed to more abuse which may endanger both physical and emotional welfare. The cumulative effects of abuse may lead to death or to total separation from reality and an inability to relate to and cope with others. The lack of policies simply contribute to a continuance of abuse's life cycle or may help to assure that the child joins the ranks of abusers upon reaching adulthood.

STEPS IN POLICY DEVELOPMENT

"The first step is for those on the staff who recognize the importance of dealing with child maltreatment to get together and discuss two broad areas of concern: (1) how to achieve a workable policy and (2) the important elements that the eventual policy might include" (Erickson, McEvoy and Colucci, 1984, p. 56). Such a body will hopefully be representative of all facets of the Recreation and Leisure Services agency, and have the active participation or sanction of the administration officer— director, superintendent, chief, etc.

The second step in policy development involves the realization that extra-agency resources are available to assist or to consult in formulating up-to-date, enforceable policy. The policy committee should, with administrative consent, request input from (a) a local child protective service representative, (b) local law enforcement officials, (c) local medical leadership, (d) a local self-help group (Parents Anonymous, etc.),

(e) local school officials (which will likely have a policy in existence), and (f) the agency's legal counsel. Such input has several advantages:

  (a) may prevent unwarranted conflict
  (b) may prevent duplicity of effort
  (c) may open lines of communication leading to mutual benefit
  (d) may enhance the Recreation and Leisure Services agency's professional stature in the professional community
  (e) may result in the agency's enhanced public image
  (f) may lead to the agency's acceptance as a contributing member of the comprehensive community abuse task force.

This input will, in all likelihood, assist in the definition of the specific areas to be covered in the policy—scope as well as language.

Step three is to consider (a) available literature, (b) the input from the multidisciplinary advisory group, (c) the concerns of the agency personnel, (d) the administrative structure or hierarchy, (e) the formal and informal agency communication networks, and (f) the specific nature of the agency's program and clients in the formulation of the initial draft of the policies. The drafting responsibility should be delegated to a staff member who is both interested in and capable of the task in terms of communication skills. It is also desirable for the person to have had prior experience in policy development, as well as intimate knowledge of the mission and operations of the agency.

The draft should include the following elements:

  (a) Agency's "Statement of Principle" (see Appendix K) or philosophical position related to abuse prevention, intervention and/or treatment.
  (b) Specific statement(s) pertaining to the agency's mission related to the combating of abuse (see Appendix K).
  (c) Awareness of the mandates at the state and national levels that support the development and subsequent enforcement of policies.
  (d) Definitions of the types of abuse/maltreatment and/or neglect.
  (e) Persons required to report.
  (f) Penalties for failing to report—internal and external.
  (g) Steps to be followed in reporting suspected abuse by family members, other adults or staff members.
  (h) Content of suspected abuse report.
  (i) Disposition of reports.

    (j) Screening of applicants for paid and volunteer positions (see Chapter Twelve).

    (k) Required abuse prevention/intervention/treatment training of staff and penalties for not participating.

    (l) Guidelines for interviewing suspected abuse victims in order to determine whether report is warranted (see Appendix J).

    (m) Methods of evaluating timeliness and effectiveness of policy and procedures—should provide for both internal and external review.

The fourth step should be the review of the initial draft by the advisory group. The multidisciplinary body should review the document to assure that it is consistent with mandates and current practice. The advisory body should also be requested to respond to the syntactical development and format of the draft.

The next step involves a review of the revised draft (resulting from step four) by a representative body of agency employees. The purpose of this review is to assure that staff will be able to comprehend the substance of the policies. Consequently, it is essential that the document be composed using language that the part-time teenage employee, the janitor, the playground leader, the division/unit/area supervisor, and the chief administrative officers will comprehend. It is advisable, therefore, that the policy be prepared not only in English but in whatever other language that may be predominant among staff. For example, in Santa Fe, New Mexico it would be advisable to publish the policy in both English and Spanish.

Step six involves the advisory body's final review. They should assure that the revised document, which may now be in more simplified terminology, does not compromise the goals of the policy, the mission of the agency, current child protective policies, or conflict with state or national mandates.

The final step, if no further revisions are suggested by the advisory body, is the publication and distribution (both with administrative consent) of the final, adopted policy. All staff should be required to read the policy and then sign a statement declaring that he/she read the policy on the specified date and that he/she understands its content, particularly related to procedures and penalties for violation. This statement should then be placed in either the employee's permanent file or in the policy file. A listing should also be maintained by the agency administration which upon a minute's notice will inform the administrator who has and who has not been advised of the policy.

THE REPORTING OF SUSPECTED CHILD ABUSE

It is essential that documentation of suspected abuse be on a standardized form and as complete or descriptive as possible. The standardized form not only reflects a degree of commitment by the agency to abuse intervention, but it also provides essential direction to reporting staff as to the content of the report or the information they need to observe or acquire from the child. It is needless (hopefully) to say that (1) staff need training as to form completion, (2) the form should be in adequate supply and readily available to staff, and (3) the form should be evaluated periodically as to its effectiveness in the agency's mission against abuse.

As mentioned previously, the form needs to be structured so as to provide all the necessary information the child protective service representative will require to begin the initial phases of the investigation. A tenet in abuse report should be to provide the "who, what, where, why, when and how" of the incident.

Who

The "who" aspect of the report should provide the following information:

- Name of the child (full name)
- Age of the child
- Sex of the child
- Home address of the child
- Name of the parents, guardians
- Phone number of the family
- Name of person suspected of inflicting abuse (according to the child or witnesses)
- Name of person who first reported the abuse to the staff member (the child, another child, a volunteer).
- Name of individual completing the report (name printed or typed, signature, title, phone number)
- Name of individual receiving report (name printed or typed, signature, title, phone number)

The name of the individual who first made the staff member aware of the suspected abuse is optional. If the person wishes to remain anonymous, the reporting staff member may simply relate how he/she initially became aware of the potentially abusive situation. For example, "I was advised by two other children close to John that they thought he was being beaten regularly by his mother."

What

The "what" aspect of the report form should provide specific information as to the nature of the abuse. The form should cause the reporter to relate the:

- kind of abuse suspected: neglect, physical/sexual/emotional abuse
- physical indicators that led to suspicion or warrant the report
- behavioral indicators that led to suspicion or warrant the report

Where

"Where" provides additional information as to the nature of the injuries, as well as to the staff-child relationship. The report form should provide information as to:

- where on the child's body are the physical indicators
- where were the staff member and child when the injuries were noted
- where the child or witness says injuries were inflicted

Why

Frequently, abuse is not reported by others, it is denied by the child, and no obvious injuries are viewed by the staff member. Yet, there may be some behavioral patterns which cause the staff member to suspect possible abuse. In such instances, the report form should provide the opportunity to specify why abuse is suspect, even in light of the absence of any overwhelming physical evidence or substantiation by the suspected victim or witnesses.

It may be, however, that abuse has been confirmed by the child. If so, it may be helpful to the eventual investigating official to have some knowledge as to the child's understanding of why the abuse was inflicted. The recreation worker is not encouraged to pursue this aspect of the report beyond simply asking, "Why did your dad hit you so hard?" For other types of abuse, it is advisable to avoid asking why the abuse occurred.

Emotionally and intellectually, many children may not be capable of responding as to why a father fondles genitals, doesn't provide for daily living needs, or emotionally abuses them.

When

The "when" aspect of the report is addressed in a variety of ways. The report should respond in some manner to:

- when the suspected abuse was noticed
- when the child was questioned
- when the parents were notified of the suspected abuse (by the agency administration)
- when the child said the injuries were inflicted
- when the report was completed and submitted to the agency administration by the reporting staff member
- when the report was reviewed by the designated agency official
- when the report was forwarded to the appropriate child protective service.

The above items of information should be depicted by the month, day, year and time of the action, particularly that action taken by agency staff.

How

Finally, the "how" of the suspected abuse report needs to be encouraged by the adopted, standardized form. This will, along with the other report elements, provide a basis for decisions to be made later in the intervention process by the protective services agency. The worker completing the form should convey the following information:

- how the suspected abuse came to the reporter's attention; i.e. it was brought to the staff member's attention by a volunteer
- how the information was obtained from the suspected victim (the victim initiated the disclosure or the victim responded to staff inquiries)
- how the injuries were inflicted; i.e. bare hand, hair brush, cigarette, hot iron, etc.
- how the parents were notified of the staffs' suspicions; i.e. by phone or in person

Finally, the works of Erickson (p. 205), Harrison and Edwards (pp. 116–117), Mayhall and Norgard (pp. 243–244) as well as others, and a review of the policy in Appendix K when viewed collectively, suggest that compliance with the "who, what, where, why, when, and how" approach will assure that the necessary information to serve as the basis for further investigation will be provided. It should also assure the protection of the rights of the agency, staff member, child, and parents in the event further action is deemed necessary. Such a comprehensive approach should be viewed positively by reporting staff, in that it discourages reports submitted in anything other than good faith. This should also be a source of comfort to administrators and particularly to parents.

The form depicted allows for the disclosure of all of the recommended information. This form or others should be completed solely by the staff member suspecting abuse—with exception of those items requiring the signature of others. Also, the welfare of the suspected victim requires that the form be completed, if at all possible, before the child departs the recreational setting.

Some Recommendations for Reporting

Whether reporting the suspected abuse of a child or the abusive behavior of a staff member or volunteer, there are several general guidelines which should be followed:

- All staff are responsible for reporting suspected abuse.
- Never forcibly detain a child to secure information.
- Report suspected abuse to the immediate supervisor first.
- Report the suspected abuse to next available level of supervision in event of immediate supervisor's absence—never wait to report.
- Complete the written report immediately.
- Submit reports only on approved or adopted agency forms.
- Always make a copy of the completed form for personal records.
- Always report suspect abuse!
- Agency administration should establish a means of recording referral cases of suspected abuse to the appropriate child protective service.
- A copy of the employee completed form should always be retained by the agency.
- If law permits, take a picture of the suspect victim to record physical abuse.
- If there are questions, agency administration should consult the child protective services for guidance.

Illustration XI-I. A SAMPLE FORM FOR REPORTING ABUSE

The City of Anytown
Department of Parks and Recreation
5555 Fifth St.   55555   (555) 555-0000

<u>Report</u> <u>of</u> <u>Suspected</u> <u>Child</u> <u>Abuse</u> <u>Form</u>

Name of Suspected Victim: _____
Age:
                         First   MI   Last
Sex: _____   Address of Victim: _____
                                    Number   Street

                                    _____
                                    City
Name of Parent(s)/Guardian(s): _____

Address of Parent(s) or Guardian(s): _____
                                     Number   Street

                                     _____
                                     City
Parent(s)/Guardian(s) Phone Number: (   ) ___ - _____
Type of Suspected Abuse: _____ Neglect _____ Physical Abuse _____
Sexual Abuse _____ Emotional Abuse
Describe the physical and behavioral indicators that led to
suspicion of abuse: _____
_____
Time & Date Suspect Abuse was Noted: _____
Place Suspected Abuse was Noted: _____
Suspected Victim's Account of Injuries/Abuse (Place, Date, Time of
Infliction; Who Inflicted Injuries; Weapons Or Instruments Used,
etc.): _____
_____
_____
Other Observations/Information Which You Feel Warrant Futher
Investigation: _____
_____
_____

Person Making Report: _____ Person Receiving Report: _____
                      Signature   Signature

_____   _____
Printed or Typed Name   Printed or Typed Name

_____   _____
       Title   Title

_____   _____
Date   Time AM/PM   Date   Time AM/PM
             Circle   Circle

_____   _____
Phone Number (Office)   Phone Number (Office)

SUMMARY

Knowing the physical and behavioral indicators of abuse, knowing the definitions of the types of abuse, and knowledge of the dynamics of abuse and its costs can benefit the child most effectively when a policy for applying such information is deliberately designed and disseminated to agency personnel. The policy must be explicit and address those elements discussed. Caution and consultation are the keys to the formulation of a child abuse policy. Caution must be exercised in order to prevent conflict with existing laws and accepted practice. Consultation with other child protection professionals will prevent such conflict and also assure the timeliness of the policy, as well as its resulting procedures. Consultation will also likely result in a more comprehensive community confrontation of abuse through the increased cooperation and respect of the numerous agencies.

Yet, for a policy to have the desired result staff should also be involved and committed to combating abuse. Staff should be encouraged to participate in policy development and be given the opportunity to respond to the policy prior to formal adoption. Policies must be written in such a manner they can be readily comprehended.

Staff cannot approach abuse reporting in a cavalier manner. To take action that may result in the separation of a family and the criminal conviction of a parent or guardian requires a thorough and objective reporting of suspected abuse. Care must be exercised to avoid the violation of the rights of the suspected victim and the perpetrators and/or parents/guardians. A thorough, objective report should address the "who, what, where, why, when, and how" of the suspected abuse. Administrators should also take care to follow other general guidelines when reporting suspected abuse.

Chapter Twelve

SELECTION OF RECREATION STAFF

INTRODUCTION

The needs of abused children and abusive parents are truly unique. The abusive environment results in, among other debilitating emotions, poor self-concept, fear, distrust of adults, distrust of all others, shame, frustration, hostility, depression, defeatism and other attitudes which may tax the reserves of even the most exceptional recreation programmer. Yet, on the other hand, the abused child and even the parents may demonstrate a strong need for bonding with the recreation specialist. The kindnesses, shared laughter, shared successes, and pleasant surroundings may well result in a participant's strong dependency upon the recreation specialist. The recreation leader, the teacher or counselor may be the only contact with a non-hostile, non-aggressive, supportive, and pleasurable world, and the urge to "hold on" may become strong and uncontrollable.

Needless to say, the recreation administrator must use caution and exercise exceptional judgment in hiring and training personnel in order to not exacerbate an already painful existence. As might be expected, the same caution and judgment should be likewise exercised by the recreation program leadership in the acceptance of volunteers. The essential nature of the personnel function has been pointed out by numerous management authorities and Recreation and Leisure Service scholars, including Rodney and Toalson. "Personnel practices and policies determine in large measure the effectiveness of any recreation and park system. Indeed, the success of any recreation and park program is dependent upon the quality of its staff" (*Administration of Recreation, Parks, and Leisure Service*, 1981, p. 150). Whether the administrator is in a community-based or institutional-based program, in a profit or not-for-profit agency, in a leisure services program for able-bodied or providing a therapeutic recreation program for impaired clients, or concerned with abuse prevention, intervention or treatment, she/he will perform no more potentially beneficial or deleterious duty than the recruitment, selection, training and placement of staff. Few would argue with the statement that "more than any other factor, staffing is the major element of an organization's success."

Whether the concern is prevention, intervention or treatment of child abuse, staff that relate directly to children should possess sensitivities and strengths beyond an extensive repertoire of activities and a desire to work with children. In fact, it is the desire to work with children that must now, regrettably, flag caution amongst Recreation and Leisure Service administrators. According to Doctor W. Walter Menninger, an eminent psychiatrist and dean of the Karl Menninger School of Psychiatry and Mental Health Service, "Some abusers are drawn to occupations and activities involving children" (*Scouting,* Sept. 1986, p. 37). Pedophiles, in particular, may seek out employment that offers opportunities for close or intimate contact with individual or small groups of children. What better opportunities than those offered to recreation leaders in scouting, YMCA's, treatment centers, community playgrounds, after-school programs, or in any recreational setting offered by a broad range of leisure service agencies and programs? How to ensure against such a deviant personality being appointed as an employee or volunteer will be addressed later in the chapter.

EMPLOYEE CHARACTERISTICS

What then are the characteristics the recreation administrator should look for in the potential employee or volunteer if the program is to adequately address the child abuse issue in its community? Some of those that are essential for the recreation agency's participation in abuse prevention, intervention and treatment are:

(a) sensitivity to the needs and feelings of others
(b) ability to accept displaced hostility
(c) awareness of age-appropriate behaviors
(d) awareness of child-rearing practices amongst the community's ethnic groups
(e) commitment to role model responsibilities, particularly in relation to response to frustration and hostility
(f) advocacy for the rights of children
(g) awareness of own strengths and weaknesses
(h) ability to project an aura of optimism at all times

(i) strength and ability to allow appropriate bonding by the abused child

(j) awareness that, though a child has been abused, the need for structure and discipline still exist; i.e. empathy cannot be confused with sympathy.

(k) happiness and stability in their own lives so the abused child or abusive parent isn't viewed as a way of satisfying personal needs

(l) ability to reinforce and foster positive attitudes and behaviors

(m) patience in working with people, awareness that immediate and positive response may not be realized without extended effort

(n) willingness to commit excessive time and emotional energies

(o) willingness to work within a team approach framework

(p) awareness and commitment to the role of leisure services in fostering human growth and development, family unity, and self-esteem

(q) awareness of what constitutes appropriate personal interaction with children of the same and opposite sex

(r) awareness of age-appropriate sexual behaviors and the impact of sexuality on a child's patterns of social interacting

(s) understanding of the elements of a "helping relationship"

Sensitivity to Needs

Sensitivity to the needs and feelings of others should be a characteristic of all human services professionals, including and particularly those in Recreation and Leisure Services. The art of recreation programming is to fabricate an atmosphere where enjoyment is a major outcome. This can satisfactorily be accomplished only by ascertaining the present needs and feelings of the participant. An activity that causes an adverse reaction as a result of inappropriate stress is counterproductive. This premise is old news to seasoned recreation professionals and may, in some opinions, be too elementary to warrant mentioning. Yet, with respect to the abused child and the abusive parent, this sensitivity is more critical than with the non-abuse involved participant. Both parties are emotionally walking a tightrope and the least bit of insensitivity may cause them to slip irrevocably into the abyss of distrust, apathy, and physical separation. Those surrounded by and victimized by abuse will often consciously and unconsciously erect barriers that will impede the staff member's attempts to be sensitive to their needs. These barriers may be characterized by denial, withdrawal, over-dependency, or hostility. Unique methods of testing the recreation leader's commitment to their personal welfare may be devised as well as strategies to redirect the leader's efforts to address wants as opposed to needs.

It may be helpful to advise (or to remind) recreation personnel of the personal needs of the family in crisis. Table XII-1 identifies the needs of the parents and of the children. In addition to these, Pringle (1975, p. 159) has added the child's needs for new experiences and for a sense of responsibility. A review of Table XII-1 makes obvious the essential distinction between wants and needs. For example, a child may actively seek opportunities for belittlement, particularly if it's all she has ever known. Likewise, the abusive parent may want "punishment" or denial because of their strong feelings of guilt. The dynamics of the family in crisis are complex and require exceptional sensitivity by all staff committed to a comprehensive, community-wide abuse prevention, intervention, and treatment.

Accepting Displaced Hostility

A frequently displayed behavior by the abused child is open hostility, both physically and verbally. The hostility may be generalized and not relate to a specific event or staff member. This notion may help prevent an inappropriate reaction on the part of the recreation leader. The abused child may simply be angered by any interaction he perceives as having potential for degradation or by anyone he perceives as being in an authoritative position. The child may, in fact, be openly hostile to any adult, particularly to one of the same gender as the abusive parent. The staff member may also be viewed as simply another part of "the system" that has allowed the abuse to continue.

The parents may, likewise, direct hostility towards the recreation leader. The parent may become both verbally and physically threatening to the staff member who reports suspected abuse. Even though the agency administrator may not disclose the source of the report, it is likely that the child will, if under duress, disclose to the parent who either observed the physical and behavior indicators, asked about rumored abuse, or who he or she disclosed the abuse to. Parental hostility may also be directed to the recreation leader as a result of the child's obvious preference for the recreation program over the home or for the recreation staff member over the parent. The inadequate parent may become jealous and quite threatened by the perceived intrusion into the sanctity of the

Table XII-1

PERSONAL NEEDS OF THE FAMILY IN CRISIS

Parents *	Children
1. to feel good about themselves, to compensate for the belittling throughout their lives	1. to develop trust in adults
	2. to develop basic socialization skills
2. to be comforted when they hurt, supported when weak, and liked for their good qualities	3. to develop a positive self-image
	4. to have opportunities for normal physical growth
3. to trust someone, to have someone to lean on and put up with their bad days	5. to develop positive peer relationships
4. to have someone who will not accept their low self-esteem	6. to recognize there are other than violent means to cope with frustration
5. to have someone who will keep faith in them when they fail	7. to feel loved
6. to have someone to help them meet their practical needs, to direct them to community resources	8. to feel adequate and independent
	9. to have opportunity for age appropriate behaviors
7. to have someone who will not criticize them, even when they ask for it	10. to identify support systems and caring individuals outside of the home
8. to have someone who will help them understand their children without making them feel stupid	11. to develop social and sexual identities
9. to feel valuable and to feel they are helping others	12. to learn there are non-painful forms of physical contact--touching
10. to have someone who does not need to use them for selfish purposes	13. to sense support and understanding
	14. to sense stability and consistency (security)

*Source: The Role and Responsibility of Professionals: The Problem and Its Management: 4-5.

family. Tertiary, the parent in a treatment structure may, as the child, demonstrate open hostility out of frustration with a system that has disrupted the family, threatened familial and social status, and not delivered on previous promises. The recreation worker may be seen simply as an extension of that intrusive and faulty system.

Awareness of Age-Appropriate Behavior

Intelligent interaction and participation in a treatment framework mandate an awareness of age-appropriate behaviors of the recreation program's youthful clientele. The issue of child abuse is highly emotional and the element of chance needs to be removed to minimize the opportunity of uninformed reporting. To base a report of suspected abuse on inappropriate behaviors and to base the observations on only personal opinion can have dire consequences. First, the family may be needlessly disrupted and emotionally devastated. Secondly, the professional stature of the staff member and of the image of the total department or agency may be blemished amongst the other members of the professional community, i.e. children and family services, law enforcement, etc. Even more damaging may be the image projected to the lay community. Parents will likely be reluctant to encourage their child's participation in a recreation agency where the staff are reputed to report suspected abuse solely on the basis of personal opinion as to the appropriateness of a child's behavior. Thirdly, such irresponsible action by staff is potentially litigious, since uninformed opinion could well be viewed as negligent if staff cannot document formal training vis-à-vis college course work, conference attendance or agency-sponsored in-service training in child development, developmental psychology, or other related instructional programs. It behooves the agency administration to (1) review applicant transcripts for evidence of such course work, (2) question applicants as to such knowledge, (3) acquire such knowledge themselves in order to facilitate staff selection, (4) require all staff to participate in related in-service training, and (5) keep formal records reflecting such training.

Awareness of Ethnic Child-Rearing Practices

A reality of contemporary American society is that most communities, particularly those in metropolitan areas, are populated by numerous ethnic groups. Often, these families are well integrated into the community's socioeconomic structure and subsequently their ethnicity is frequently overlooked. One of the distinguishing factors of ethnic groups is child-rearing practices, including the mode of physical and verbal interaction between parent and child. The recreation leader, particularly one working in a multicultural community or in one which is alien to the recreator, must become acquainted with the various and diverse practices. The perception of abuse may otherwise be nothing more than the imposition of the worker's particular values when, in fact, the behavior is perfectly acceptable within the specific ethnic community. It is particularly essential for a member of the Recreation and Leisure Services professional community to be cognizant of culturally or ethnically sanctioned play patterns—those among siblings and peers, and between parents or adults and children. Not only is this awareness necessary for a clearer perception of abuse, but it is also relevant in terms of the community's acceptance of the recreation program and the perceived appropriateness of the staff member's interaction with its children.

Role Model Responsibility

Perhaps the recreation leader has no more important task with respect to child abuse intervention and treatment than the development of a positive social climate for the family members in crisis. A positive social environment, one that provides opportunities for character growth and development, can be realized only by staff that recognize the impact of their own behaviors. The staff member's responsibility as a role model to both the child and the adult takes on increased importance when the element of abuse is interjected. The staff member, when relating to those involved in abuse, must be constantly aware of the need to exhibit alternative means of dealing with frustration, means other than verbal tirades or violence. This is, of course, true even when abuse is not a factor. The recreator has a responsibility to: (1) inspire participants to respond in a controlled, non-violent or non-abuse manner to frustration; (2) promote the development of positive interaction skills; (3) demonstrate the value to diverse leisure interests; and (4) demonstrate that people in authority can accomplish as much with benevolence as with physical or emotional intimidation. This can be accomplished most effectively when the staff member models his behavior in accordance with these values or responsibilities.

Advocacy for Children

Recreation administrators should be particularly sensitive to the need for all staff relating to youth to be advocates for the rights of children. These rights may frequently need to be defended vigorously and vociferously. A staff member who views children as having fewer rights than adults or as the "property" of the parents cannot be relied upon to (1) recognize or suspect abuse, (2) report suspected abuse, or (3) relate to the child as an individual with unique needs. Child advocacy also includes the ability to recognize the nurturance of the child as the primary task and to prevent the subjugation of the child's needs by the needs of the program or the staff. Child advocacy does not, however, involve abdication of authority or control to the child. Empathy, respect, structure, discipline and firmness need not be sacrificed. Many abused children are victims of anarchistic families and do, consequently, need a disciplined environment but one that is consistent, kind, and aware of the rights and needs of children.

Awareness of Own Strengths and Weaknesses

Insight into personal strengths and weaknesses is a desirable characteristic in most employment settings. It is more than desirable when working in a human services setting—it is essential. Recreation leaders have a particular need to look within, particularly those that are developing programs to benefit those in crisis. To adequately fulfill the function of leadership, i.e. inspiration, instruction, guidance, organization, and evaluation (Carlson, Deppe, and MacLean, 1963, pp. 334–335), is demanding in and of itself; but it is particularly demanding when those you hope to serve may exhibit short attention spans, distrust, strong dependency, developmental lags, open hostility, poor self-concepts, resentment of authority, fear, and a variety of disruptive or asocial behaviors. The recreation leader attempting to benefit a clientele under such potentially stressful conditions should be able to identify his or her own points of weakness, vulnerability and strength—whether it be repertoire of facilitation skills, sensitivity to specific behaviors, counseling skills, attitudes towards children, management/discipline style preference, etc.

Aura of Optimism

Most individuals choosing a career in Recreation and Leisure Services can be characterized as "upbeat." Those who do not like people and do not have a commitment to enhancing the quality of life via enjoyable activity will either never select such a career, or function for a very short, non-productive period of time. Yet, in most situations "having a bad day" may have only short-term deleterious effects. Yet, for some of the aforementioned reasons, a "bad day" may be much more injurious to the child victimized by abuse. A point of clarification: by "upbeat" is meant an optimistic, not Pollyanna approach to recreation leadership. The optimistic or upbeat leader "expects the best, but if the results in followers or programs are less than the best, he is patient and tries again; or better still, he tries a different method" (Carlson et al., 1963, p. 329). Upbeat also refers to a sense of humor. The ability to capitalize in a light moment can ease situations encumbered by stress and controversy. The gift of being able to elicit laughter is a particularly desirable attribute when relating to abused children, many of whom have had little humor in their lives.

Allowing Appropriate Bonding

Perhaps the greatest need of most abused children is to feel that someone cares. This need is frequently so strong that the child will develop a strong bonding with an adult that demonstrates an interest in his welfare. The recreation worker may notice that a befriended child will repeatedly offer to assist with tasks, constantly volunteer in activities, consistently stay late at the recreation facility, repeatedly ask for rides home, begin asking personal questions about the recreation leader's relationship with his/her family, and generally attempt to spend more time with the leader than with peers. As suggested in Chapter Seven, this is particularly true of the emotionally abused child. The recreation leader is then confronted with the dilemma of determining when this dependency upon the leader exceeds the boundaries of appropriateness and how to establish a mutually agreeable relationship. Needless to say, the staff member needs to possess certain qualities in order to keep the bonding from becoming detrimental to the child, the remaining youth, him- herself, and to the program. First, the staff member needs to recognize the signs of bonding; secondly, a sensitivity to needs of abused children is required; tertiary, a sense of timing is critical so the appropriate time to address the issue can be recognized; and finally, the staff member must recognize the need to seek outside assistance from trained clinicians to deal with the issue. Under all circumstances the staff member should guard against the child feeling rejected. A situation handled inappropriately may well drive the child beyond the grasp of child protective services and result in irreparable harm to the child's self-esteem and attempt to establish a liaison with a caring world.

Awareness of Need for Structure and Discipline

Upon hearing that a child who is a participant in programs has been identified as a victim of abuse, staff may have a variety of reactions. Among these may be shock, anger, denial, and sympathy. As more evidence is produced to substantiate the rumor the first three reactions will usually diminish in intensity or disappear entirely. However, with respect to sympathy the inverse relationship between substantiation and intensity of emotion may result. Staff will likely become more sympathetic as they become convinced of the brutal reality of the child's abuse. Staff may need to be reminded that abused children are still in need of structure and discipline. Regardless of the type and intensity of abuse the child still has the need to comply with rules and to exhibit socially appropriate responses to authority and frustration. The neglected child may particularly need to be made aware of the importance of controls. As with other children, the recreation leader's responsibility is to assist the abused child to become adjusted, happy, and a productive individual. To accomplish the task or to assist him in realizing his potential, inappropriate behaviors which may act as barriers to potential must be addressed but not only by the social worker or other child protective service workers.

This commitment to structure and discipline must, however, be exercised with judgment. Recreation workers cannot afford the luxury of being inflexible in rule enforcement. When working with children and families whose lives read like a Hollywood horror movie script, judgment in administering of agency rules, policy and disciplinary procedures must be a major concern. The staff, without abdicating all control, will likely be called upon to reach into the inner depths and ever-growing bag of tricks to creatively cope with the unique behavioral issues that will arise.

Awareness of Need for Personal Stability

One of the greatest needs shared by abused children and their families is that of stability. Stable environments are difficult to assure if the staff themselves are not stable or do not have control in their lives. Staff whose lives are stable are typically happy and do not view the abused child or abusive parent as only a way to meet or satisfy their own needs. Staff with motives other than to make the participant's lives more enjoyable and alleviate the incidence of abuse cannot provide the stable, congenial atmosphere necessary. The employee unhappy with his/her own life or whose personal life is in turmoil will very likely find it difficult to put the needs of clients first.

Awareness of Need for Positive Response

Working with individuals in crisis, including abused children and abused parents, requires the ability to recognize and reinforce positive behaviors and to discourage behaviors that disrupt programs or that will result in less successful life-styles. However, whether or not an action is reinforcement or discouragement is determined solely by the appropriateness of the behavior in question. Consequently, a recreation staff member must be willing to invest more in the job than simply planning and leading activities. A more personal investment must be made; the staff member must be willing to devote time and energy to getting to know what "makes the client tick" and what staff reactions may result in the desired responses and behaviors. When dealing with physically, sexually and emotionally abused and neglected youth some "traditional" staff responses may have little positive effect and, in fact, result in the withdrawal of the child from the protective network. For example, a premature hug or pat on the back may be misperceived by a child who has experienced these acts as preliminaries in sexual abuse. Likewise, the ill-timed threat of withdrawal of affection may be irreparably devastating to the child on the brink as a result of long-term emotional abuse. Therefore, the staff member needs not only to understand what constitutes appropriate reinforcement but must also be the possessor of a good sense of timing with respect to application.

Patience

Those working with children and other members of abusive families should be prepared to "wait it out." Patience is not only a virtue but a necessity when relating to the victims and perpetrators of abuse. Abused children will likely be apprehensive and distrustful and possibly unwilling to respond positively to the initial approaches of the recreation leader. They have often lived their lives under the veil of fear and may have been prevented by the parents from ever developing play skills and trust in other adults. Abusive parents are likely to encourage their child's distrust of other adults in order to prevent the disclosure of the evidence of abuse. This effort to prevent disclosure may also include the denial of opportunities to interact, i.e. play with peers. Consequently, the abused child may well possess neither the trust, social and activity skills, or appreciation to respond positively upon program initiation. The evolution of a frightened, withdrawn, distrustful, unskilled and hostile child into an eager, outgoing, accepting, contented, skilled and congenial individual will undoubtedly consume a significant amount of the recreator's time and energy.

Likewise, the parents of abused children are likely to be even less responsive than their children. This is particularly true of the perpetrators, who may well have been abused children that experienced the same circumstances as described above. The parents will likely be resentful of agency intervention and express this by only passive cooperation. They express hostility towards all they perceive as disruptive of their family or as threatening to their security and stature in the community. They will, in all probability, also lack the social and activity skills that will facilitate an immediate positive response to the recreation leader's efforts. The recreation leader requiring immediate, positive responses from participants in order to maintain initiate is advised to seek employment in an agency other than one addressing the issue of child abuse.

Commitment of Time and Energy

Due to the aforementioned reasons, the individual working in a recreation program whose administration is committed to addressing abuse must be willing and capable of devoting extra time and energy, physical as well as emotional. From the prevention perspective, the staff must be constantly aware of socioeconomic patterns and population dynamics which, if unaddressed, may lead to abusive situations. Staff should be cognizant of individual familiar crises and keep an eye and ear open to conversations and behavioral patterns which may suggest a family in crisis.

Intervention is stress-producing, in that the staff must remain constantly alert to the indicators of abuse as discussed in Chapters Five through Eight. The greatest potential for stress, however, lies in the discovery of the indicators. The reporting of suspected abuse is an anxiety-ridden process in which such questions as, "Do I have enough evidence to suspect abuse?" "What will be the reaction of the child and family?" "Will the parents take it out on the child?" or "How will this affect my job?" are likely to plague the staff member. Other staff may contribute to the stress with advice to overlook the indicators. The allegedly abused child may also add to the emotional drain by pleading with the staff member to not report the findings. Obviously, with these potential deterrents to intervention (and only few have been mentioned), the staff member must have a strong commitment to abuse intervention and the time and emotional reserves to act as a vigorous advocate for children.

Recreation specialists working in a treatment setting are, with their other colleagues, charged with the monumental responsibility of re-mediating the family in crisis and of meeting the needs of the primary victim, the other family members, and the perpetrator. "Treatment is aimed at helping people move out of their isolated, trapped, hopeless patterns of living into a greater sense of self-esteem. Ideally, treatment can enhance the ability of a person to find gratification in the world. The helper acts as a catalyst to this process and encourages and allows the child or adult to try out new ways of relating to other people and to the world" (Mayhall and Norgard, 1983, p. 337). To help individuals who feel trapped, isolated, hopeless, unloved, and victimized requires an inordinate amount of conviction, energy, time and creativity. The afore-mentioned lack of trust in adults and of "the system" only add to the potential for emotional drain. A great deal of time will likely be consumed in the formulation of ploys or strategies to first gain trust and to then involve the child or adult into recreational programs that will help them work through feelings and step into the mainstream of life.

A Willing Team Member

The issue of child abuse is no longer solely in the domain of social work or of any other single discipline. It has become evident that the only effective means of addressing abuse is through a comprehensive community approach and involving all agencies addressing the needs of children and families. Therefore, if such an approach is to be successful all parties must be committed to the team concept. Being a team player in this respect requires a thorough understanding of the roles and responsibilities of other concerned agencies, a receptivity to suggestions for programs and other interventions, and a willingness to share information freely. A true team player must also be aware of his or her own limitations and be willing to seek appropriate assistance and opportunities to eliminate the limitation. A commitment to continuing education or staff development is paramount; this is true regardless of the primary emphasis—prevention, intervention, or treatment—or of the setting—a hospital, community recreation, a correctional center, a day treatment center, etc.

Awareness and Commitment to Role of Leisure Services

Being a team member has at least one additional essential requirement: a commitment to the role of leisure services in the fostering of human growth and development, family unity, and self-esteem. Recreation departments may be required to demonstrate that they, indeed, have a significant contribution to make. Programs may have to be marketed, not only to the recipients, but to other concerned agencies as well. The commitment cannot be expressed in esoteric terms which will likely lead to only more confusion. It must be expressed primarily by means of knowledge of the stages of human development and of the inherent characteristics of activities provided and of the potential benefits to be derived. An accompanying awareness of the social dynamics of families and of the principles of motivation is also a key ingredient in the demonstrated commitment. A lack of this commitment will likely result in the recreation program's delegation to only the fringes of the front in the battle against child abuse.

Awareness of Appropriate Personal Interaction

A concern of any agency providing services to children is that its staff use good judgment in its interaction with its youthful clientele. Staff should use caution to not in any manner exacerbate further the stress or conflict the child may be experiencing. It is particularly important that all staff be aware of what constitutes appropriate interaction with children, particularly those who may be victims of abuse. Discretion and good judgment are essential when relating to all children from the standpoints of both the agency and the child. A well-meaning staff member who is perhaps guilty of nothing more than being overly demonstrative can cause unfavorable attention to the agency by inappropriate hugging, patting or other forms of expressing affection. The appropriateness may be determined by the immediate community, and the range of its acceptable behaviors may be significantly narrower than society as a whole. Parameters of acceptable behavior, particularly those related to sexuality, must be defined and respected. To exceed the boundaries may result in unwanted publicity to the agency, to say nothing of the effects on the staff member and the child.

From the child's perspective, an ill-timed physical demonstration of affection may be the cause for additional hostility, fear, or distrust. This is particularly true if the child has been sexually abused by an adult and the abuse is prefaced by a similar physical act.

Awareness of Appropriate Sexual Behavior

As noted in Chapter Five, one of the indicators of possible sexual abuse is inappropriate sexual activity or sophistication on the part of the child. Therefore, staff should be aware of what constitutes appropriate behavior. Staff should possess knowledge of human sexuality and of the differing sexual mores of the predominant cultures or ethnic groups in the catchment area. Ignorance of these essential pieces of information may result in the staff member's misassessment of the child's sexuality and overall maturation.

Understanding a Helping Relationship

Finally, for recreation staff to effectively cope with the issue of child abuse and to be proactive, as well as reactive, advocates for the rights of children, they must understand and support the elements of a helping relationship. Besides having an expanded repertoire of activities, staff should recognize that to be a participant in a helping relationship and partnership in the battle against abuse they must be committed to:

- reporting abuse whenever it is suspected
- learning about all services available for abusive families in the community
- encouraging troubled families to seek help
- providing support, encouragement, and understanding to children who have been abused, and to their families
- never using physical force in their program, other than to prevent injury to another child

(Broadhurst, *Educators, Schools, and Child Abuse,* 1986, p. 25)

- educating the community as to the dynamics of abuse
- guarding against circumstances that may lead to institutional abuse
- maintaining an objective, supportive, and honest relationship with children and other family members
- demonstrating by personal life-style the value of recreation and other meaningful leisure pursuits
- always endeavoring to discover and build upon the family's strengths
- complying with professional standards for programming and personal behavior

Summary

A recreation program or agency staffed with individuals adhering to these principles, as well as those discussed previously, should be well suited to join in the battle against child abuse. Admittedly, staffing with personnel possessing such insights, sensitivities, and programming skills may sorely limit the pool of suitable candidates and frequently conflict with a pressing need to fill a position. Nonetheless, the war against abuse cannot afford a compromise on personnel standards; likewise, the recreation and leisure services cannot afford to compromise if they are going to honor the traditional tenets to foster human growth and development, social skills, and the perpetuation of culture.

SCREENING PERSONNEL

All agencies involved in direct services to children have an obligation to their clientele to assure the availability of the best-qualified staff and a safe, secure program environment. Administrators can ill-afford to hire personnel without first challenging the credentials proffered. The term "challenging" denotes an active, deliberate and quasi-adversarial process and is intended to do so, particularly in the context of staffing of programs for children. Furthermore, the fragile nature of the youthful participants and today's legal climate or society's litigious inclinations requires that those charged with the staffing of programs not hire solely on the basis of the resumé, interview and letters of recommendation from individuals selected solely by the applicant. The comment by Doctor Menninger in the introduction of this chapter makes a painful, dramatic and truthful point: pedophiles and other child abusers are naturally drawn to career fields that offer opportunities for close, personal relations with children. What better way to establish a child's trust and foster dependency than through enjoyable activity? With this distasteful reality in mind, the administrator should be guided by "measured paranoia" and establish rigid and searching procedures for screening all individuals seeking either employment or volunteer opportunities. This is particularly true for those agencies whose clients may be receiving treatment for dysfunctions resulting from abuse. Following are some recommended guidelines pertaining to the development of a screening process that should ensure the selection of staff well suited for working with children, regardless of the leisure service setting. The recommendations will address (1) position advertisement, (2) the search, (3) the application form, (4) the interview process, (5) criteria for letters of recommendation, and (6) background checks.

Advertising the Position

The first step in the staffing process after the determination of the position's need and requirements is to advertise or attract candidates. Often, and regrettably, more attention is given to attracting the greatest number of marginally qualified personnel. Frequently, the position announcement includes minimal insight into educational and experiential requirements, job requirements, and rarely the fact that the applicant will be subject to a thorough background check by the agency or a law enforcement agency. This lack of definitive job or position description can result in a large number of applications, but it may also result in (1) an exorbitant amount of time spent with inquiries for additional information, (2) lost time and money in reviewing credentials of unqualified applicants, (3) unwarranted postponement of hiring, and (4) poor public relations for the agency.

Meyer and Donaho provide some guidelines for writing job advertising copy which should be helpful to the administrator or the agency's search committee. They suggest the following questions be considered:

- Is it clear which job or positions are available? (Responsible party should make certain that both the position title and the description are clear.)
- Is it clear what the work entails? (This should include the working conditions.)
- Have you indicated only which candidates should apply via bona fide qualifications?
- Has the deadline date for application been set? (Deadline should provide for adequate time for the securing of all required supporting documentation and consider media publishing schedules.)
- Have the correct name, address, times, and phone numbers for response been indicated?
- Has the salary or range been indicated? (This will possibly limit the number of applicants and discretion should be used; a knowledge of the employment pool would be helpful in deciding whether or not to include salary information.)
- Does the announcement specify the types of information and enclosures the applicant should supply or have forwarded?
- Is the position announcement free of prejudice and fair to minorities? (It is wise to include in the ad the statement "Equal Opportunity Employer.")

(Meyer and Donaho, 1979, pp. 42–43)

It may also be helpful to include (1) job advancement opportunities and (2) a statement that all applicants may be subject to a background check by a law enforcement agency (or another investigative body).

The Search

"Acquiring outstanding prospects (applicants) improves the odds of finding that best person for the job. Granted, prospects are everywhere—but the best prospect must actively be sought out" (Meyer and Donaho, p. 44). Yet, the unique needs of children, particularly those victimized by abuse, and the need to provide a safe, secure environment dictate particular caution in the search process. Consequently, agencies should select cautiously the avenues for seeking qualified candidates for positions at all organizational levels, but particularly at those that require frequent interaction with youthful participants. Some recommended avenues for recruiting qualified applicants are:*

(1) High school teachers and counselors. Both may well be aware of current or former students who are suited for leadership positions at camps, day camps, playgrounds, pools, or community centers. Such school personnel are often aware of the interests and behavioral characteristics of students and may be helpful in the search process.

(2) Current employees. Staff can be requested to convey to individuals they believe will be interested and who are qualified the availability of positions. The staff, who are also likely to be committed to protecting their positions, will in all probability be quite selective in who they inform of the position.

(3) Student employment offices. Area colleges/universities will likely maintain employment referral services for their students, particularly for those who are not eligible for financial aid or for those who require supplemental income. Employment counselors should be advised of the necessary performance and behavioral requirements for the position and requested to inform only those students well suited for working with children.

(4) Professional Job Bulletins. Professional organizations at national, state, and local or regional levels often publish job bulletins listing employment opportunities or position announcements; for example, the National Recreation and Parks Association's *Job Bulletin.* Such publications offer some assurance that resulting candidates are likely to be better prepared academically and experientially in the recreation and leisure services and with children.

(5) Academic Departments. An estimated 260 colleges and universities offer undergraduate professional preparation programs in Recreation and Leisure Services. In addition, there are an estimated 200 community colleges offering associate degree programs in recreation leadership. The faculty of academic programs are frequently queried by current and former students as to available positions. They can be quite helpful in the search process by posting copies of position announcements and by advising suitable candidates. When an academic department's reputation is at stake, to say nothing of personal credibility, faculty are likely to advise and recommend

---

*Taken in part from Meyer and Donaho, pp. 45–52.

only those individuals they believe to be well suited for working with children.

(6) Conventions, Symposia, Workshops. A frequent feature of such professional gatherings is a portion of the display area, the convention floor, or the hotel lobby devoted to a "Job Mart" posting career opportunities. At such gatherings the potential employer can post any and all available positions with a reasonably strong assurance that most of those reviewing the postings are likely to be (a) interested in a Recreation and Leisure Services career, (b) academically and experientially qualified, and (c) able to provide suitable credentials and references. This search resource can be capitalized on even further if the agency sends a representative to the gathering to personally confer with candidates to implement the application and screening process.

(7) "Pirating." Unfortunately, this term has a negative connotation to many; yet, as a common practice it can be quite productive if done diplomatically and openly. The practice involves notifying employees of other Recreation and Leisure Service agencies that a position is available. In order to preserve a stable professional community, however, there are two recommended procedures for "pirating." First, the management of the neighboring agency or the management contemporary could be advised of the opening with a request to notify those he or she (a) knows is looking for a change and (b) could recommend for the position. Secondly, if a manager learns of a likely candidate presently employed by another agency contact could be made through the current employer. The current employer could be asked for permission to speak to the employee or to convey your interest. Employers will often be cooperative, particularly if the position offers advancement opportunities to the employee that he or she cannot provide.

(8) Agency Cutbacks. Recreation managers would do well to keep appraised of agencies that are being forced to cut back services either due to funding cuts or diminished need for services. These agencies could be rich with qualified, experienced staff hoping to relocate.

(9) College/University Placement Offices. Placement offices can serve two functions in the search process. First, they may be able to put the agency in touch with likely candidates and supply resumés for

review, as well as letters of recommendation. Secondly, placement personnel can make referrals to appropriate faculty of related academic departments.

(10) Cooperative/Experiential Education Coordinators. Numerous colleges/universities have active programs in cooperative-experiential education. Such programs are likely to be characterized by centralized coordination. The Coordinator may be helpful in the search process. He or she can often match appropriate students seeking opportunities for credit-bearing practical experience opportunities with agencies searching for semi-skilled, skilled, or paraprofession level personnel. The co-op has the advantage of providing the agency the opportunity to "field test" the candidate prior to an employment commitment. Here, too, the Coordinator is going to be conscious of the need to preserve the reputation of the school and the program's credibility. Great care is usually devoted to ensuring appropriate placements.

(11) Practicums/Internships. The typical academic program of Recreation and Leisure Studies requires a supervised fieldwork experience, one that is closely supervised and coordinated between the placement agency and the academic department. Managers seeking position candidates may do well to look to their own student affiliates or to other agencies. University/college supervisors will in all likelihood be willing to advise managers of sites which are currently supervising students that are likely candidates. Managers could then decide to either contact the student via the agency or the college supervisor.

(12) Employment Agencies. For smaller agencies professional employment agencies may prove invaluable. For a fee, such agencies will assume many of the time-consuming search activities; and since they want satisfied customers they can usually be relied upon to be quite thorough and efficient.

(13) Civil Service. A large number of recreation agencies rely on civil service systems for the search process. National, state, county, and many municipal agencies must hire from a central registry. There are some obvious advantages to the employer. First, there is likely to be a constant pool of candidates who meet the minimal educational and experiential requirements. Secondly, the scope of the search may attract more candidates, depending upon the nature of the governing body. There are problems with civil service searches,

however. The lists are often out-of-date. People may be qualified for eligibility for reasons not directly related to job requirements, i.e. veteran's status, minority membership, minute differences in examination scores. Finally, some managers express concern that civil service (in their specific settings) prevents them from hiring those they feel will fit into the organizational mainstream because of their social skills and attitudes; many managers believe these to be more, or at least equally, important than position on the list, test score, or other weighted factors.

(14) Newspapers. Perhaps the least desirable means of conducting a search is through the printed news media. Even as a search supplement, the newspaper approach can be expensive and inefficient. The ad, if it can be located, is often too brief (the cost factor) and results in the manager being inundated with inquiries at all times of the day. Also, newspapers are read by the general public, including pedophiles and others who may want to work with children for all the wrong reasons.

Summary

In summary, the recreation manager should realize the scope of search avenues available. Many of those mentioned have an obvious advantage: built-in screening for appropriate candidates. College/university faculty, high school counselors and teachers, professional colleagues, and current employees are going to use discretion in conveying position information and are going to pay particular attention to a candidate's behavioral and emotional qualifications. They have two important commodities at stake: their professional reputations and the reputations of their agencies. Professional publications and gatherings provide some assurances that candidates are academically and experientially suitable. Professional employment groups also have two essential commodities at stake: reputation and income to continue business.

Finally, the search process must in the context of the child abuse issue be more than simply a means of attracting applicants. The process must emphasize the screening of applicants with respect to professional credentials (including experience) and the equally (if not more) important aspect of behavioral and emotional suitability for close, intimate contact with children.

The Application Form

"An application blank usually serves two purposes: as a tool to predict on-the-job success and as a source to provide preemployment information for administrative purposes" (Meyer and Donaho, p. 57). For the two purposes given, one thing should be obvious, namely: standardized forms should be avoided, since each agency is likely to be different in terms of specific goals and administrative concerns and connotations. Yet, this is not to suggest that the individual agency has carte blanche when it comes to the inquiries it can make on the application form. Regulations established at the national level were designed to protect the rights of individuals and to assure equal employment opportunities for citizens, to prohibit inquiries into certain facets of a person's life and mandate careful attention to the content of application forms, as well as to interview format. Because of these guidelines certain questions need to be avoided in the application form (and during the interview). Some questions which may be considered suspect and leading to unlawful discrimination in hiring are:

(1) What is your religion?
(2) What is your marital status?
(3) Have you ever been arrested?
(4) Have you ever been convicted of a crime?
(5) What is your race?
(6) What is your ethnic origin?
(7) What is your political affiliation?
(8) Are you disabled/handicapped?
(9) What are the ages of your children or dependents?
(10) What was your place of birth?
(11) What are your physical characteristics?*
(12) What is the lowest salary you will accept?*
(13) What is your age?
(14) What is your financial status?
(15) Is a friend or relative a former or current employee of this agency?*
(16) Will you work weekends?
(17) Are you a naturalized or native citizen of the United States?
(18) Have you ever been treated for mental illness?

*(Horine, 1985, p. 44)

What Can Be Asked?

Remaining faithful to the conviction that agencies should not adapt a standardized application but develop one germane to their own needs and organizational goals, only areas of appropriate inquiry will be mentioned. Under most conditions, employers may ask for the following information:

(1) Name
(2) Current address
(3) Phone number(s) at home and at work
(4) Social Security number
(5) Education—level, location, degree, area of specialization
(6) Current employment—location, type of work, name of supervisor
(7) Previous employment—location, type of work, name of supervisor
(8) Professional credentials—licensure, certification
(9) Special skills—activity and technical
(10) Languages other than English spoken and proficiency level
(11) U.S. citizenship—yes or no. If no, type of visa and registration number
(12) The contributions the applicant believes he/she can make to the agency
(13) Hobbies or special interests
(14) Workshops, conferences, symposia attended in last (?) years
(15) Names and addresses of possible references

It is recommended that all applications be closed with the applicant's signature beneath a brief statement which:

(a) provides permission to do a background check on their work history;
(b) provides permission to check with references and other sources related to candidate's background;
(c) witnesses the understanding that any falsification of information or deliberate omissions is justification for refusal to hire or, if employed, termination of employment.

(Meyer and Donaho, p. 81)

Administrators are urged to require applicants to forward additional documents with the completed application form; namely, a resumé and an official transcript from the high school, community college or college/university. These documents will serve the purpose of confirming (in part) information on the application form. Transcripts without the raised, official seal of the school should not be accepted.

The Interview Process

"The interview process is important because the program manager and other interested individuals have an opportunity to meet the candidates and make decisions about their attitudes, capabilities, temperament and other characteristics that may be pertinent in making the final selection" (USDHHS, *Recruitment and Selecting of Staff,* 1985, p. 2). Furthermore, Rodney and Toalson (p. 155) state, "The purpose of the personal, or oral, interview is to see if a candidate has the personal qualities needed for the job to be filled. Strictly speaking, it is a person evaluation of a candidate's appearance and personality." The interview has an extensive history in the hiring practices of Recreation and Leisure Service agencies. It is through the interview that managers can either confirm or test for qualification of the candidate depicted on application materials and those desirable to the agency. Yet, the interview can lead to unfavorable results if not properly planned and conducted. When hiring personnel who will be interacting with children it is particularly important to create an environment that will allow for the disclosure of pertinent information relative to their professional qualifications and personal suitability.

The interview is conducted after the review of application forms, letters of recommendation, and other appropriate materials which have led to the subsequent selection of finalists. However, none of the aforementioned should lull the manager into complacency or into "letting down the guard." The interview will lead to the hiring decision. Therefore, it must have sufficient time allocated and be well planned as to content and climate.

Time

Providing adequate time may necessitate the cancellation or postponement of other administrative duties, programmatic tasks, and personal activities. Positive interaction is unlikely to be a result of a hurried interview. The interviewer should guard against rushed questions, omission of questions, or "spoon-feeding" answers to candidates in order to "move on" to the next item. A sense of importance and relevance should be transmitted to the candidate and he/she should be given adequate time to respond. Likewise, the manager needs adequate time to listen or reflect on each response. A "machine gun" approach to questioning will not allow accurate impressions to be formed as to candidate attitudes and interests or the candidate's personality.

Time relates, as well, to the time of the day of the interview. The interviewer is likely to be more informative if the candidate can select a time that will provide adequate opportunity to respond. The manager may be wise to allow sufficient latitude to the candidate to select a day and time within parameters established for the interview phase of the hiring process. Candidates whose only options are to interview after a day's work or during a break in his or her workday may not be fresh or relaxed enough to project a truthful or accurate image.

Planning

"Off the cuff" interviews may be relaxed, but rarely are they productive. Yet, a well-planned interview may appear relaxed and also provide the desired information. A planned interview is characterized by a set of standardized questions which will allow for the disclosure of a central body of information on all the finalists that can serve to screen both for personal and professional characteristics. Standardized questions should relate to items as mentioned previously, as well as cover such professional concerns as education, past work experience, credentials, leadership skills, desired working conditions, and career goals. Managers must, however, remember to keep in mind the necessity of abiding by the EEO and Affirmative Action recommendation discussed earlier.

Climate

Interview climate refers to the atmosphere of the interview. The interview atmosphere is influenced by the interviewer, freedom from distraction, privacy and other environmental factors.

First, if the chief executive of the leisure agency chooses to delegate responsibility for interviewing finalists the individual chosen should be organized, speak clearly and with inflection, and be personable. Good candidates may form negative impressions of the agency if the interviewer is unorganized, hard to understand, or abrasive. Needless to say, the person conducting the interview should have adequate knowledge of the agency to respond to the interviewee's inquiries.

Interviewers should leave instructions with the agency secretary that there are to be no interruptions during the interview. Constant, or even occasional, interruptions can disrupt the candidate's and the interviewer's concentration and convey the impression that the process is not taken very seriously by the agency.

Privacy and confidentiality must be guaranteed the interviewee. It is imperative that a location for the interview be selected that will prevent third parties from "listening in" to the deliberations. Few individuals feel comfortable discussing themselves behind room dividers or in a common office area.

Applicants should be assured that their comments will be used only for hiring purposes and not be conveyed beyond those immediately concerned within the agency. A candidate may not wish for the current employer to know of the interview or of the reasons for wishing to change employment.

Environmental factors also play an important role in the interview process. A comfortable setting is a must for an effective interview. The room temperature should be in a comfortable range (68°–75°). The room should be well lighted. Comfortable seating should be provided. The interviewer should not be seated behind a desk. The room should be free of outside distractions (lawn mowers or air conditioning compressors outside the window). The room should be pleasantly furnished. Coffee or other liquid refreshment such as water should be available. Tape recorders and video recorders should be used only with the candidate's knowledge and permission. Smoking should not be permitted. And, finally, the room should be well ventilated.

It is important to remember one thing: do not make commitments to a candidate immediately following or at the end of the interview. The candidate should be informed that his responses and credentials will be reviewed, along with those of the other finalists, and that notification of the decision will be rendered by a specified date. Candidates should also be reminded that a background check must be completed prior to employment.

Finally, it may be helpful to list the specific purposes of the employment interview. The interview should be structured to accomplish these purposes of both the agency and the candidate:

(1) To confirm/discover the candidate's related work experience.
(2) To confirm/discover the candidate's related training and education.
(3) To discover the candidate's personality characteristics.
(4) To confirm/discover the candidate's special skills and interests.
(5) To advise the candidate of the specific nature of the agency.
(6) To inform the candidate of the agency's working conditions and expectations.
(7) To respond to inquiries the candidate may have about the agency.

(8) To familiarize the candidate with the physical plant—a tour should be a standard part of the interview procedure.

(9) To persuade the candidate that the agency is competitive in terms of salary, perks, personnel policy, advancement opportunities and concern for employee welfare.

(10) To persuade the candidate that the agency's programs are of the highest quality.

(11) To convince the agency that the candidate has the background, desire and initiative to do the desired tasks.

(12) To convince the agency that the candidate has personality traits suitable for fostering desirable participant behaviors and attitudes.

(13) To persuade the agency that the candidate has the skills (leadership and activity) to foster the growth and public perception of the agency.

(Meyer and Donaho, p. 155)

In closing, the interview is crucial in the process of assuring a safe, supportive program atmosphere for the recreation and leisure services agency. It should be approached seriously and structured to result in the candidate's perception of its seriousness. Yet, a balance is essential. The candidate should also be made to feel that the agency is equally concerned for his/her comfort and welfare. This balance is critical for the free exchange of information and reliable decision making by both parties.

Letters of Recommendation

Unfortunately, letters of recommendation are often overlooked as a viable method of screening applicants. A conversation with the administrator of a large community recreation agency about letters of recommendation resulted in the following comments:

> Letters of recommendation? Sometimes. I really don't put much faith in them. You know, most of the time they don't tell you much. Unless the competition for a job is really heavy I'll usually forget about them and go with the results of the interview. Besides, we rarely have the time to wait for the letters. We need to fill these jobs so we can keep our programs up and running.

Such an attitude about any phase of the staffing process is analogous to playing Russian roulette with all the pistol's chambers loaded. In this instance, the reason for the lack of confidence in the references lies with the administrator. He simply did not ask the right questions of the reference concerning the referent or, to put it another way, did not provide guidelines for letter content.

The administrator's first task is to identify the references to be used. References may be selected from a listing provided by the applicant. However, this may not be the most reliable source, since applicants tend to identify references they believe will have positive things to say. Another ploy is to contact former employers as opposed to current employers. Current employers could become disturbed to learn an employee is contemplating leaving his or her agency and be less than fair in the reply. The applicant's employment could also be jeopardized. On the other hand, former employers can afford to be much more honest in their replies. They may not be as hampered by the possible repercussions of the Freedom of Information Act and can, therefore, feel free to be candid in their assessment of the applicant.

Another possible source of information is college/university faculty. Using the application form and the resumé as sources, the employer can identify the school and major department and then contact the appropriate faculty for letters. But, here too, some caution should be exercised. As one of the author's colleagues stated, "If a student is good enough to graduate from our program, he deserves a positive letter of recommendation to help him gain employment." Such an attitude is reckless and does not take into consideration the dire consequences to the academic unit, the agency, and agency clientele of an ill-conceived letter of applicant support. Fortunately, most faculty are aware that graduation may reflect nothing more than academic performance and relate little to emotional suitability for a particular agency. Many faculty are responsible enough to not write letters of recommendation unless asked to respond to specific inquiries. This leads to the next item of discussion.

Questions to Ask

For a letter of recommendation to be helpful to a specific setting or population some guidance needs to be provided to the reference. Before posing specific questions for response, the agency should provide a brief description of the agency—its programs, goals and clientele. Following the description, the respondent should be asked to reply to some site-specific questions, and in the instance of youth-serving agencies some of these questions should relate specifically to the candidate's suitability for working with children. Following are some questions which should be posed:

(1) Would you be reluctant to employ this individual for a position involving close, intimate contact with children? If yes, for what reasons?

(2) In your opinion, what are the applicant's qualifications for working with children?

(3) How do children respond to the applicant?

(4) For what youth-oriented programs do you believe the candidate to be most suited?

In addition to these questions, the employer may wish to formulate inquiries specific to items as mentioned previously. Other questions related to education, professional credentials and skills may also be appropriate, as would questions related to such generic qualities as cooperation, punctuality, initiative and reliability.

At the end of the reference criteria sheet, the reference should be thanked and reminded of the agency's concern over assuring its clientele of a safe and secure setting. Finally, it is suggested that the employer call each reference to cite specific items from the criteria sheet for the purpose of emphasizing the importance of a candid reply and to authenticate the process.

It is unlikely that an individual will knowingly falsely respond to specific questions. That should not, however, cause the employer to be the least bit reluctant to institute the final screening procedure, one which can be conducted prior to or following the personal interview. Since the process does require the cooperation of an outside agency, it may be reduce the potential work load and request the final screening after the final candidate has been selected but prior to employment.

Background Check

The final screening process referred to is a background check by a law enforcement agency, the municipal or agency legal counsel, the state attorney general's office, or a contracted and licensed investigator. Of special interest would be any history of behaviors which may endanger children. To reiterate, applicants should be advised via the job announcement, the application form and the interview that background checks will be conducted and that misrepresentation of information is cause for disconsideration for employment.

The investigators have at their disposal, if adequately armed with the applicant's name and social security number, public records at the national, state, county or parish, and municipal levels. These records should be reviewed closely for any incidences of arrest and conviction for child sexual and physical abuse or for the trafficking of controlled substances. If the individual was arrested but not convicted, the evidence of acquittal should be reviewed closely. In addition, further checks should be made to determine if there is evidence of subsequent behavior which may suggest that the applicant is likely to place children at risk. The investigators should endeavor to use all records available to determine an applicant's suitability and should pay particular attention to unaccounted-for periods (school, military service, employment) in the candidate's life. If no records can be found or if the candidate refuses to disclose his or her whereabouts for such a period, then employment must be denied. Do not be intimidated by threats of legal action into hiring staff whose backgrounds are not vividly clear.

Some Additional Screening Possibilities

Employers may wish to consider testing as a part of the screening process. A college degree in Recreation and Leisure Studies does not, unfortunately, mean that the candidate is best suited for leisure services or for working with children. Depending upon the individual setting and resources available, the employer may seek additional assurances by requesting the candidate to submit to a battery of tests, making certain that such testing falls within the allowable parameters of the Civil Rights Act. The battery may include psychological, aptitude, and intelligence tests. Qualified testing professionals should be consulted prior to instituting such a battery for advice on test suitability or selection. Such personnel should also be available for administration and interpretation of tests.

A Final Word on Personnel Selection

It may be trite, but it bears repeating. Personnel or staff are the heart of a program. People, more than all other factors combined, determine the success or failure of a program. Yet, in reference to the maintenance of a safe and secure environment, staffing is often underconsidered or not considered at all. It is a known fact, one that is demonstrated almost daily in the news media, that people who abuse children gravitate to occupations that will permit close or intimate contact with children. Recreation is such an occupation.

The personnel or staffing process, if conscientiously approached, can provide opportunities to inhibit the aforementioned gravitation. Administrators cannot afford to be overwhelmed by lengthy and impressive resumés or by flowery letters of recommendation. Neither can the administrators allow themselves to be swept off their feet by dynamic candidates during interviews. No aspect of the hiring process can be neglected or diminished if there are to be assurances of the hiring of suitable personnel or the selection of appropriate volunteers. The safety and welfare of children cannot and must not be compromised by soft staffing practices.

Finally, if the administrator is not inspired to follow the procedures which have been recommended in this chapter for reasons of professional and personal ethics or a concern for child welfare, there is a remaining reason to be cautious and thorough. The legal concept of respondeat superior relates to an agency's susceptibility to litigation for the actions of its employees. Under this principle, an agency that cannot demonstrate responsible hiring practices to manage risk to its clients or participants may find its position as a defendant jeopardized. Agencies are encouraged to consult legal counsel with respect to the relationship between staffing policy, procedures and risk management. The trend, however, suggests that administrators and their agencies may be found liable for gross negligence in matters of personnel practices. Administrators have a duty to their service recipients to assure a safe environment; this duty includes the availability of competent and suitable personnel. A proactive staffing procedure can significantly diminish the need to appear before a court and result in a positive perception by the courts, the general public, applicants and those being served.

Chapter Thirteen

ABUSE, RECREATION AND THE LAW

INTRODUCTION

The previous chapters have made one truth apparent; namely, the world is a dangerous place for today's children. The contemporary child does not, unfortunately, live in the ideal world described by Caulfield (1979, p. 4) where "all children would receive just what they need in the way of nurture and love; none would be victim of abuse or neglect." What's even more unfortunate is that today's child does not live in a world that could be described as even just slightly less than ideal where "abuse and neglect might exist but when they were recognized, all people would make every effort to solve the problem in a humane and effective manner" (Caulfield, p. 4). Utopia and Shangri-la were not characterized as places of diverse child-rearing practices, of single-parent families of unbearable economic and social stress, of racial discrimination, of diverse cultures, or of primary concern for the self. In these ideal settings the child would be revered, those who harbored thoughts of abusing children would actively seek help for themselves and their families and there would be no need for laws to protect children. In this far-from-ideal or real world, however, laws are regrettably needed to protect our children from their parents, guardians, teachers, ministers, scout leaders, and others who have been entrusted with their care and nurturing. Many of these individuals have chosen to exacerbate even further the lives of children growing up in a world of increasing stress by imposing on them the physical pain, shame and burden of child abuse. As a result, it has been necessary to enact laws for the protection of our children from the abusers. One such category of laws are referred to as reporting statutes or laws.

REPORTING STATUTES

Currently, all fifty states, as well as the U.S. territories and the District of Columbia, have laws that mandate the reporting of child abuse. As might be expected, these laws differ from one state to the other; yet, they all address common elements, namely:

- definitions of abuse
- types of abusive behaviors which must be reported
- means of reporting
- who must report
- time frames for reporting
- who is to receive the report
- content of the report
- protection (immunity) provided the reporter.

Due to the overriding concern for the welfare of the child it should be noted that no state requires that there be absolute proof of abuse before a report is made. Rather, most require the reporting of suspected abuse. "The law may specify reporting of 'suspected' incidences or include the phrase 'reason to believe'" (Heindl et al., p. 33). The common thrust, however, is to convince potential reporters that suspected cases of child abuse should be reported immediately.

Who Reports?

The majority of states as well as territories require the reporting of suspected incidences of child abuse (including neglect) by all of those who work directly with children or who may be in contact with children in some other capacity. A review of the state statutes as of 1986 does not reveal that in any is the Recreation and Leisure Services professional specified as one who must report suspected child abuse. This, however, should not be interpreted as freedom from legal responsibility to report. Each state's statutes do, however, identify categories of professionals and paraprofessionals that may well include the Recreation and Leisure Services provider. What follows is a state-by-state identification of categories of individuals, which may well include Recreation and Leisure Service providers, that are required to report suspected abuse in their respective states or territories:

1. Alabama: day care workers; mental health professionals; school officials.
2. Alaska: school staff members of public or private schools; officers of institutions; child care providers.

3. American Samoa: hospital personnel engaged in the admission, care or treatment of patients; school official or employee; worker in a family care home or child care center; mental health professional.
4. Arizona: school personnel; counselor or any other person having responsibility for child care.
5. Arkansas: hospital personnel; school official; day-care center worker; child care worker; mental health professional; member of the staff of any public or private agency.
6. California: any child care custodian; employee of any public or private school; administrator of a public or private day camp; employee of a community care facility; employee of a child care institution; any person who has reason to believe that a home or institution is unsuitable.
7. Colorado: hospital personnel engaged in the care or treatment of patients; school official or employee; worker in a family care or child care center; mental health professional.
8. Connecticut: mental health professional; any person paid for caring for children in a day-care center; any person having reasonable cause to suspect a child is in danger of being abused or neglected.
9. Delaware: any person in the healing arts; any other person who knows or reasonably suspects child abuse or neglect.
10. District of Columbia: person involved in the care and treatment of patients; school official; day-care worker; mental health professional; member of the staff of a school, hospital, social agency or similar institution.
11. Florida: all employees or agents of the district school board; every staff member of every general or specialty hospital; mental health professional; day-care worker; other professional child care, residential or institutional worker.
12. Georgia: day-care personnel; school personnel.
13. Guam: any person who in the course of employment or practice of his profession who comes into contact with children; hospital personnel engaged in the care of children; child care worker; mental health professional.
14. Hawaii: any health-related occupation who examines, attends, treats, or provides specialized services to minors; employees or officers of any public or private agency or institution providing

social, medical, hospital or mental health services; employees of any licensed or registered child care facility.

15. Idaho: day-care personnel; person having reason to believe that a child has been abused.

16. Illinois: personnel engaged in the care of persons; director or staff assistant of a nursery school or a child day-care center; field personnel of the Illinois Department of Mental Health, Developmental Disabilities, Corrections, Children and Family Services.

17. Indiana: any person who has reason to believe that a child is the victim of abuse or neglect; an individual as a member of the staff of a medical or public or private institution, school, facility or agency.

18. Iowa: employee or operator of a licensed day-care center; staff of a mental health center.

19. Kansas: other employees of a school; employers of child care services.

20. Kentucky: any person (responsible for the care of children).

21. Louisiana: other persons or agencies having responsibility for the care of children.

22. Maine: homemaker; child care personnel, mental health professional.

23. Maryland: a person other than a health professional . . . who has reason to believe that a child has been subject to abuse; "educator or social worker" means any professional employee of any correctional, public, parochial or private educational, health, juvenile service, social, or social service agency, institution or licensed facility.

24. Massachusetts: hospital personnel engaged in the care or treatment of persons; day-care worker; any person paid to care for or work with a child in any public or private facility or home or program funded by the Commonwealth. . . .

25. Michigan: only regulated child care provider.

26. Minnesota: a professional . . . engaged in the healing arts, social services, hospital administration, psychiatric treatment, child care.

27. Mississippi: child care giver; any other person having cause to suspect that a child brought before him for . . . care or treatment or of whom he has knowledge; member of the staff of a hospital, school, child care center or similar institution.

28. Missouri: hospital and clinic personnel; mental health professional; day-care center worker; other child care worker; person with responsibility for the care of children.

29. Montana: member of hospital staff; health or mental health professionals; other school officials; employee of any registered or licensed day-care facility; institutional worker.

30. Nebraska: any other person who has reasonable cause to believe that a child or an incompetent or disabled person has been subject to abuse or neglect.

31. Nevada: any person engaged in . . . care of persons; any person who is employed by a facility or establishment that provides care for children; children's camp or other public or private facility, institution or agency. . . .

32. New Hampshire: hospital personnel; school official; day-care worker; any other person . . . shall report.

33. New Jersey: Any person having reasonable cause to believe that a child has been subjected to child abuse. . . .

34. New Mexico: any other person knowing or suspecting that a child is an abused or a neglected child.

35. New York: hospital personnel; school official; day-care center worker; mental health professional; member of the staff . . . or other public or private institution, school, facility or agency.

36. North Carolina: any person who has cause to suspect child abuse or neglect; any person or institution.

37. North Dakota: mental health professional; day-care center or any other child care worker.

38. Ohio: health care professional; administrator or employee of a child day-care center; public or private children services agency.

39. Oklahoma: every other person. . . .

40. Oregon: employee of the Department of Human Resources, county health department, community mental health program, a county juvenile department, or a licensed child-caring agency; employee of day care.

41. Pennsylvania: any persons who, in the course of their employment, occupation or practice of their profession, come into contact with children.

42. Puerto Rico: professionals in health and education . . . and persons working as directors or employees of institutions or centers for the care or rehabilitation of children.

43. Rhode Island: any person who has reason to believe. . . .
44. South Carolina: mental health or allied health professional; child care worker in any day care center or child-caring institution.
45. South Dakota: mental health professional; school official.
46. Tennessee: mental health professional; day care center worker; school official or personnel; residential or institutional worker; any other person. . . .
47. Texas: any person having cause to believe. . . .
48. Utah: any person who has reason to believe . . . or observes. . . .
49. Vermont: day care worker; mental health professional.
50. Virgin Islands: hospital personnel engaged in . . . care or treatment of persons; mental health professional; other school personnel; day care worker.
51. Virginia: other person employed in a public or private school; person providing full or part-time child care for pay on a regularly planned basis; any professional person . . . employed by a private or state-operated hospital, institution or facility. . . .
52. Washington: professional school personnel; child care facility personnel; anyone engaged in a professional capacity during the regular course of employment in encouraging or promoting the health, welfare, support or education of children; an employee or agent of any public or private organization or institution.
53. West Virginia: other school personnel; child care . . . worker.
54. Wisconsin: medical or mental health professional; child care worker in a day-care center or child-caring institution; member of the treatment staff employed by or working under contract with a county department. . . .
55. Wyoming: any person who knows or has reasonable cause to believe or suspect. . . .

The primary source for all of the aforementioned information on who is required to report in each state and territory is *State Statutes 1986: Who Must Report* which was compiled by the Clearinghouse on Child Abuse and Neglect Information. Only those segments of the reporting laws that most likely relate to Recreation and Leisure Services personnel were mentioned.

What is apparent from a review of the state reporting statutes is that the Recreation and Leisure Services professional is not exempt from reporting suspected child abuse (or neglect). What is also apparent is that the specifics of the reporting process likely differ from state to state. Therefore, it is strongly advised that the Recreation and Leisure Service administrators and staff members consult the statutes of their respective states for additional information. However, it should be remembered that "currently many states require staff of early childhood programs to report suspected child abuse and neglect directly to a specified agency. While program policy may require reporting to a child abuse coordinator or program director, this does not eliminate the need for the worker to ensure that a report is filed with CPS. Thus, if the staff member who is designated by the program to report fails to do so, the early childhood worker should report directly" (Broadhurst, Edmunds, and MacDicken, 1979, pp. 31–32). Finally, the literature does not suggest that the advise proffered by Broadhurst, Edmunds and MacDicken is not applicable to all other staff and in all other settings where children are participants. Quite simply, the responsibility for protecting the welfare of our children cannot be abdicated. The ultimate responsibility for making a child protective service (CPS) aware of the possible abuse and neglect of a child has lies with the individual suspecting or observing the abuse or neglect.

Why Report?

Aside from the obvious moral and professional reasons to report suspected or observed incidences of child abuse there are legal incentives to do so as well. The professional who does not find abuse to be personally abhorrent or who is fearful of "getting involved" should be advised that there are legal consequences or penalties for not reporting. The penalties are most certainly to be imposed against the professional personally and, perhaps, against the employing agency. Because of the possible consequences to both employees and the agency, the administration of the agency has an obligation to not only require reporting but also to make individuals aware of the possible criminal and civil penalties which may likely be imposed upon them if it should become apparent that they had knowledge or evidence of the abuse of one of their youthful charges.

It may be worth noting here, before discussing penalties any further, that the Recreation and Leisure Services professional in most states and jurisdictions cannot seek refuge under privileged communication. The recreator is strongly advised to review his or her own state's statutes for information and guidance related to exclusion of privileged communication with a child or the perpetrator.

Penalties

As with most state statutes there are penalties for non-compliance. As suggested earlier, so is the case with child abuse and neglect reporting statutes. "The typical penalties range from a low of 5 to 30 days in jail and/or a $10 to $100 fine to as high as a year in jail and/or a $1,000 fine" (*Child Abuse and Neglect: State Reporting Laws,* p. 15).

Caulfield reports: "In 26 states a person who suspects abuse or neglect but does not report it may be criminally prosecuted for failure to do so. The punishment for conviction ranges from a $25 minimum fine in New Mexico to a $500 fine and/or six months in jail in Alabama and Louisiana" (1979, pp. 20–21). She also advises, "In 18 states, if you encounter a reportable case of abuse or neglect, you may be convicted for not reporting it, whether or not you knew a report was required and regardless of whether the failure was deliberate or a case of negligence" (1979, p. 21).

The Recreation and Leisure Services professional may well, depending upon state law, be facing civil action in addition to criminal litigation in the event suspected abuse is not reported, particularly if the absence of a report leads to the additional injury or death of the child. The failure to report the suspected or confirmed abuse may be viewed as cause to presume or confirm negligence on the part of the individual. This is particularly true in states having mandatory reporting laws (1979, p. 21).

Unlike criminal action, civil action will not result in the imprisonment of the negligent staff member or agency. It will, however, likely result (if the plaintiff's action is successful) in a sizable financial or cash award. This is particularly true if the failure to report results in further injury to the abuse victim. For example, in 1976 a $200,000 claim for damages was won against a California physician and his employing hospital when he failed to report obvious abuse (Broadhurst and MacDicken, p. 2). This settlement is worth noting, in that it demonstrates that the employing agency can as well as the employee be found negligent and liable in civil action resulting from failure to report abuse and neglect. Considering the litigious nature of contemporary society and the tendency of generous court decisions, the 1976 decision would likely today be larger — maybe much larger. This assumption is supported by a statement made as long ago as 1979 by Broadhurst, Edmunds and MacDicken; they stated, "In some states, recent court decisions have resulted in civil judgments in excess of one million dollars" (1979, p. 10).

In summary, the failure to report suspected abuse and neglect can be, and will likely be, expensive to both the professional and the employing agency in terms of dollars and time—time spent in defense against civil and/or criminal litigation or in jail or prison. Agencies can protect themselves as well as their employees by (1) demonstrating the existence of agency policies that are compatible with state statutes that mandate reporting and that outline or specify reporting procedures; (2) providing comprehensive staff training as to indicators of abuse, appropriate and inappropriate staff-client behaviors, and reporting mandates and procedures; and (3) keeping up-to-date records of staff training and attempts to screen new staff and volunteers as to their appropriateness to work directly with children (see Chapter Twelve). Such steps by agencies are supported by Stavis when he states, "And as most people know, under our laws the liability or responsibility for an injury does not always remain confined to the actual perpetrator. Just as likely, a supervisory authority is held equally responsible under the legal doctrine of respondant superior (the master is liable for acts of his servant) or other legal principles, such as a board of director's statutory responsibility for mismanagement by employees of a not-for-profit corporation" (Stavis, 1988, p. 1). Again, the individual is urged to refer to state statutes and agency administration for specific procedure and penalties relating to the reporting of child abuse and neglect. Likewise, administrators are urged to consult state statutes and legal council as to appropriate steps to be taken for the protection for the agency against successful litigation for child abuse—reporting as well as perpetration.

Immunity

Every state, territory, and the District of Columbia provides immunity from criminal penalty and civil liability for all of those required (and those not required) to report suspected or confirmed incidence of child abuse and neglect if the report is made in good faith. "To be acting in good faith, when you report a suspected case of child abuse or neglect, you must have 'reasonable grounds' to support the belief that the child has been abused. Good faith does not mean that you personally are required to believe beyond a doubt that abuse or neglect has occurred" (Caulfield, 1981, p. 19). This condition of immunity requires that the individual reporting do so without malice. "In legal terms, to say that a person acted with malice is to attempt to prove that the person acted with spite or an improper motive. Malice is a specific intent to harm, a state of mind that is difficult to prove" (Caulfield, 1981, p. 19).

Immunity, it must be emphasized, does not mean that the professional cannot be named in a lawsuit. A lawsuit is always a possible consequence of reporting suspected abuse and neglect. It is a regrettable fact that a suspecting staff member can be sued if he does report and if he does not. The angered parent or any other suspected perpetrator very well may file suit for defamation of character, harassment, or invasion of privacy. Yet, "The risk of being held liable in these actions are slim, however, since in each of the above legal actions the person bringing the lawsuit must prove that you acted with malice or perhaps with extreme negligence" (Caulfield, 1981, p. 22).

The best immunity against criminal and civil liability in reporting is in the report itself. The reports should be made in such a manner to simply report the child's appearance, behaviors or explanation for injuries or behaviors and not to accuse the parents. A report should state or suggest only "that a child may be an abused child, not that the parents are child abusers" (Heindl et al., 1979, p. 33). The reader is urged to refer to Chapter Eleven and specifically Illustration XI-1 for guidance on the report content.

Other Legal Considerations

Screening of Personnel

As mentioned previously in this chapter and elaborated upon in Chapter Twelve, the screening of personnel prior to employment is one means of preventing the abuse of youthful program participants. This means of preventing abuse by recreation and leisure services staff, as well as by other child care personnel, has been mandated by some states; for example, Maryland, New Jersey, and New York.

Maryland's H. B. 528, Criminal Background Investigation—Child Care Facilities, was introduced to the Maryland House of Delegates on January 17, 1986. The bill requires that applicants for employment in certain types of agencies that care for and supervise children undergo a thorough background check by federal and state law enforcement offices. The purpose is to determine if the applicant has a history of conviction

Illustration XI-I. A SAMPLE FORM FOR REPORTING ABUSE

The City of Anytown
Department of Parks and Recreation
5555 Fifth St.   55555   (555) 555-0000

Report of Suspected Child Abuse Form

Name of Suspected Victim: _____
Age:
                          First   MI   Last
Sex: _____   Address of Victim: _____
                                  Number   Street

                                  _____
                                  City
Name of Parent(s)/Guardian(s): _____

Address of Parent(s) or Guardian(s): _____
                                      Number   Street

                                      _____
                                      City
Parent(s)/Guardian(s) Phone Number: (   ) ___ - _____
Type of Suspected Abuse: _____ Neglect _____ Physical Abuse _____
Sexual Abuse _____ Emotional Abuse
Describe the physical and behavioral indicators that led to
suspicion of abuse: _____

Time & Date Suspect Abuse was Noted: _____
Place Suspected Abuse was Noted: _____
Suspected Victim's Account of Injuries/Abuse (Place, Date, Time of
Infliction; Who Inflicted Injuries; Weapons Or Instruments Used,
etc.): _____

Other Observations/Information Which You Feel Warrant Futher
Investigation: _____

Person Making Report: _____ Person Receiving Report: _____
                      Signature   Signature

_____   _____
Printed or Typed Name   Printed or Typed Name

_____   _____
       Title   Title

_____   _____
Date   Time AM/PM   Date   Time AM/PM
              Circle   Circle

_____   _____
Phone Number (Office)   Phone Number (Office)

or a conviction pending any of a variety of crimes including murder; rape; child pornography; child abduction; child kidnapping; a sexual offense involving a minor, a non-consenting adult, or of a person who is mentally or physically incapable of adequate self-defense against such an assault. The bill not only requires agencies which will employ Recreation and Leisure Services personnel to comply with the background investigation requirements, but actually specifies recreation. Specifically, it states, "A recreation center or recreation program operated by state or local government primarily serving minors; or a day or overnight camp . . . primarily serving minors" (see Appendix I). The bill also states that the check or investigation is to extend to individuals who may be seeking volunteer opportunities in such organizations.

New Jersey's proposed Bill S-2512 deals specifically with the certification of Recreation and Leisure Service professionals. The bill is directed to the establishment of a certifying board to administer a plan of professional certification for both the public and private sectors of employment; certification of the public sector to be mandatory and permissive in the private sector. It further stipulates that the board is to have conducted by the State Bureau of Identification and the Federal Bureau of Investigation a background investigation to determine if the candidate "has been convicted of a crime involving moral turpitude, violence, sexual assault or neglect which relates to the exploitation of any child or adult, is a drug addict or alcoholic or is mentally incompetent . . . " (see Appendix H). The bill stipulates that such evidence is to result in the denial of the candidate's application for professional certification.

Chapter 677 of New York's Child Abuse Prevention Act of 1985 specifies that agencies that employ individuals who have the potential for regular and substantial contact with youth who are provided care by the agency should consult the "department" to determine suitability for such contact. Specifically, each employee and volunteer should be screened for evidence of previous involvement in activities which might place the children at risk. The law specifies that any individual applying for a license to operate a child care facility or program (including a camp) shall be screened, as well as the employer, prior to the license being granted (*New York Consolidated Laws Service*, 1985, pp. 1732–1780).

Obviously, the consequences of not complying could be devastating to an agency or program. The message is clear: the administration of such programs (Recreation and Leisure Services included) have not just a moral or professional obligation to screen staff and assure a safe environment but a statutory one as well. Should a program staff member abuse one of the program's youthful participants, and were it disclosed that he or she had a prior history of such activity and that no background investigation was conducted, the results are predictable. Not only will the abuser be persecuted, but it is quite likely that the agency will be found both criminally and civilly negligent. The consequence to the agency and the program are obvious. The same is true for the careers and reputations of the administrator and program employees. All Recreation and Leisure Service administrators and employees should consult both with their legal councils and state statutes to determine the existence of such mandates. If in existence, personnel practices should then be reviewed as to agency or program compliance. For specific guidelines consult Chapter Twelve.

Training

There are state statutes which mandate the training of individuals who are responsible for the direct care of children. The training responsibility is usually charged to the state CPS. The statutes may require the CPS to:

- prepare and disseminate educational programs and materials on child abuse and neglect
- provide educational programs for professionals required by law to make reports

(Broadhurst, and MacDicken, 1979, p. 3)

The state statutes may also require that the administration of agencies providing services to children make child abuse and neglect training available to all direct-care staff. It is likely to be stipulated that the training shall include such components as abuse and neglect identification, orientation to reporting laws, agency reporting responsibilities and procedures, and the prevention and treatment of abuse. Here, too, the Recreation and Leisure Services profession should consult state statutes and agency policies to determine compliance.

SUMMARY

The legal aspects of child abuse are not solely the concern of law enforcement, the municipal or agency legal council or administration, or the social worker. The concern must be shared by all professions and professionals who provide direct services to children. A review of state statutes reveals that Recreation and Leisure Services personnel have as much legal responsibility to intervene in the cycle of abuse and neglect as does the physician, nurse, or social worker. Ignorance of that responsibility is indefensible and will eventually result in severe criminal and civil penalties. More importantly, it could well result in the additional injury or even death of a child.

Chapter Fourteen

PROGRAMMING FOR ABUSE PREVENTION AND TREATMENT

INTRODUCTION

Having reached this point in the text, the reader has hopefully made the commitment to become a fervent advocate for children by assuming an adversarial posture against child abuse. The preceding chapters have addressed such issues as the dynamics, costs and indicators of abuse; the extent of the problem; the nature of its perpetrators; the selection of personnel; the development of abuse policies; rationale for recreation's active role in a comprehensive community approach; the needs of the victims; and the legal mandates for intervention through the reporting of suspected and confirmed abuse. There should be no doubt at this point that responsibility for the intervention in and prevention and treatment of child abuse does not fall solely within the domain of therapeutic recreation practitioners; rather, all Recreation and Leisure Service practitioners who work directly with children have equal responsibility. Testimony has also been provided from other professions supporting recreation's active participation in the efforts to combat abuse. And, there have been reminders of the historical and close ties between the development of Recreation and Leisure Services and the concerns for child welfare. In addition, by now it should be obvious that the problem of child abuse cannot be adequately addressed by developing programs to meet the needs of only the children; the needs of the abusers must be met as well if the cycle of abuse is to be broken.

So, what additional information may be necessary for the Recreation and Leisure Services agency to undertake an active role in confronting the child abuse issue in its community? The Recreation and Leisure Services professional may find helpful some recommendations as to activities and programs to offer in both the prevention and treatment efforts. It is not suggested that the activities and programs that follow are the only ones worthy of consideration or that they will be successful in all instances. The recreation programmer is limited only by his or her creativity and initiative. Also, the selection and success of each activity or program will be determined by:

- The interests of the child or adult
- The needs of the child or adult
- The perceived appropriateness by the clinical team
- The current and foreseen resources of the family

Finally, the purpose of this chapter is to generate creative ideas for recreation programs that may be of value in the prevention and treatment of abuse. Programs and activities are offered in the hope that they may not only be implemented but that they will result in additional innovative programs as a consequence of their consideration.

APPROACHES FOR PREVENTING CHILD ABUSE

The first step in the development of recreation and leisure programs to assist in the community's joint efforts to prevent child abuse is to identify those families that are at risk. The most meaningful way to accomplish this task is through networking with others concerned with abuse prevention. Chapter Ten addresses becoming a member in a comprehensive community approach to combating abuse. The social service agencies and school systems can assist in the identification of families at risk. Though specific characteristics may differ from community to community there are some general characteristics which Cohn and others (Cohn, 1983, p. 4) offer which warrant consideration. The recreation agency should be alert for family situations where the following conditions exist:

- extended unemployment
- history of alcohol abuse
- lack of social support
- inaccessibility to community services
- crowded living conditions or inadequate housing
- large single-parent households
- disabled child in the household
- history of drug abuse
- history of illiteracy or low academic achievement
- low socioeconomic status
- large families with closely spaced siblings
- teenage parents of lower socioeconomic status

It should be mentioned again that due to the complex nature of child abuse that it is not possible to accurately predict who will abuse their children. However, "it is possible to do a pretty good job of identifying groups of people in which the risk is much greater or much less than average" (Cohn, 1983, p. 7). Some of these characteristics are reflected in the above listing. It goes without saying that a family may have two or more of these characteristics and never become involved in abuse activity. However, what research does tell us is that if these conditions exist and persist, the likelihood is greater that abuse will occur. Perhaps Cohn best defines the task of professionals concerned with the prevention of abuse. She states:

> A strategy for prevention clearly must concern itself with characteristics or circumstances that increase the likelihood of abuse. If possible, all families should have "enhancing" services available, but the target is always subgroups within the population who are classified as high-risk. In this, the political and moral risks in falsely identifying nonabusive but at-risk parents can be great in any response that can adversely label those so identified. The best course seems to be to do all possible to create supportive climates for all families while always seeking to identify and meet special needs.
>
> (Cohn, 1983, p. 7)

Here, too, it goes without saying, the recreation agency leadership and staff must, therefore, totally familiarize themselves with the community and families they serve as well as with the dynamics of child maltreatment.

COMPONENTS OF A PREVENTION PROGRAM

As discussed in Chapter Ten, the task of preventing the abuse of children is far too monumental for any one community agency. What is required is a comprehensive community approach. The recreation agency, as a part of the comprehensive approach, may discover that it can contribute to one or more of the preventative program areas identified by Cohn, namely:

- support programs for new parents
- education for parents
- early and regular child and family screening and treatment
- child care opportunities

- programs for abused children and young adults
- life skills training for children and young adults
- self-help groups and other neighborhood supports
- family support services.

(1983, p. 25)

Perhaps one additional program component should be mentioned in addition to those identified by Cohn. Jenkins, Salus and Schultze discuss the importance of the advocacy role for preventative efforts. This role goes beyond simply providing programs that may involve those areas identified but extend to the political arena through the vocal and active support of changes in the community's social, economic, and other conditions which lead to "dysfunctional family life" if left unaddressed. Programs, however, that are provided as part of the advocacy role should lead to new patterns of intervention and prevent problems in the family (Jenkins, Salus, and Schultze, 1979, p. 84).

Support Programs for New Parents

It has often been said that the most important job a person ever has is the one for which there is the least training or preparation. This job is, of course, parenting. Parenting is difficult even under the most ideal conditions, but imagine assuming the role if you're only a teenager, if you will not have a spouse, if your parents refuse to provide assistance, if your own parents were ineffective or unavailable during your development, if you have no social support, or if you have limited leisure interests or recreation skills. If these conditions exist in part or in total, the necessary positive bonding between the new parent and child will be difficult to accomplish without support programs that will provide opportunities for the development of supportive relationships and the acquisition of coping skills.

These young soon-to-be parents should be targeted as early in the pregnancy as possible to alter social or life-style patterns that may lead to abusive behaviors once the child is born. The prenatal emphasis takes into account the realization that the young parent will be detracted from preventative efforts by the demands of parenthood. The emphasis in the prenatal approach should be upon where to go for support, who to call or where to go when a respite from being a parent is necessary, where to go to satisfy recreational interests, and on the development of interests that can be pursued once the child arrives.

There are several things the recreation agency, particularly the community parks and recreation department, can do to provide support for these ill-prepared parents-to-be. Jenkins, Salus, and Schultze make reference to a "block parent system" (1979, p. 89) when they discuss the advocacy role. We could provide such a system of neighborhood support by opening up our community centers with a variety of programs and services designed specifically for the soon-to-be and new parents. Needless to say, the atmosphere must be accepting or such to assist the parent in coping with her feelings of isolation, frustration, and shame or embarrassment. Working in conjunction with health and social service agencies the community centers could offer support programs where the new parent could get assistance with medical and financial problems. A variety of club activities could likewise be developed around special interests. The community recreation agency could provide child care services during the activities, the cost of which could be covered entirely or in part by fees paid either by the young parent or a social service agency. This may, however, be an excellent way to utilize members of a core of responsible, experienced volunteers.

Education for Parents

To be an effective parent today one has to rely on more than instinct. Effective parenting is primarily a function of learning, learning from our own parents how to prepare for various stages of child development; how to respond in certain crises; how to cope with the various social expectations; and how to interact appropriately with the child to foster its psychological, physical, and social development. But, what if the young parent was either raised in a dysfunctional family or in the absence of positive parenting role models? Such is the situation for many of today's youthful parents. Perhaps they were born to ill-repared teenage parents; perhaps their parents were substance abusers; or perhaps they were raised in a single-parent family where 90–100 percent of the parent's energy was devoted to avoiding starvation or having to live on the streets or in the family automobile. In such situations children are taught little about how to be effective parents and they are, consequently, in dire need of education in effective parenting skills. The Recreation and Leisure Services agency should be able to make some significant contributions in the education of parents, particularly in the area of social interaction with the child. Typically, the child of a dysfunctional family has deficiencies in the area of play and often are uninformed or misinformed about recreational opportunities available within the home and within the community in general. What follow are a few suggestions as to how the Recreation and Leisure Service agencies in the communities may assist in the education component of abuse prevention.

First of all, the agency may do something as simple as make space and resources available for education programs conducted by other health and social agencies. For example, there may be a need to provide classes in newborn care, infant nutrition, or in home management. At-risk parents or parents-to-be are likely more willing to attend such classes if they do not involve expensive and complicated transportation arrangements or require venturing into unfamiliar neighborhoods. A familiar community center may be an ideal setting.

Secondly, other than simply providing space and resources the recreation agency may be able to encourage participation in the educational programs by providing on-site child care during the class times. This could alleviate the concern the parent may have over securing a babysitter. Here, too, this may be an ideal way for the recreation agency to utilize responsible and experienced (and screened) volunteers.

A third service or program that may be of value is that of leisure referral. As suggested previously, part of the anxiety about becoming a parent may well relate to the child's impact on how the parent pursues leisure time. This, of course, relates to informing the parent of alternatives to abuse. The ultimate goal of networking the new parent with the appropriate recreational resources, program or agency may be as uncomplicated as simply making her or him aware of those programs where child care is available or those that are available at times and locations convenient with child care arranged by the parent. The process, however, may be much more complex than simply informing the parent of available, appropriate recreation programs. If the parent has come from a dysfunctional family there may be the need for a structured program of leisure education and counseling. It may well be that the new parent is unaware of the impact of leisure time and the value of recreational pursuits to family unity. It may also be possible that a history of inappropriate leisure time pursuits is present. Quite simply, the new parent may not only not know the impact and value of recreation, but not know how to play or recreate. Therefore, the recreation agency may be called upon to provide a structured, comprehensive program of leisure counseling and education.

The goal of meeting the education needs of the family at risk may be satisfied by borrowing a program concept from the Joseph P. Kennedy, Jr. Foundation. Let's-Play-to-Grow was developed "to bring the physical and spiritual delights of play to all the parents and teachers who so deeply wish to reach special children and share with them a close and creative relationship," according to Eunice Kennedy Shriver (*Let's Play to Grow*, 1977, p. 1). Though the program was developed primarily to assist the parents and teachers of disabled children to foster a positive relationship in the family unit and the growth or development of the child through play, its structured program of instruction is readily adaptable to the situation under consideration. There are implications both pre- and post-natally. The expecting parent or parents could be referred to or volunteer to participate in order to acquire elementary play skills, and from that joint effort experience and develop a closer relationship. Then, upon the birth of the child, the parent or parents could again go through the program with the child. Not only will the child benefit in terms of acquired skills, but from the bonding that will likely result between the child and the parent(s).

The Let's-Play-to-Grow instructional packet consists of twelve booklets or guides. They are:

1. For the Special Child who is Very Young or Severely Handicapped
2. Fun with Rhythm, Movement and Dance
3. Fun with Seeing and Creating
4. Walking, Running, Jumping and Fun with Ropes
5. Fun Outdoors: Hiking, Camping, Picnics
6. Fun in the Water
7. Basic Ball Skills
8. Fun with Bowling
9. Fun with Volleyball
10. Fun with Basketball
11. Fun with Soccer and Kickball
12. Fun with Softball

For use in the preventative format the instruction could be conducted in sequence or based on specific needs and deficiencies. Recreation agencies wishing to consider adoption of the Let's-Play-to-Grow approach to play instruction should contact:

Let's-Play-to-Grow
Joseph P. Kennedy, Jr. Foundation
1701 K Street, N.W.
Washington, D.C. 20006

Child and Family Screening

As pointed out previously, not only expecting or new parents are at risk of abusing their children. Other events occur which can result in enough stress to lead to child abuse. The recreation leader can play an important role in the screening of children and families by being alert for behavior patterns which may suggest the family is at risk. During recreational activities, when defenses may be down, participants may express concerns over conditions within the home or demonstrate marked changes in behavior. For example, if a father who has always emphasized participation with his children begins to express strong preferences for those activities which exclude his children or which his children dislike, there may be cause to suspect that the family may now be at risk. Also, if a child who has always seemed content suddenly begins expressing a concern over a mother's increased drinking, this too may be cause to suspect the family is at risk. Being an advocate for children requires the recreation leader to be alert for such changes and to report such changes to the appropriate child protective service. Advocacy also involves keeping informed of changes in neighborhood demographics which may suggest a greater likelihood of the presence of at-risk families.

Child Care (Respite)

Many families are under severe stress due to unemployment, divorce, crime, alcohol and drug abuse, unwanted pregnancy, or chronic health problems. Often, such parents may be aware that they are losing control over their emotions and may be unaware of alternatives to abuse. Perhaps they are new to the community and are unfamiliar with its programs. Perhaps the child is simply in the wrong place at the wrong time and would not be abused if some respite were available to the parent. Perhaps there is not a safe playground where the parent can send the child in order to diminish the tension. The problem is exacerbated when the child is disabled and requires additional parental attention or cannot independently utilize facilities that may be available. In situations such as these one of the most beneficial services the recreation agency can provide is respite services. The respite services may be provided in a variety of program offerings, some of which are suggested below:

(1) Itinerant Recreator—a service that could be limited to at-risk homebound children. The recreator could make periodic visits—scheduled or on a crisis intervention basis—to the child's home. The purpose of the visit would be to entertain the child in play activity and to provide relief to the parent. During the visit and with agency approval the parent may be able to leave the home for a brief period of time. Also with both parental and agency approval the recreator may be able to remove the child from the home in order to utilize agency or community facilities. This option would provide both the child and parent respite and also provide the opportunity for the parent to address a neglected household task. Eligible homes for such a unique and specialized service could be identified by the local child protection service or the local health and social services officials.

(2) Fun Bus—on a recent trip to Leeds, England a brightly painted bus was observed participating in the Lord Mayor's parade. The double-decked bus was painted with cheerful caricatures and flowers. It was the property of the city's leisure services department. It was literally a community center on wheels. The bus would make scheduled visits to neighborhoods that were somewhat removed from one of the city's numerous leisure and sports centers. Typically, these neighborhoods were characterized as being crowded with lower socioeconomic families. Recreation agencies here may want to consider the adoption of such a unique approach to provide services to at-risk families. Like the Leeds bus it could be staffed by department personnel plus volunteers and be outfitted with play-room materials and games and be equipped for arts and crafts activities. Brief visits one to two times weekly to neighborhoods designated as being at risk would provide valuable respite for the parent being stressed by economic woes, crowded living conditions and other factors which place the family at risk. The visits could give both parents and children something to look forward to. It may, also, serve as a social focus for the parents who may wish to accompany their children to the activity site.

(3) Day Camp—the recreation department could periodically schedule day camping programs for residents of high-risk neighborhoods or for families referred by local health and social service officials. The camp's staff could be composed of recreation personnel and volunteers as well as personnel from child protective services

and health, social service, and education agencies. The camps should be structured to provide a relaxed setting for family recreation, adult and youth recreation, parenting skills training, nutrition education, vocational counseling, etc. Extended sessions with unstructured evenings could present the opportunity for staff and families to interact informally, thereby establishing a sense of community.

(4) Crisis Play Centers—neighborhood or community center staff could be trained to care for children whose parents need a temporary respite. Parents who are under a great deal of stress may appreciate having a place where they could "drop off" a provoking child when they feel the pressure building. This is similar to the crisis nursery concept, but twenty-four-hour care and infant care would not necessarily have to be provided. The emphasis would be on giving the child some room to be a normal child and on giving the stressed parent an option to abuse and time to seek assistance in resolving the crisis.

Programs for Abused Children and Young Adults

As has been stressed repeatedly in this text there is one regrettable fact about this insidious social malady referred to as child abuse. That is, abuse begets abuse. Invariably an investigation of an abusive parent's history will disclose that he or she was abused as a child. In the literature the phrase "cycle of abuse" is discussed as is the reference to the "intergenerational nature" of abuse. To break this cycle prevention must be concerned with the treatment of children identified as victims of abuse. Treatment and prevention consequently must go hand-in-hand. More will be discussed later in terms of treatment; yet, an important part of the treatment process must involve emphasis on alternatives to abuse in order to prevent the abused from becoming an abuser. For example, the teenage or young adult victim via the counseling process may be assisted in identifying recreational activities that may be pursued by either him/herself or by his/her child when abusive impulses arise. For such a comprehensive program structure as is being suggested here, the community recreation agency should definitely consider the employment of a therapeutic recreation specialist with academic and professional background in counseling. Participants already involved in the cycle of abuse will require attention from a staff member trained in therapeutic interventions and behavior altering, or goal-oriented recreational programming. This staff member should have direct and open communication with officials of the local child protective services and substantial control over referral case load.

Life-Skill Training for Children and Young Adults

The literature in education, recreation and leisure studies, psychology, child development, and sociology offers substantial support for the role of play activity in teaching skills required for successful human endeavors. Play or recreational activities can provide, if properly supervised or structured, opportunities for children to learn how to cooperate, to be responsible, to learn impulse control, to acquire decision-making and problem-solving skills, to become self-confident, and to acquire a variety of other skills necessary for citizenship or living in and contributing to the community. None of this is new information for Recreation and Leisure Services personnel, but it never hurts to be reminded of the benefits our services can provide if we are prudent or judicious in conducting our programs.

Self-Help Groups and Other Neighborhood Supports

As mentioned previously, it is Jenkins, Salus, and Schultze who support such a role for our centers. "A block parent system can be initiated so as to reestablish the 'neighborly' attitudes that are rare in modern neighborhoods. Also neighborhood centers, where families can go just to socialize or to receive services, can be encouraged" (1979, p. 89). We should open our centers to Parents Anonymous, Alcoholics Anonymous, Parents Without Partners or any other self-help groups that are confronting issues that contribute to the likelihood of child abuse. We should also seek out opportunities for cooperative endeavors with volunteer groups that address other issues, such as illiteracy or health care, and offer meeting space and child care in support of their efforts.

Family Support Services

"Lacking anywhere to turn in times of crisis puts families at significantly greater risk for abuse or neglect" (Cohn, 1983, p. 28). The message embodied throughout these last few pages is that Recreation and Leisure Service agencies, if they are going to be effective agents in preventing abuse, have to do more than only offer recreational activities. They have to integrate recreational activities into a comprehensive and cooperative approach to abuse prevention. Community, activity, or neighborhood centers and all recreational facilities need to be perceived as integral parts of the neighborhoods where people can go for assistance, where there will be sensitive and helpful staff to assist in crisis resolution. This does not mean that the recreation profession needs to be all things to all people, but it does mean that if the center is located in a predominately Spanish-speaking neighborhood that some of the staff should speak Spanish. It does mean that all of the staff should be well versed in how to network the person in crisis with the appropriate health or social service agency. It does mean that the center should have services available that can allow the child to be temporarily removed from the crisis in a manner to not threaten the family's unity or the child's sense of security. What could be less threatening than providing the child the opportunity to have fun in one of the program options discussed?

Additional Components and Suggestions

From the aforegoing discussion it could mistakenly be assumed that Recreation and Leisure Services personnel have responsibility to provide preventative services to only those children and families identified as being at risk. In fact, as a human service we have a responsibility to all children and families, regardless of life condition. What follows are three suggestions for additional measures we can take to assure we are fulfilling our responsibility to all of our citizens.

Abuse Awareness

One program area Cohn did not identify in her 1983 text is abuse awareness. As professionals entrusted with the care of children we have an obligation to teach our youthful clients their rights and how to recognize, resist, and report abuse. In doing so we must keep in mind that "Kids can be taught to protect themselves—without scaring or confusing them, without prompting them to 'embellish' the truth" (Ray-Keil, p. 2). We have to admit to a regrettable fact of contemporary

American life; namely, what our children do not know can hurt or quite possibly kill them. We must also come to grips with the realization that everyone who works with children needs to assume the responsibility of making children aware of the perils they face and how to prevent and cope with them. Everyone concerned with a child's welfare should be responsible for assisting that child in distinguishing exploitation from affection and good touching from bad touching, and in understanding when it is okay to say no to adults or older children. The recreational setting may well provide an effective and minimally stressful opportunity to provide children the chance to develop such valuable insights. One source for educational materials that may assist in developing abuse awareness is the Seattle Institute for Child Advocacy. Requests for information should be addressed to the Institute's Committee for Children at:

172 20th Ave.
Seattle, WA 98122

Other books and audiovisual aids are also available. An example of a book which may easily be utilized in an awareness program was discovered while browsing through a bookstore in the train station in Leeds, England. Entitled *It's O.K. to Say No!*, the book consists of a number of scenarios that can be read through aloud by adults and children. These scenarios could also serve as bases for a series of short dramatic presentations or skits depicting examples of potentially abusive situations. Each of the situations depicted by Levett and Crane end by asking the question "What would you do?" Following the dramatic depiction, the adult leader could conduct a brief discussion with all children present, asking them to respond to the aforementioned question. The authors relate that the awareness of such situations presented in their book "offers no guarantees, but it at least reduces the risks" (Levett and Crane, 1986, p. 8). Recreation and Leisure Service professionals should attempt to do no less.

Area Safety

Another means of preventing abuse is to take measures to assure the safety of our recreational or activity areas. As mentioned previously, child abusers, particularly pedophiles, are attracted to areas frequented by children. Chapter Twelve relates to steps we can undertake to assure that appropriate personnel are available to supervise our areas, but there are two additional measures that may be taken.

First of all, the physical structure should be such to discourage frequenting by potential abusers. There should be limited access to the facilities. Only authorized parents, agency staff and volunteers should be admitted through supervised entrances. All hallways and restrooms should be adequately lighted. Ideally, lighting for all areas not under constant staff supervision should be controlled centrally. All playgrounds and parking lots should be lighted. In parks, restrooms should be appropriately located. Concerning the consideration of location, Williams and Holcomb state, "Previously, play areas were located near restrooms, and where possible trees or woodlands were used as buffers between play areas and picnic areas. Aesthetics, accessibility, and user patterns remain important considerations in designing park facilities. However, further consideration must be given to the fact that deviant behavior may be most prevalent in restrooms and that wooded areas provide ideal cover from which potential abusers can observe children at play without being seen, and that such areas provide secluded places for abuse to occur" (Williams and Holcomb, 1985, p. 60). Parks should, therefore, be designed so all play areas and restrooms can be adequately supervised or observed by park personnel, group leaders or parents. Williams and Holcomb further recommend, "Areas surrounding those used intensively by children should be thinned and trimmed in a manner that ensures visibility. Undergrowth, particularly in isolated areas or along riverbanks, should be controlled so that abuse cannot take place unobserved" (1985, p. 60). The physical and staffing arrangements should be such to assure that each child can be adequately supervised and protected from the abuser that may be lurking around the corner or behind the shrubs.

Secondly, all staff, volunteers and participants should be aware of the potential for abuse. Specifically, everyone in the recreation area should be alert to the appearance of unfamiliar personages in or around recreation areas. Administration, following consultation with local law enforcement, should establish policies and procedures related to the reporting and possible confrontation of unauthorized and unfamiliar individuals.

These additional measures may not only reduce or eliminate the incidents of child abuse in our facilities, but they may likely reduce the likelihood of criminal or civil litigation against our agencies. However, our primary responsibility is to assure the safety and well-being of our youthful participants and to honor a trust bestowed upon us by their parents and the community as a whole.

Latchkey Programs

Since the end of World War II the number of mothers of minor children who are in the work force has been on a steady rise. "In 1947 less than one in five mothers of minor children (18%) were working outside the home. By 1980 nearly three out of every five mothers with children under eighteen years of age (57%) were employed. The figures are even more dramatic for mothers of preschoolers since they account for the fastest growing segment of this country's work force" (Coolsen, Seligson, and Garbarino, 1986, p. 4). The predictions are that by the end of this decade the number of working mothers of minor children may approach 70 percent. These figures and the fact that 22 percent of today's children live in single-parent households make one fact obvious. Namely, a large number of American children return from school to homes that have no adult supervision. One estimate is that 25 percent of the nation's children in the six to fourteen years age range are responsible for their own care after school. "Most studies report that about half of the children thirteen and younger whose parents are employed full-time are in self-care" (Coolsen et al., 1986, p. 8).

It should be a source of professional pride that numerous community recreation agencies have assumed leadership responsibilities in providing latchkey or after-school programs to address the risks related to the latchkey phenomenon. The risks or possible negative consequences to the child that have been specified are that the child will:

- feel badly (feel rejected, afraid, alone)
- be harmed physically (accidents, physical and sexual abuse)
- develop poorly (poor school performance, not develop proper social skills)
- demonstrate deviant behavior (delinquent, criminal behavior)

(Coolsen et al., 1986, p. 9)

The February 1988 edition of *Parks and Recreation* magazine identifies several communities where recreation and parks or leisure service agencies are assuming key roles in safeguarding against such risks. Some of the communities mentioned are Cincinnati, Ohio; Washington, D.C.; Austin, Texas; Richland, Washington; Albuquerque, New Mexico; and Jackson, Tennessee. These communities and others have developed interagency programs or programs in cooperation with local churches, schools, area colleges, and YMCA's and YWCA's.

Among the examples of programs offered is the Washington, D.C. Recreation Department's extended-day program for school-aged children who are five to fourteen. "In 13 facilities throughout the District, a staff trained in early childhood education, recreation and/or therapeutic recreation involves the children in recreational activities, takes them on field trips, and helps them with their homework. The staff/child ratio is 1:15, and the department limits enrollment to 385 (50 of whom are disabled). Participants must be D.C. residents whose parents are working or in school, and their fee ranges from free to $6.50 per week, depending on family size and income" ("Issue Update: Latchkey Children," 1988, p. 50).

Another example is Albuquerque's extended-day and after-school programs administered by the Parks and Recreation Department. The department's supervisor of playgrounds reports that "for a $10 fee parents can enroll their children in an extended-day program in one of nine public schools from 7–9 a.m. and 3:30–6 p.m. on weekdays (7–9 a.m. and 1:30–6 p.m. on Wednesdays) or in PlayScape, a free after-school program offered on weekdays. Both extended-day and PlayScape run with the cooperation of the Albuquerque Public School System, offering games and special activities to children 9 to 13 years old. The staff ratio ranges from 12 to 15:1 and consists primarily of recreation department staff and recreation majors from local colleges" ("Issue Update . . . ," 1988, pp. 50–51).

A third example of recreation's leadership in a cooperative community effort is described in an article by Campbell in the same issue of *Parks and Recreation.* In "Latchkey Children: Meeting the Need in Tennessee" she describes the history and the progress of the Jackson After-School Program. The program is a cooperative effort between Jackson City Schools and the Jackson Recreation and Parks Program. The program emphasizes homework assistance and the offering of stimulating recreational activities. According to Campbell, "In a recent survey, parents expressed their approval of the minimal fees, enjoyable recreation, and, most especially, the fact that their children did not have to be transported to another location after school. 'We have one fifth-grade parent who could make other arrangements for her child after school,' says Allen, 'but chooses this program because of the help her child receives with homework, something that his parent feels she is not qualified to do'" (Campbell, 1988, p. 54). Allen is the coordinator of the program.

These are only three examples of community efforts to address the issue of the latchkey child and to prevent their possible abuse. The programs these and the other agencies mentioned in the latchkey articles range anywhere from coordinating hot-line and block parent programs to comprehensive programs of recreational activities after school for both disabled and non-disabled students of elementary and middle school ages. These communities are examples of what recreation and leisure professionals who are true advocates for children can do to prevent the abuse of their communities' children.

A Final Note On Abuse Prevention

Recreation and Leisure Service agencies can provide not only a wide variety of recreation or activity programs to prevent abuse but they can also allow their facilities to be utilized for a variety of preventative services. They can encourage or require their staff to be aware of the needs of families at risk and of the characteristics of the adjacent neighborhoods. They can demonstrate that they are committed to fulfilling recreation's role in child development, family management, self-development, self-actualization, and in the advocacy of each child's right to grow up in a family free of the threats of sexual, physical, and emotional abuse and neglect.

RECREATION AND THE TREATMENT OF ABUSE

Just as child abuse is a complex or multifaceted issue, so is its treatment. Treatment of the parties involved, the abusers and the abused, may take place in a variety of settings; i.e. mental health centers—day treatment or residential programs, special schools and homes, correctional centers, or outreached programs supported by combined community agencies. And as discussed in Chapter Ten, it is now recognized that effective treatment can be delivered only through a multidisciplinary approach.

The same chapter provides ample support for recreation's role in the treatment of abuse. Prescott tells us that experiencing pleasure will make family members less violent. Furthermore, he proposes that dull or numbing counseling sessions be replaced by such recreation activities as camping or swimming. He believes that if families could learn to have fun together that there may be less violence (Straus et al., 1981, p. 236). Mayhall and Norgard also support the use of recreational activities as a means to work through the feelings and problems abused children experience (Mayhall and Norgard, p. 345). In addition, Elkind expresses the opinion that recreational or play activity may be the most effective way to combat the effect of childhood stress (Elkind, 1981, pp. 192–198). Wayne and Avery also addressed the important role of recreationally oriented activities in the group therapy process for abusive mothers (Wayne and Avery, 1980, p. 65).

Treatment Goals for Recreational Programming

The goals of recreational programming for abused children and their abusers must, as with other clientele or special populations, be in keeping with the overall treatment goals for specific individuals. These goals are likely to be determined by a team of qualified professionals who are concerned with comprehensive or wholistic treatment. However, there are some overall or universal goals for abusers and their victims which have been identified in the abuse and recreation literature. Recreation agencies in the variety of settings may find an awareness of these goals to be helpful when establishing goals specific to their individual settings and clientele. An awareness of these general or universal goals, if used as guidelines, should provide some assurances that what the recreation staff is attempting to accomplish will find acceptance amongst other child protective services (CPS) professionals and result in the life enhancement of the program's participants.

Treatment Goals for Abusers

Again, the specific treatment goals for abusers will be determined by the structure of the specific agency and the individual needs of the abuser or his/her dynamics. Yet, regardless of the specific setting or individual, there are general goals the recreation specialist should attempt to meet individually or in cooperation with other CPS professionals. These are as follows:

- assist the abuser in understanding age-appropriate behaviors of children and to then establish appropriate limits
- assist the abuser in meeting their unsatisfied dependency needs
- assist the abuser in improving self-concept by providing opportunities for success
- assist the abuser in diminishing the sense of social isolation from other family members and the community in general
- asist the abuser in identifying available life-support services, agencies, or programs

- assist the abuser in establishing appropriate interactional patterns with children and other adults
- assist the abuser in identifying and means of pursuing appropriate options in relieving stress
- assist abusive parents in finding means by which they can enjoy one another in order to diminish demands upon their children to satisfy adult needs
- assist the abusive parent in developing leadership skills and assertiveness in order to prevent sole power delegation to or acquisition by any one adult
- assist the abuser in acquiring appreciation for and skills in cooperation, responsibility and acceptance of individual differences
- assist the abuser in the acquisition of appropriate verbal and non-verbal communication skills
- assist the abuser in developing realistic expectations for themselves and an awareness of their existing physical, social and intellectual skills
- assist the abuser in developing an appreciation for the necessity of structure or rules
- assist the abusive parent in developing a sense of their child's needs and knowledge or resources available for meeting them

(Mayhall and Norgard, 1983, pp. 337–340)

- assist the parents or abuser in recognizing the importance and means of enjoying their lives and their children in socially appropriate endeavors
- assist the parent in recognizing the importance and means of the child finding enjoyment and gratifying relationships outside of the central family unit

(Martin, 1979, pp. 54–55)

- assist parents in comprehending the role of leisure activity and fun in fostering family unity and communication

(Edwards, 1988, p. 47)

Treatment Goals for the Abused

As with the abuser, the specific treatment goals for abuse victims will be determined by a variety of factors. Such factors as type of abuse, age of the victim, duration of abuse, victim physical and mental status, victim interests, and agency structure will be among those considered by the treatment team in establishing individualized goals. Yet, here too, general or universal goals have been identified which can be used as guidelines in establishing individual goals and in selecting programs and activities to benefit the victim of abuse. Some of these are as follows:

- assist the child in improving self-concept by providing opportunities for success
- assist the child in the development of appropriate interaction skills, with adults and other children, inside and outside of the family unit
- assist the child in the development of age-appropriate behaviors
- assist the child in expressing feelings about abuse by providing a non-threatening, supportive, and safe activity environment
- assist the child in developing appropriate expectations of family life and an awareness of his/her rights as a child
- assist the child in the acquisition of the appropriate skills to express his/her needs and frustrations
- assist the child in diminishing or eliminating the sense of social isolation which may result from the abusive situation
- assist the child in the prevention of future abuse by developing an awareness of appropriate child-adult interaction
- assist the child in the development or re-establishment of trust in adults (particularly of the offending gender) by the recreator's function as a positive adult role model

(Mayhall and Norgard, 1983, pp. 337–342)

- assist the child in combating physical, social, and intellectual delays which may result from abuse
- assist the child in developing an awareness of community resources available for life enhancement

Some Suggested Programs and Activities

What follows is a discussion of some specific programs and activities the recreation professional may wish to implement in a program of abuse treatment. The absence of a program or activity is not necessarily an indication of its inappropriateness. Rather, the programs and activities discussed are, when the needs and characteristics of abusers and their victims are considered, thought to be particularly fitting for a program of abuse treatment.

Some of the discussion may appear to be repetitious. It is and rightly so. Earlier a reference was made to the cycle of abuse and the need for prevention and treatment to go hand-in-hand in breaking the cycle or in addressing the intergenerational nature of abuse. It will come as no particular revelation to the recreation worker, particularly the therapeutic recreation specialist, that an activity or program can be both remedial and preventative. For example, sports activities are utilized to both prevent and remediate juvenile delinquent behavior.

Finally, and it goes without saying, the selection of activities or programs will depend on numerous factors. Among these are staff and facility resources available, the needs of the adult or child (client), and the interests of the client.

Therapeutic Child Care

The program should provide a supportive environment that is free of regimentation and encouraging of the child's exploration and adaptation to the environment. It should be staffed by personnel that can, through the use of activities, foster the child's positive self-concept and trust in adults. "A wide range of activities similar to those in general programs should be offered, including such things as water play; paints and dough; a housekeeping area with dolls, kitchen equipment, and 'dress-up' clothing; indoor and outdoor gym equipment; and moveable props which allow children to create their own environment" (Broadhurst, Edmunds and MacDicken, 1979, p. 51). This program could be held in conjunction with the counseling professional working with abusing parents; the recreation leader could conduct activities for children. This will prevent parents from having to secure baby-sitting services and at the same time present an excellent opportunity to observe the children. The recreation leader could take note of the children's behavior while in a low-stress leisure-play setting. These groups and the parent therapy sessions could be conducted in one of the recreation centers, community centers, or neighborhood centers—thereby eliminating some of the stigma of going to the mental health center, counseling center, etc.

Toy Library

Such a program could be provided through the cooperation of the city, town, or village library and the department of recreation. The service could be limited to abusing parents or families in crisis in the lower-income levels. Children from such families often provoke their parents into violent acts by constantly demanding toys and games they see advertised on television or in magazines. This may simply add to the feelings of inadequacy, which may eventually result in abuse of the demanding child. The toy library could make available such toys and games on loan to the parents on a limited basis. The loan could be extended for a small fee, or the toy or game purchased by the parent for a small, affordable monthly installment. Funding could possibly be shared by the municipal library, the recreation department, and the social services agency concerned with child protection. Additionally, loans could be limited only to families referred by the child protection agency.

Therapeutic Day Camps

The recreation department could schedule day or weekend camps for families in crisis. The staff could be composed of recreation personnel and other child protection or abuse prevention personnel. The camps could be structured to provide a relaxed setting for family recreation, parenting skills training, counseling sessions, nutrition education, vocational counseling, youth recreation, therapeutic play, etc. Extended sessions, with unstructured evenings, could present the opportunity for staff and families to interact informally and thereby establish a sense of community. The camp planning should be with the guidance of the primary therapist, since the principle goals are to unify the family and to protect the health and welfare of the child.

Leisure Counseling

This should be a parent-centered program. The goal would be to assist the parent in realizing the importance of productive, low-stress leisure pursuits in maintaining family unity. Parents would be referred to the department of recreation, therapeutic recreation services, etc., by the social services agency working with the family. The leisure counselor, with client knowledge, could provide feedback to the primary therapist on a periodic basis so an overall assessment could be made as to the parent's suitability to continue as the child's caretaker.

Itinerant Recreator

This is a service that could be extended to the abused as well as the at-risk homebound child. The recreator would make periodic visits to the child's home to play with the child and to relieve the parent of the stress of constant care. Such homes would be identified by the child protection agency.

Place-to-Meet

This is a support service that may facilitate the beginning of new chapters of such organizations as Parents Anonymous and Mothers'

Anonymous. Often, such groups need a place to meet, and one that has supervised play areas for their children may be ideal. Recreation centers and their adjacent playgrounds and playrooms may be the most suitable.

Neighborhood Block Clubs

Often, abusive parents are residents of either transitory or anomic neighborhoods where there is little opportunity for interaction and linkage with the total community. This simply exacerbates the feelings of isolation and frustration. Neighborhood clubs could ease these feelings by providing social support and regular opportunities to get away from the pressures of too many children, children who are disabled or children demonstrating undesirable behavior. Involvement in club leadership could provide status in the neighborhood and also provide the opportunity to become involved in service functions for the neighborhood and the community as a whole. Such clubs serve as the foundation for a large variety of recreational and service activities, and once established they may only require occasional consultation by a representative of the Recreation and Leisure Services agency. Such support systems that may develop could well interrupt the cycle of abuse by alleviating precipitating stress and teaching options to abusive behaviors.

Outdoor Adventure Activities

Though the following chapter presents an in-depth review of the applicability of adventure games and activities in the treatment of abused children, particularly as related to self-concept, it may be helpful to briefly review some of the general benefits participants have mentioned. Darst and Armstrong report testimony as to the following benefits:

- Escape. A number of people see in these activities an escape from the complexities of modern life, a release from the tensions and anxieties of living in a sometimes dehumanizing society.
- High-risk, experience. Some individuals feel that participation in stressful activities that border on the physically dangerous will help them overcome fear, gain self-confidence, obtain emotional stability, and successfully cope with additional responsibility.
- New experience. Many feel that these activities provide a new and exciting experience filled with adventure, fun, and challenge.
- Success. Many people who have limited athletic ability seem to experience a certain amount of instant success in these activities . . . for a

small investment of time and limited amount of physical effort, a person can achieve a highly personal sense of accomplishment.

- Knowledge. Some people point out that they participate in outdoor activities to learn more about the earth's environment as well as more about themselves. These activities enable people to reflect upon their goals, strengths, weaknesses, and limitations. Many feel that this knowledge enhances their feelings of personal worth.
- Physical fitness. Many people participate in wilderness activities because they promote cardiovascular-respiratory fitness.
- Socializing. Because of the social opportunities presented by these activities, many people see them as a chance to meet others who have similar interests.
- Unity. Some people feel that outdoor adventure activities promote unity and cohesiveness among people and groups.
- Cooperation and trust. Still other people feel they participate because of the development of cooperation, trust, and appreciation of other people.
- Minimal financial investment. Some people claim that one of the prime reasons for their participation in these activities is the small—in some cases, negligible—financial investment required to pursue them.

(Darst and Armstrong, 1980, pp. 6–7)

One such outdoor adventure program is entitled Project Adventure (PA). PA, by utilizing such low and high rope elements as Beam, Criss Crotch, Mohawk Walk, Burma Bridge, Running Zip, Pamper Pole, and other events such as Trust Dives and Trust Falls, targets individuals who exhibit:

- low self-esteem
- low sense of control over themselves and their environment
- confused and defensive self-concept
- fantasy-ridden goal-setting behavior
- high need for adventure
- low physical fitness skills
- marked emotional withdrawal
- drug involvement
- disruptive behavior

As to goals, PA is designed to develop or remediate:

- psychomotor/perceptual motor skills—balance, strength, coordination, kinesthetics, auditory/visual motor memory
- decision making/problem solving
- interpersonal communication skills
- impulse control, trust, coping mechanisms, autonomy

- attitudes/appreciation of self and others
- enjoyment of physical education/outdoor leisure time experiences
  (It's Happening! Project Adventure, 1988)

For more information on program development, staff training, etc., interested parties should contact:

Project Adventure
P.O. Box 100
Hamilton, MA 01936

Animal/Pet Therapy

Much has been written about the benefits of pet ownership in relation to physical and mental health. Mather has identified some benefits that may be derived from having an animal in the home or treatment environment. Some of these benefits are as follows:

- Physical contact: Owners can hug, kiss and caress their pets without too much sexual guilt. This is a psychological service performed by pets.
- Understanding: Many pet owners report they derive much satisfaction out of feeling that their pets understand them. Animals seem to gauge the emotional state of a human. . . .
- Giving and receiving of love: Animals are dependent on us. Psychologists report that young girls growing up deprived of love and feeling unwanted and worthless, develop a craving to look after other people's babies—to be needed is gratifying. The pet's dependence makes us feel needed.
- Security: Real or imagined physical dangers can be warded off by a pet.
- Play: Play is relaxing, but when people become adults they tend to play less. The only chance an adult has to play silly, uninhibited games is either with children or adults. For children a pet may allow the development and exploration of thoughts. They are also safe to talk to and can serve as a non-threatening focus of conversation.
- Ownership: Control of an animal can boost the ego. The dog exhibitor, the greyhound owner, the racehorse owner are like the knight in armor and the modern man in his Aston Martin—egotistical, but therapeutic.
- Redirected aggression: Redirected aggression is of great therapeutic value when an animal is used, although it may not be too good for the pet.
- Psychiatric element: Animals bring considerable comfort to children. The relationship is unconditional, the pet does not mind human inadequacies or peculiarities. An example of their therapeutic effectiveness was observed in a Boston psychiatric unit for severely disturbed children. Many of the children had refused to respond to medical treatment. The

first positive responses were noted when the head nurse brought her dog onto the unit.

(Mather, 1981, pp. 22–23)

There is additional support for the introduction of pets into recreational programs or facilities or into the homes of abuse victims. Begley and Fitzgerald (1987, p. 20) report a study conducted by Hubert Montagner of the Universite de Franche-Comté in Besancon, France. He studied both children reared with dogs and those who were not. He found those with dogs tended to be less aggressive with their peers.

Another study by Michael Levine of Pennsylvania's Bloomsburg University compared college students who grew up with dogs and those who did not. He found that the college women who had grown up with dogs in their homes "score higher on tests of self-reliance, social skills, sociability and tolerance than petless women did. Men felt a greater sense of personal worth and of belonging and had better social skills if they'd had a dog" (Begley and Fitzgerald, 1987, p. 20).

Perhaps it is Mather who provides the best summary of the benefits to be derived from the presence of animals. She concludes:

- Animals give us tactile comfort.
- They enhance our importance.
- They help us drop our social facades and become ourselves.
- They give us a feeling of companionship and security.
- They can boost our ego.
- They act as scapegoats for our hostilities.
- They increase our self-confidence by submitting to our authority.
- They play with us and allow expressions of the eternal child inside the adult.
- They play with children and allow the child to develop his fantasies and thoughts and gain a sense of responsibility in its care.
- They act as a go-between in human relationships.
- They allow us to love and be loved.
- They forgive us our weaknesses and faults.
- The greatest psychotherapeutic service which they can give us is the feeling of being loved.
- As a companion they are most supportive especially to the old and the lonely.

(Mather, 1981, p. 23)

It may be worthwhile getting to know owners of local pet shops and the administrator of the humane society.

Puppetry

"Puppetry, which represents the integration of sculpture, design, movement, expression and other elements of the arts, has almost unlimited potential as a teaching and therapeutic tool" (Renfro, 1984, p. 16). Renfo, likewise, identifies goals which can be attained via the use of puppetry:

- Developing language and communication skills. Puppets can put a child at ease and make the development of skills less threatening. Since the child may view the puppet as "saying it," it may make the expression of inner feelings easier. Puppetry can also foster development of non-verbal communication.
- Overcoming emotional and physical isolation. Puppetry may be an ideal way to introduce appropriate emotional and physical contact since the activity requires either puppet-child, child-child, child-therapist-puppet, or therapist-child interaction.
- Building self-esteem. Creative puppet design and use can provide positive audience feedback.
- Encouraging emotional release. Scripts can be developed around the child's or adult's life and provide rich opportunities for role playing. Anger can be appropriately vented through the use of aggressive characters — wolves, lions, bears, tigers, sharks, etc.
- Making decisions. A puppetry program can provide numerous opportunities for individual and group decision making and problem solving, particularly through puppet and scene design and script or skit development.
- Physical therapy. Puppetry provides non-threatening opportunities to develop fine and gross motor skills; i.e. digital coordination, eye-hand coordination, and speech-manual coordination.

(Renfo, 1984, pp. 16–21)

Philpott provides additional support for the inclusion of puppetry. He includes testimony proffered as to the psychotherapeutic benefits as long ago as 1944 by Marks in the 1944–1945 *EPA Year Book*. She stated, "Its scope as a curative and recreative medium, already sensed by many professionals and amateur puppeteers, becomes increasingly apparent. The school teacher who employs puppetry as an educational medium finds backward pupils reacting spontaneously to puppet suggestions; the entertainer in hospital, club, school and elsewhere, feels the release of suppressed instincts and emotions" (Philpott, 1977, p. 101).

In the same edition of the *EPA Year Book* Bender and Woltman testify to the effectiveness of puppetry on Bellevue's Children's Observation Ward. They stated that the children needed assistance in working out "The problems arising from unfavorable home or school situations, or from unhappy emotional experiences, and to gain relief from sullen or aggressive feelings or fear and shame.... To this end, puppets proved superior to other treatment, largely because the emotional feelings of the individual are released verbally and physically, more unrestrainedly in a crowd. Glove puppets are used exclusively, being found more direct and convincing, and capable of more aggressiveness" (Philpott, 1977, p. 101). The last sentence suggests that puppetry need not be a complicated or expensive program (see Appendix M).

More current testimony as to the therapeutic potential of puppetry in the treatment of abused children is also available in the literature. Burch, for example, provides testimony relating to his experiences with a 13-year-old boy, Carl D. He describes how Carl recreated in four puppet dramas the memories and emotions related to his background of abuse, deprivation and rejection (Burch, 1980, pp. 79–89).

The recreation worker is urged to consider the implementation of a program of puppetry in the program of abuse treatment. There is ample evidence to warrant the effort.

Dance/Movement Activities

Evidence suggests that dance may result in a lost or confused body image being regained that can result in an improved self-concept at a "pre-verbal level" (Levanthal, 1980, p. 4).

Espenak identifies some of the goals which may be realized in a program of dance or movement. They are as follows:

- The stimulation and release of feelings through movements and gestures.
- The release of communication and contact through non-verbal activity.
- The reduction of anxiety through noncritical aspects of the therapeutic setting and through the suspension of self experienced in dance.
- The experiencing of physical and emotional joy through the impact of auditory stimuli (rhythm) together with freedom of movement.
- The use of innate human response to rhythm in order to generate both individual movement and participation in simultaniety with others.

(Espenak, 1981, p. 7)

There appears to exist ample evidence suggesting the value of including dance as a key component in a leisure services program hoping to combat the effects of an abusive environment. There are significant physical, emotional, and social benefits to be derived. It goes without saying that these benefits may be further enhanced by the employment of an individual with training and/or background in dance therapy.

Drama

Pigeon, when speaking of drama as a creative art, states, "The expression of emotion, and with it the control of emotions through appropriate and understandable forms of communication, must be considered as important as the cognitive factors. Both are aspects of personal growth and are essential in the development of a balanced personality" (p. 33).

Additional testimony supporting the inclusion of drama in an abuse treatment program is offered by Wethered. She states, "Within the structure of some dramatic situations, particularly when people are at least partly responsible for its creation, they can act out difficulties and learn to adapt through interaction with one another. They have the support of the story or scene, and can learn to fit in with, and get on with, others in its context. One of the main problems with patients is their inability to relate, so to have the change to experience emotion and speech playing, imaginary people may help them to be able to emerge from the shell in which they are imprisoned" (Wethered, 1973, p. 61).

There are numerous forms of drama activity. Some of those which the recreation agency or department may want to provide are:

- play composition
- character development
- acting in a play
- mime
- set design and construction
- improvisation
- play reading
- role playing
- impromptu acting

Finally, drama, as puppetry need not be an expensive programmatic endeavor. Many set and costume pieces can readily be found in closets, attics, and thrift stores. Its creative potential is limited only by creative limits of the staff.

SUMMARY

The aforementioned programs, activities, and support services are presented for the purpose of stimulating the Recreation and Leisure Service professionals to think about ways they can assist in the prevention and treatment of child abuse—its victims and its perpetrators. The suggestions, though numerous, are not all-inclusive. Specific sports or physical activities, other than outdoor adventure and Project Adventure, were not mentioned as were not a number of creative activities; but this should not be interpreted as a suggestion that they have no value or merit in abuse treatment. Also, it should be obvious that such a program as Let's-Play-To-Grow may be equally valuable for abuse treatment as prevention. Any activities which can enhance self-concept, foster trust, or develop social skills (new games, for example) have merit in combating the deleterious effects of abuse. However, the prevention and treatment of abuse requires the recreation staff to extend their programmatic efforts beyond the traditional sports, arts and crafts, and music programs.

The key to the success of these and other possible efforts is the recreation leader's attitudes towards the targeted citizens. Programs that are conducted in anything other than a spirit of acceptance and support will fail. It is not an exaggeration to state that a failure to project that spirit could result in the continued abuse and even death of a child. The other option, to continue doing nothing, will have the same results. If, as members of a profession, recreators are what they claim—advocates for children and for human dignity, growth and development—isn't it time to act decisively?

Chapter Fifteen

ADVENTURE GAMES IN THE TREATMENT OF ABUSED CHILDREN (A STUDY)

ROBERT G. MCDONALD, JR.

INTRODUCTION

The developmental sequencing of self-concept supports the generally held view of personality theorists that a positive self-concept is integrally related to experiences with success (McFern, 1973). A development in contemporary education is the emphasis being placed on students' subjective and personal evaluation of themselves. Brothers (1975) indicated that the starting point for both success and happiness is a healthy self-image, and that self-concept affects every aspect of behavior: the ability to learn; the capacity to grow and change; and the choice of friends, mates, and careers.

Abused children typically have a lower self-concept than non-abused children (Burgess and Conger, 1978). Hjorth and Ostrow (1982) compared 30 abused adolescents, aged 12–16 years, with 30 non-abused adolescents from similar backgrounds. The abused subjects showed, among other impaired attitudes, poorer self-concept. Oates, Forrest, and Peacock (1985) in a study comparing 37 abused children with 37 non-abused children found that the abused subjects saw themselves as having significantly fewer friends than the comparison subjects. They were also significantly lower in self-concept. Kazdin, Moser, Colbus, and Beel (1985) in a study of 33 physically abused children found that when compared with 46 non-physically abused children the abused children evidenced significantly lower self-esteem. Hjorth (1982) found that physically abused adolescents had an overall lower self-image than did adolescents from similar backgrounds who had not been abused. Kinard (1980) in a study of 30 abused children matched with 30 non-abused children found the results supported the hypo-

227

thesis that abused children have significantly more negative self-concepts than non-abused children. Buckner (1986) in a study of 39 abused children and 103 non-abused children found that the abused children had a lowered self-reported (Piers Harris Children's Self-Concept Scale) self-concept than non-abused children, particularly on the anxiety cluster scale. Low self-concept and child abuse have been identified so often as correlates that Dean writing in *Children Today* (1979, p. 18) defined emotional abuse as "acts on the part of a parent or caretaker that prevent the development of a positive self-image in the child."

If a positive self-concept is important for children to develop successful and happy life-styles, and if abused children typically have lower self-concepts than their non-abused cohorts, then an important research question would be: What type of treatment would enhance the self-concept of abused children?

Orlick (1978, p. 5) said "Children nurtured on cooperation, acceptance, and success have a much greater chance of developing strong self-concepts." Orlick (1978, p. 5) also suggested that the activity children do most, play, when it is competitive might be aiding in the destruction of self-concept rather than its enhancement: "Pitting children against one another in games where they frantically compete for what only a few can have guarantees failure and rejection for the many."

A STUDY

A study was conducted to investigate the effect of organized involvement in cooperative, non-competitive, initiative and challenge games (hereafter called adventure games) on the self-concept of abused children. These adventure games have as an inherent part of the activity the processing or debriefing of the games and the players' attitudes.

The primary research hypotheses were that there are statistically significant differences in the global and cluster scale self-concept scores of abused children who have participated in an adventure games program and abused children who have not participated in an adventure games program, as measured by the Piers Harris Children's Self-Concept Scale (PHSCS) posttest scores; and that there is a statistically significant difference in the self-concept of abused children related to the demographic characteristics of sex, age, and lapse of time since the last reported incidence of abuse.

Terms

The following operational definitions will assist in understanding terms as they were used in the study:

• *Adventure games.* "Adventure games" is used synonymously with terms such as: cooperative games, non-competitive games, challenge games, new games, developmental games, initiative games, and low element or low ropes games. These games usually present a problem or task that involves the children interacting together to achieve a solution. The players in the game must help one another by working together as a unit, with each player being a necessary part of that unit. Each person is to make a contribution—and no one is to be left out of the action waiting for a chance to play (Orlick, 1978). In this study, adventure games also included a debriefing session after each adventure game. The debriefing consisted of a discussion led by the leader about the game that had just been completed.

• *Debriefing.* Debriefing occurs after an activity when the details of the activity are discussed by all the people involved in the activity with the focus of the discussion centered on the interaction of the participants. Debriefing is the examination of what and how decisions are made, what the results of the decisions are, and how they impact the persons involved.

• *Discounting.* Discounting is "putting down" or ridiculing a person's ideas, comments, or actions. Also, in the study, discounting was the interruption of a person who has the floor for discussion.

• *Expressive activities.* Expressive activities are those activities that allow persons to express their feelings through an activity instead of through words or pictures. Expressive activities are often used to allow non-verbal persons to act out their feelings but can be considered an activity allowing for individual feelings to be expressed.

• *Residential abused children.* Residential abused children are those children who have been abused in the past and owing to the threat of continued abuse have been removed from the living arrangements where the abuse occurred. They are living in a substitute care facility offering 24-hour care for such dependent children.

• *Self-concept.* Self-concept is the evaluation an individual makes concerning his or her worth. Self-concept conveys a disposition of approval or disapproval and signifies the degree to which an individual considers himself or herself to be able, important, successful, and valuable. Self-concept is a subjective experience expressed to others by verbal means and other expressive behaviors (Coopersmith, 1967). For the purposes of the study, self-concept was operationally defined as the score on the Piers Harris Children's Self-Concept Scale (see Appendix L).

• *Traditional recreational games.* Traditional recreational games are commonly known group activities that are usually done in a competitive team atmosphere and are typical to most community centers and youth-serving agencies. Such activities include basketball, dodgeball, football, kickball, soccer, softball, and volleyball. While this is not an all-inclusive list of possible traditional recreational games activities, it represents the types of activities included in this definition.

Assumptions

Certain assumptions underscored the study. It was assumed that:

1. The standardized instrument measuring self-concept (the PHSCS) was appropriate for the population studies and the construct presumably being measured.

2. The population under study responded to the various measures of self-concept in an unbiased manner.

3. No abuse occurred during the treatment period.

4. The decisions made by the courts to remove the children from their homes based on findings of abuse were correct, and therefore the children in the study were, in fact, abused children.

5. History, maturation, testing, instrumentation, regression, and selection were controlled by the random selection and assignment of subjects with a pretest-posttest control group design (Campbell and Stanley, 1963) conducted as a field experiment.

Delimitations

The scope of the study was delimited to the examination of the self-concept of abused children living in a residential facility that was outside their home environment. This population was chosen to control for abuse during the treatment program (involvement in adventure games) and so that all general recreation activities apart from the experiment could be monitored during the course of the study. The study was also delimited to the abused children residing specifically at a state residential school for dependent and neglected children. Because it was a state agency rather than a private one, children residing at the selected site tended to be from a lower socioeconomic background. While abuse has not been shown to be more prevalent, neglect has been determined to predominate in poorer homes (Burgess and Conger, 1978). Also, the level of positive reinforcement for esteem-building activities is found to be lower among families in lower socioeconomic homes (Trowbridge, 1972). Further, only one person (the researcher) was providing the real and placebo "treatments" to both the experimental and control groups. Thus, the results of the study could have been affected by the lack of a blind or double-blind situation. However, as a trained and experienced therapist, the researcher attempted to display equal affect and behavior towards the two groups.

Limitations

The following limitations applied to the study:

1. The study was limited to the abused children living at a small residential school for dependent and neglected children in the Piedmont area of South Carolina. The school is a state-owned and operated residential school serving children between the ages of 6 and 18 years. While the small number of students available (N = 38) limits the generalizability of the findings, the data with an N this small could be statistically treated (Crosswhite, 1970).

2. Since the subjects included in the study were only those abused children available in residence at the South Carolina school, the results are generalizable only to that group or to similar groups of residentially housed abused children.

3. The treatment was conducted by only one researcher. Thus, the possibility of difference in the self-concept of various leaders and/or various effects of different leadership styles could not be tested in this field experience.

4. Because two of the subjects did not have reading skills necessary to complete the PHSCS alone, questions were read to them by the researcher. In light of this, some of their responses might have been given by them incorrectly in an attempt to impress the researcher.

Significance of the Study

As stated previously, children who have been abused generally have lower self-concepts than children who have not been abused. A positive

Table XV-1

SUBJECT CHARACTERISTICS

Variable	Category		n	%
Treatment	a.	Experimental	18	47
	b.	Control	20	52
Sex	a.	Females	19	50
	b.	Males	19	50
Age	a.	8 - 11 years	10	26
	b.	12 -1 4 years	14	37
Lapse of Time Since Last Incidence of Abuse	a.	less than 1 year	15	39
	b.	more than 1 year but less than 2	11	29
	c.	more than 2 years	12	32

self-concept tends to enhance a child's ability to succeed in a number of important developmental areas. For children who have a lower self-concept, professional ethics mandate that some method of intervention should be attempted to enhance their self-concepts. Research results suggest that Outward Bound type programs will enhance self-concept in some but not all groups of individuals (Kimbell, 1980). These types of programs are expensive and take highly trained staff. Chase (1981), in attempting to justify Outward Bound as an adjunct of therapy, gave the integral elements of the Outward Bound program that his research had led him to conclude enhanced self-concept. He listed the elements as: a natural physical environment, a small social environment, and the challenges of coping with both the physical and social environments, and debriefing the activities after the group concluded each challenge. The problem-solving setting evokes and reinforces coping rather than defensive behaviors. The activities themselves become the therapy because consequences are direct, immediate, and impartial. In small groups of 9 to 12, individuals learn to communicate, cooperate, depend on, and trust each other when faced with challenges. Successfully met challenges lead to self-confidence. The study attempted to determine if adventure games with the key elements of the Outward Bound program (a physical environment, small trusting social environment, and challenge and problem-solving activities plus debriefing) would enhance self-concept without the expenses associated with the Outward Bound type of wilderness experience. Since little experimental research has been done to determine the most effective ways to ameliorate low self-concept in abused children, the study was concerned with testing one treatment technique: the use of adventure games as a means of enhancing positive self-concept.

Recreational Activities and Self-Concept

Various recreational activities have been tried as treatments for improving low self-concept. Outdoor challenge programs (Benson, 1981; Brown and Simpson, 1979; Marsh, 1984; Martin, 1983; Stogner, 1979; Wright, 1982); summer camps (Miller, 1978; Thacker, 1979); wilderness experiences (Bertolami, 1981); canoe trips (Bosse, Durand and Beaumont, 1984); and rock climbing (McClary, 1984) have been tried as possible treatments to enhance self-concept.

The effectiveness of these treatment techniques is mixed, with the results showing the greatest rise in self-concept scores coming from wilderness experiences and outdoor challenge courses. Brown and Simpson (1979) in a six-week outdoor challenge program for juvenile offenders found that the outdoor experience was effective in providing improved self-confrontation, self-concept, and understanding of others. Bertolami (1981) investigated the changes in self-worth and self-reliance in young adults that participated in a 26-day Outward Bound course. The subjects showed significant increases in self-concept after participating in the high-risk wilderness program. Bertolami concluded that the structured wilderness experience provided an important medium for enhancing the personal development of young adults. Further, he attributed the changes in self-concept to the successful accomplishment of different activities, a supportive group environment, and intense personal interactions. Wright (1982) found a significant improvement in posttest scores on the Tennessee Self-Concept Scale after a nine-week High Adventure experience for 57 males and females aged 14–18 years. O'Conner (1983) found that a one-week residential outdoor education program significantly enhanced the self-esteem of fifth and seventh grade children.

Marsh (1984) administered questionnaires to 361 participants of outdoor challenge programs (a high element course) conducted at an Australian Outward Bound facility. The participants (aged 16–31 years, 75% males) completed a self-description questionnaire one month before going through the challenge course and one day after the program ended. Findings showed that participation in the 26-day program produced increases in the multiple dimensions of self-concept, suggesting the program's effectiveness.

Kimbell (1980) surveyed more than 80 wilderness/adventure programs serving juvenile offenders. Most of these programs, lasting 14–30 days, did not consistently test for enhancement of self-concept, making definitive findings scarce. However, the programs that did use pretests and posttests found that in more than one half of the cases, significant $(p < .10)$ positive self-concept changes occurred at least in the short run. Richards and Richards (1981) in a small study of 12 underachieving boys (average age 15 years) found that an adventure program of expeditions, ropes courses, and rafting brought about significant positive changes in personality in general and self-concept and self-esteem in particular. The greatest enhancement of self-concept seems to have occurred in those programs where a debriefing session followed the activity.

While some studies indicate that participation in an adventure program is positively correlated with an improved self-concept for special children, other studies indicate no correlation between adventure programs and enhanced self-concept. Winterdyk (1980) in an experiment with 60 male delinquents, aged 13–16 years, during a 21-day wilderness adventure program found no significant relationship between exposure to the program and self-esteem measures. Washburn (1983) found no significant difference between the pretest and posttest self-concept scores among college students who participated in high-risk ropes course activities which were thought to improve individual self-concept.

The mixed findings about outdoor challenge programs enhancing self-concept provided a rationale for further study. A number of contributing factors might explain these inconsistencies in the findings. Among these factors could be that different self-concept scales were used, different levels of significance or different levels of involvement in the outdoor programs were present in the studies, different spans of time for treatment were involved, differences in the time that the tests were administered before and after treatment, and/or the wide range of types of subjects used. It has not been demonstrated that every disadvantaged group of individuals as a whole suffers from low self-concept. It was the thrust of the field experiment to work with abused children who had consistently demonstrated, as a group, generally lower self-concept (Hjorth, 1982; Burgess and Conger, 1978).

Length of Treatment in a Wilderness Outdoor Program and Self-Concept

Most studies found in the literature showed a two- to four-week treatment period. The researcher found no rationale for why the two- to four-week length of time was the most commonly used. Kelly and Baer (1968) reported a significant positive change ($p < .07$) in adolescent delinquents in present and ideal self-concept and value orientation after a 26-day Outward Bound program. Stimpson and Pederson (1970) reported significant changes in self-concept after a three-week wilderness program. Collingwood (1972) conducted a three-week camping program for delinquents and reported several significant results including positive changes in self-concept, locus of control, and behavior. Two evaluations of the 19-day Connecticut Wilderness School program for adolescent delinquents (Cytrynbaum and Ken, 1975) reported significant positive changes in self-concept, behavior, locus of control, self-confidence, and problem-solving ability at the end of the program. Porter (1975) evaluated an eight-day wilderness experience program for youth with adjustment problems. Porter found that at the end of the program the experimental group was significantly higher in self-concept and social acceptance than the control group. At a six-week follow-up, the experimental group showed significantly higher scores on self-concept, social acceptance, and self-concept than the control group. The experimental group when compared with the control group also showed a significant increase in esteem behavior and a significant decrease in defensive behavior both at the end and at six weeks after the program concluded.

The study compared the self-concept of an experimental group of residential abused children in grades three through twelve who participated in a treatment program of adventure games with the self-concept of a control group of residential abused children who did not participate in the adventure games program.

Further, differences in pretest self-concept scores were compared to the demographic characteristics of sex, age, and elapsed time since the last reported incidence of abuse.

Null Hypotheses

The following null hypotheses were established and tested. Hypothesis 1 through 5 were tested using the following measures as dependent variables: (a) Piers-Harris Children's Self-Concept Scale (PHSCS) pretest scores and (b) Piers-Harris Children's Self-Concept Scale posttest scores.

(1) There is no difference ($p < .10$) between global self-concept score, as measured by the PHSCS posttest scores of residential abused children who participated in adventure games with scores of abused children who were not involved in an adventure games program.

(2) There is no difference ($p < .10$) between cluster self-concept scores as measured by the PHSCS posttest scores of residential abused children who participate in adventure games with scores of abused children who were not involved in an adventure games program.

(3) There is no difference ($p < .10$) in the self-concept of residential abused children related to the demographic characteristic of sex as measured by the pretest scores on the PHSCS.

(4) There is no difference ($p < .10$) in the self-concept of residential abused children related to the demographic characteristic of age as measured by the pretest scores on the PHSCS.

(5) There is no difference ($p < .10$) in the self-concept of residential abused children related to the demographic characteristic of elapsed time since the last reported incident of abuse as measured by the pretest scores on the PHSCS.

Population

The population for the study consisted of abused children residing at a small residential school for dependent and neglected children in the Piedmont area of South Carolina during the summer of 1987. The population included all of the abused children ($N = 38$) between the third grade and the twelfth grade who had been removed from their homes because of abuse.

Children who live in a residential substitute home were used in the study because the actual determination of abuse by parents of children living in the community was impossible. Also, because child abuse is often a continuing problem, a study to show ways to enhance the self-concept of children who are continuing to live in an abusive home environment would not be effective. The children selected were enrolled in grades three through twelve in order to ensure the reading ability necessary to complete the self-concept scale. According to Piers and Harris (1969), the scale is designed primarily for that age range.

Instrumentation

The instrument used to collect the data on the subjects' self-concept was the Piers-Harris Children's Self-Concept Scale (PHSCS). The selected instrument (PHSCS) was judged to be appropriate for use in the study because of the practical utility of administration with children of this age group and its psychometric characteristics.

According to Piers (1969), the 80-item scale was developed using subjects in grades three through ten. Piers reported that the development of the PHSCS consisted of a derivation from an item pool and an initial pilot study. A content-valid self-concept scale for children was logically inferred to consist of items reflecting the concerns the children have about themselves. Building content validity into the scale was a concern at the outset, according to Piers (1969), and was resolved by defining the universe to be measured as the areas about which children reported qualities they liked or disliked about themselves. Piers and Harris used Jersild's (1952) collection of children's statements about what they liked and disliked about themselves as in the following examples: "I am strong," "I am lucky," "I forget what I learn," and "I am smart." Items were scored in the direction of a positive self-concept according to judges' ratings of what constitutes a self-favorable image. Piers and Harris then grouped these items into the following categories:

a. physical characteristics and appearance
b. clothing and grooming
c. health and physical soundness

    d. home and family

    e. enjoyment of recreation

    f. ability in sports, play

    g. ability in school, attitudes toward school, etc.

    h. intellectual abilities

    i. special talents (music, art)

    j. just me, myself and

    k. personality, character, inner resources, emotional tendencies

Support for the Piers-Harris Children's Self-Concept Scale validity rests in the attempt of the authors to build-in content validity through the Jersild's (1952) items and also in empirical evidence. Piers (1977) reported the findings of factor-analytic studies (Michael, Smith, & Michael, 1975; Piers & Harris, 1964). Convergent validity was evidenced by significant correlations between the scale and the Coopersmith Self-Esteem Inventory, Lipsitt's Children's Self-Concept Scale, and the Tennessee Self-Concept Scale as reported in Piers (1977) and in Piers and Harris (1969). Reviews of the validity of the Piers-Harris Children's Self-Concept Scale were generally positive in terms of other self-concept instruments. Bentler, writing in Buros (1981), was favorable toward the scale, and Wylie (1974) considered it to be the most promising of widely used instruments for children. The scale was also the most highly recommended measure in the "Measures of Self-Esteem" chapter by Crandall in *Measures of Social Psychological Attitudes* (Robinson & Shaver, 1973).

This instrument has been used with children because of its proved reliability. In the standardization sample of 1183 children, the mean score was 51.8 with a standard deviation of 13.87 (Piers & Harris, 1969). As a measure of instrument reliability, specifically in order to judge the homogeneity of the test, the Kuder-Richardson Formula 21, which assumed equal difficulty of items, was employed with coefficients results ranging from .78 to .93. As a check, the Spearman-Brown odd-even formula was applied for half the sample, generating coefficients of .90 and .87 respectively for grade ten and grade six of the sample. A retest after four months on one-half the standardization sample resulted in coefficients of .72, .71, and .72, demonstrating the stability of the test. A test-retest reliability coefficient of .77 was reported for the current 80-item version of the test (Piers & Harris, 1969). Piers (1977) reported additional reliability studies on the 80-item scale. These studies confirm test-retest correlations of .80 or over, and a general alpha of about .90.

Experiment Design

The design of the field experiment was a pretest-posttest control group design. Through the use of an experimental design in the field setting, the researcher attempted to control the threats of history, maturation, testing, regression, selection, mortality, and the interaction of selection and maturation in terms of internal validity (Campbell and Stanley, 1963).

In implementing the study, the researcher:

1. administered the PHSCS as a pretest to all abused students who were in grades three through twelve residing at a state-supported school for dependent and neglected children during the summer term, 1987;

2. randomly assigned subjects to either the experimental (Group E) or control (Group C) group; (Since the standard deviation of the pretest scores were small, a simple random assignment procedure was used to assign subjects to either the experimental or control groups.);

3. collected the demographic data by review of documents, observation, and/or interview;

4. conducted the adventure games treatment program for a period of one hour daily for four weeks' duration with the experimental group (Group E). While this treatment program was being conducted, the control group (Group C) subjects were either swimming or engaged in supervised table games.

5. After the adventure games treatment program had been completed each day, the researcher conducted a traditional recreational games program for a period of one hour the same four weeks' duration for the control group (Group C), while the experimental group (Group E) was involved in either a swimming activity or supervised table games. While both the control group and the experimental group participated in swimming or in table game activities each day, the groups swam or played table games as groups. That is, the groups did not participate together. The control group and the experimental group did not use the pool or the game room at the same time. The traditional recreational games program was used to control for the Hawthorne Effect.

6. Then, the researcher administered the PHSCS posttest both for the experimental and the control groups at the end of the study.

Procedures

Data Collection

The PHSCS pretest was administered to all the abused children who were serving as subjects together as a group. This was done by the same researcher, in the same location, to obtain data that reflected the least variation of circumstances possible. This also enabled the questioning to have the same connotations for all subjects according to the researcher's oral expression.

At the beginning of the study, after the administration of the pretest, demographic data were collected from permanent records as well as by having the subjects answer questions related to the last time abusive action was directed toward them.

The PHSCS posttest was administered at the end of the study within one day of the last adventure game session. The posttest was also administered to all the subjects together as a group to ensure the least variation of circumstances as possible.

Treatment

The treatment program consisted of each subject receiving an hour of supervised table games or recreational swimming and an hour of structured games each day for 28 consecutive days. The supervised table games/ recreational swimming and the structured games programs were done by the subjects as a part of a group, either the control (Group C) or the experimental (Group E). The groups participated in these two hours of activities separately.

The supervised table games consisted of various quiet games such as billiards, foosh ball, card games, or checkers. These activities were chosen freely by the subjects, with a recreation worker present to provide supervision but not to provide game leadership. The swimming activity consisted of a one-hour supervised swimming experience with a lifeguard available but with no structured program occurring. Both the control and the experimental groups participated in swimming for the same length of time each day or they were free to play the same table games each day. The two groups swam or played table games separately with Group C playing the table game/swimming while Group E participated in the adventure games treatment program. Group E played table games/swam while Group C played the traditional recreational games. Group E played table games/swam the first hour and then had their adventure games treatment program the second hour 14 of the 28 treatment days. Group C played table games/swam the first hour and then had their traditional recreational games program on alternate days so that each group had an equal number of days when table games/swimming preceded the structured games program.

The table games and swimming were supervised by one of the school's recreation workers who was instructed to interact with the subjects only when necessary to maintain order. After each day's two-hour session, the subjects returned to the regular daily activity of the school. The experimental group was asked not to participate in any of the adventure games activities during the 28-day experiment treatment period other than during the one-hour treatment time each day. The experimental group was asked not to share any information about the adventure games with any other students until after the 28-day treatment program was completed.

Traditional Recreational Games Program

The structured traditional recreational games program consisted of the researcher leading the control group in the following games: basketball, dodgeball, kickball, soccer, softball, touch football, and volleyball (refer to Kirchner's *Physical Education. . . . Children* for rules). One of these games was played each day, with each of the seven games being played once before starting the rotation again. During the 28-day period of the experiment, each game was played four times. The researcher chose the game to be played each day without input from the students. Each subject daily selected a number from 1 to 25 and the researcher thought of a number prior to the activity and the two subjects whose numbers were nearest the researcher's number served as team captains and chose the teams for that day. The traditional recreational games were played on the playground area or the gymnasium area of the school's campus.

Adventure Games Treatment Program

The adventure games treatment program consisted of the researcher leading the experimental group subjects in the following games: Trash Toss, Sit Down Dodge Ball, Go Tag, Fox and Squirrel, Everybody Up, Rotation Volleyball, Moon Ball, Hunker Hawser, Togeth-Air Ball, Collective Score Towel Ball, Rope Push, Blindfold Soccer, Squat Thrust, and Punctured Drum (refer to Flugelman's New Games books for rules). All games were played once and then the subjects assisted the researcher in choosing which games were played again. The researcher's involvement with each game was to present the rules or situation and then to step back and allow the group to work through the rules or problem until the game was played or the problem solved. Interaction of group members was of interest and not how well the subjects performed physically. After the group had completed the game or problem (in some cases the problem was not completed), the last 20 minutes of each one-hour treatment period was used for debriefing. Such debriefing is an inherent part of adventure games programs. The typical debriefing protocol was followed.

During debriefing time, the details of the game or problem were discussed by all who were involved. The discussion focused on the process the subjects had experienced. They examined what decisions were made and by whom, who had ideas that were not expressed, or that were expressed but not heard. The conversations often moved into a comparison of the cooperative processes which can characterize one's functioning well in society. The following questions guided the discussion when appropriate. Was the game fun? What would make the game more fun? Who were the leaders and followers? What was the effect of group support or lack of it? Was peer pressure negative or positive? Was hostility present? How was hostility and negativism handled? Is there some carry-over from these games or problems to real-life situations? Was fear of failure present (Rohnke, 1984)? In this discussion time two rules always existed. They were clearly articulated and enforced by the researcher at each session. First, there was to be no discounting among subjects. Discounting is interrupting, "putting down," or ridiculing the ideas or comments of anyone else. Second, every subject had the right to pass (remain silent) in any discussion. The researcher recorded field notes during and subsequent to each session in order to maintain a descriptive narrative of what transpired and of the context of the debriefing sessions.

Analysis of Data

The primary research hypothesis was that there is a difference in overall self-concept as measured by the PHSCS posttest scores of residential abused children who participated in adventure games, when compared with residential abused children who were involved in a traditional recreational games program. Another level of interpretation involved the six cluster scales of the Piers-Harris Children's Self-Concept Scale. The secondary research hypothesis was that there is a difference in overall self-concept as measured by the PHSCS posttest cluster scores of residential abused children who participated in an adventure games program when compared with residential abused children who were involved in a traditional recreational games program. The six cluster scales looked at children's self-concept for the constructs of Behavior, Intellectual and School Status, Physical Appearance and Attributes, Anxiety, Popularity, and Happiness (Piers, 1977). Inherent in the use of these scales is the assumption that self-concept is not a unitary dimension. According to Piers (1977), these cluster scales may be used to generate clinical hypotheses and identify areas of relative strength and vulnerability in individual children. To validate previous findings by the researcher, three additional research hypotheses sought to determine if sex, age, and amount of elapsed time since the last reported occurrence of abuse affected self-concept. The children's pretest scores on the PHSCS were analyzed to see what effect abuse had on these three demographic dimensions.

Testing of Null Hypotheses One

The first null hypothesis was tested using an analysis of variance (ANOVA) for a one factor design with the Piers-Harris posttest as the dependent variable and the type of program (adventure games for Group E and traditional recreational games for Group C) serving as the independent variables. The results of this testing are given in Tables XV-2 and XV-3 (*denotes statistically significant differences).

Table XV-2

ANALYSIS OF VARIANCE FOR HYPOTHESIS 1

Dependent Variable: Total Difference or Gain Score

Source of Variation	DF	Sum of Squares	Mean Square	F	p-value
Treatment	1	313.83	313.83	18.86	.0001*
Error	36	599.14	16.64		

Based on this test, there was a statistically significant difference between the PHSCS posttest mean score gains between groups. An examination of the analysis led to the following conclusions:

Table XV-3

MEANS AND STANDARD DEVIATIONS FOR TOTAL
GAIN SCORE OF HYPOTHESIS I

Group	N	Mean ($\bar{x}$)	Sd
Experimental	18	9.06	3.32
Control	20	3.30	4.71

1. As already noted above, the F-value of 18.86 indicated a statistically significant difference between the means of the experimental and control groups with a probability of .0001 that an F-ratio of 18.86 or larger would occur due to chance.

2. The mean score gain for the experimental group of 9.06 was statistically significantly higher than the mean gain score for the control group of 3.30, although both the experimental and the control groups' mean scores increased during the time of the study.

Testing of Null Hypothesis Two

ANOVA was also used to test the six cluster scale scores of Null Hypothesis Two. Results are presented in Tables XV-4, XV-5, XV-6, XV-7, XV-8, XV-9, and XV-10.

Table XV-4

ANOVA VALUES FOR BEHAVIOR CLUSTER SCALE IN HYPOTHESIS 2

Dependent Variable: Gain Score on Behavior Cluster Scale

Source of Variation	DF	Sum of Squares	Mean Square	F	p-value
Treatment	1	26.85	26.85	16.51	.0003*
Error	36	58.55	1.63		

Table XV-5

ANOVA VALUES FOR SCHOOL CLUSTER SCALE IN HYPOTHESIS 2

Dependent Variable: Gain Score on School Cluster Scale

Source of Variation	DF	Sum of Squares	Mean Square	F	p-value
Treatment	1	0.26	0.26	0.16	0.6910
Error	36	59.00	1.64		

Analyses of variance were used to test Null Hypothesis Two at the .10 level of significance. As shown in Table XV-10, Null Hypothesis Two was rejected for four of the six mean scores used as dependent variables. As shown in Tables XV-4 through XV-9. Null Hypothesis Two was rejected for four of the ANOVAs used to compare dependent variable means for the cluster scale scores. That is, there was a statistically significant difference in the cluster means for all but two of the six ANOVA comparisons.

An examination of the analysis led to the following conclusions:

1. As noted above in Tables XV-4 through XV-9, the F-values of 16.51 on the Behavior cluster scale, 17.07 on the Anxiety cluster scale, 4.49 on the Popularity cluster scale and 13.08 on the Happiness Cluster scale

Table XV-6

ANOVA VALUES FOR PHYSICAL APPEARANCE CLUSTER SCALE
IN HYPOTHESIS 2

Dependent Variable: Gain Score on Physical Appearance

Source of Variation	DF	Sum of Squares	Mean Square	F	p-value
Treatment	1	0.45	0.45	0.39	0.5357
Error	36	40.95	1.14		

Table XV-7

ANOVA VALUES FOR ANXIETY CLUSTER SCALE IN HYPOTHESIS 2

Dependent Variable: Gain Score on Anxiety Subscale

Source of Variation	DF	Sum of Squares	Mean Square	F	p-value
Treatment	1	26.32	26.32	17.07	0.0002*
Error	36	55.50	1.54		

indicate a statistically significant difference between the means of the experimental and control groups with a probability of .05 or less that F-values of these sizes or larger would occur due to chance.

2. As noted in Tables XV-4 through XV-9, the F-values of 0.16 on the School cluster scale and 0.39 on the Physical Appearance cluster scale are not statistically significantly different at the .10 level.

3. The mean gain scores for the experimental group on the cluster scales of Behavior (2.33), Anxiety (2.17), Popularity (0.78) and Happiness (1.89) were statistically significantly higher than the mean gain scores for the control group on the cluster scales of Behavior (0.65), Anxiety (0.50), Popularity (0.10) and Happiness (0.55).

4. The mean gain scores for the experimental group on the cluster

Table XV-8

ANOVA VALUES FOR POPULARITY CLUSTER SCALE IN HYPOTHESIS 2

Dependent Variable: Gain Score on Popularity Cluster Scale

Source of Variation	DF	Sum of Squares	Mean Square	F	p-value
Treatment	1	4.35	4.35	4.49	0.0411*
Error	36	34.91	0.97		

Table XV-9

ANOVA VALUES FOR HAPPINESS CLUSTER SCALE IN HYPOTHESIS 2

Dependent Variable: Gain Score on Happiness Cluster Scale

Source of Variation	DF	Sum of Squares	Mean Square	F	p-value
Treatment	1	16.98	16.98	13.08	0.0009*
Error	36	46.73	1.30		

scales of School (0.67) and Physical Appearance (0.67) were not statistically significantly from the control group scores on the cluster scales of School (0.50) and Physical Appearance (0.45).

Testing of Null Hypothesis Three

The analysis of variance used to test Null Hypothesis Three is presented in Tables XV-11 and XV-12.

Based on this test, there was no statistically significant difference in the self-concept of residential abused children related to the demographic characteristic of sex as measured by the PHSCS pretest.

Testing of Null Hypothesis Four

The analysis of variance used to test Null Hypothesis Four is presented in Tables XV-13 and XV-14.

This test showed a statistically significant difference in the PHSCS pretest mean scores related to the demographic characteristic of age. To try and determine among which age groups the variations were significant, the Scheffe multiple comparison test was used to analyze the data. Table XV-15 presents the results of this procedure.

An examination of the analyses led to the following conclusions:

1. As noted in Table 13, the F-value of 24.00 indicated a statistically significant difference between the means of the pretest scores based on age with a probability of .0001 that an F-value of 24.00 or larger would occur due to chance.

2. The Scheffe test for comparisons showed that the statistically significant different scores existed between group A (8- to 11-year-olds) and

Table XV-10

MEANS AND STANDARD DEVIATIONS FOR CLUSTER SCALE SCORES

Cluster Scales		Experimental (n=18)			Control (n=20)		
		Pre-test	Post-test	Change	Pre-test	Post-test	Change
Behavior	x̄	8.83	11.16	2.33**	8.55	9.20	0.65
	Sd	2.27	2.26	1.08	2.55	2.52	1.42
School	x̄	8.55	9.22	0.67	9.00	9.50	0.50
	Sd	2.14	1.90	0.77	1.14	1.38	1.60
Physical Appearance	x̄	6.72	7.39	0.67	7.15	7.60	0.45
	Sd	1.56	1.42	0.84	1.74	1.80	1.23
Anxiety	x̄	6.44	8.61	2.17**	6.15	6.65	0.50
	Sd	2.03	2.11	1.15	2.15	2.08	1.32
Popularity	x̄	5.89	6.66	0.78**	5.95	6.05	0.10
	Sd	1.37	1.49	0.88	1.91	1.86	1.07
Happiness	x̄	5.55	7.44	1.89**	5.70	6.25	0.55
	Sd	1.42	1.53	1.08	1.79	1.89	1.19

** $p<.001$ * $p<.05$

groups B (12- to 14-year-olds) and C (15- to 17-year-olds). There were no statistically significant differences between the scores of groups B and C. This means that the younger subjects had significantly higher self-concept than did the middle or older aged subjects.

Table XV-11

ANALYSIS OF VARIANCE FOR HYPOTHESIS 3

Dependent Variable: PHSCS Pretest Scores

Source of Variation	DF	Sum of Squares	Mean Square	F	p-value
Sex	1	50.95	50.95	0.62	0.44
Error	36	2943.37	81.76		

Table XV-12

MEANS AND STANDARD DEVIATIONS OF PRETEST SCORES
FOR HYPOTHESIS 3

Sex	N	Mean ($\bar{x}$)	Sd
Male	19	43.63	8.49
Female	19	45.95	9.57

Testing of Null Hypothesis Five

The analysis of variance used to test Null Hypothesis Five is presented in Tables XV-16 and XV-17.

This test showed no statistically significant difference in the self-concept of residential abused children related to the lapse of time since the last incidence of abuse as measured by the PHSCS pretest.

Field Notes

The researcher recorded observations and comments from subjects after each treatment session. The games used with the experimental

Table XV-13

ANALYSIS OF VARIANCE RESULTS FOR HYPOTHESIS 4

Dependent Variable: PHSCS Pretest Scores

Source of Variation	DF	Sum of Squares	Mean Square	F	p-value
Age Group	2	1731.57	865.79	24.00	0.0001*
Error	35	1262.74	36.08		

Table XV-14

MEANS AND STANDARD DEVIATIONS OF PRETEST SCORES
FOR HYPOTHESIS 4

Age Groups		N	Mean ($\bar{x}$)	Sd
a.	8 to 11 years old	10	55.70	8.56
b.	12 to 14 years old	14	42.93	5.21
c.	15 to 17 years old	14	38.86	4.38

** $p < .001$

group were games selected from cooperative games books. These games were chosen because they stressed non-competitive involvement between players. These games are in contrast to the competitive games, in that the subjects played with each other instead of against each other. No one was eliminated, rejected, or intentionally hurt. These were games of acceptance, cooperation, and sharing. Some of the games posed problems that had to be solved or presented a challenge for the entire group to encounter together.

The literature supported that the opportunity provided for experi-

Table XV-15

SCHEFFE'S TEST FOR COMPARISONS OF SIGNIFICANT MEANS

Dependent Variable: PHSCS Pretest Scores by Age Groups

Age Group Comparison	Lower Confidence Limit	Difference Between Means	Upper Confidence Limit
A - B	6.41	12.77	19.12**
A - C	10.49	16.84	23.20**
B - A	-19.12	-12.77	-6.41**
B - C	-1.73	4.07	9.87
C - A	-23.20	-16.84	-10.48**
C - B	-9.87	-4.07	1.73

Table XV-16

ANALYSIS OF VARIANCE RESULTS FOR HYPOTHESIS 5

Dependent Variable: PHSCS Pretest Scores

Source of Variation	DF	Sum of Squares	Mean Square	F	p-value
Lapse of Time	2	98.74	49.37	0.60	0.5561
Error	35	2895.57	82.73		

Table XV-17

MEANS AND STANDARD DEVIATIONS OF PRETEST SCORES
FOR HYPOTHESIS 5

Lapse of Time Since Last Abuse Incident	N	Mean ($\bar{x}$)	Sd
a. less than 1 year	15	43.27	10.04
b. more than 1 year but less than 2 years	11	47.18	9.46
c. more than 2 years	12	44.50	8.75

mental group subjects to discuss their feelings at the end of the games was a key element in the self-concept enhancement process and, further, that the group also chose the activity enabled them to be a part of the decision-making process.

Because the age range was so wide among the subjects, the participants had to choose from among games that would appeal to youths between the ages of 8 and 17. If there had been a narrower age range, it is possible that different, more age-focused games would have been selected.

Another element that was observed to be critical to the treatment process (adventure games) was the debriefing sessions at the end of each game period. This time seemed especially important after the first two weeks of the study when the subjects and researcher became familiar with each other. A familiar relationship developed between the researcher and both the experimental and the control groups, but it was after the first two weeks that the researcher began to feel that the subjects "opened up" in their discussions of their feelings and more positive statements were made during the debriefing sessions. Although the non-competitive games reduced the stress level from the play situations that often accompany competitive games, the debriefing sessions seemed to be very beneficial to the self-concept enhancement of the experimental group. During the debriefing sessions, the experimental group, who had the opportunity to share their feelings about the games, appeared to develop an affinity as group members, almost to the point of developing a group identity. One subject, not knowing the purpose behind the different groups, referred to the experimental group as the "new games" group and the control group as the "old games" group.

It was noted that the experimental group did not have as many conflicts between participants as did the control group during the game sessions and the researcher noted more expression of concern among the experimental group toward the other participants than was evidenced among the control group.

It was also observed that among the experimental group, the older subjects often dominated the discussion during the debriefing sessions. The younger subjects reiterated the feelings expressed by the older subjects.

Subjects in the experimental group during the debriefing sessions tended to express more satisfaction with their home lives than with relationships at school. This was somewhat unexpected considering the fact that abuse had existed in their homes. While this observation may reflect family lives that the subjects "wished" would exist, it may also be related to the possible tendency to view their home lives more positively because of the substantial periods of separation.

Summary of Findings

Two statistical procedures were used in the data analyses, analysis of variance and the Scheffe test for multiple comparisons. The following findings relate to each of the five hypotheses:

1. Null Hypothesis One was rejected at the .10 level. There was a statistically significant difference in the PHSCS pretest and the PHSCS posttest mean gain scores between the experimental and control groups. The experimental group's mean gain scores were significantly higher than the control group's mean gain scores.

2. Null Hypothesis Two was rejected on four of the six subscale scores at the .10 level. There was a statistically significant difference in the PHSCS pretest and posttest mean gain scores on the Behavior, Anxiety, Popularity and Happiness cluster scale scores between the experimental and control groups. The experimental group's mean gain scores were significantly higher than the control groups mean gain scores on the cluster scales of Behavior, Anxiety, Popularity and Happiness.

Null Hypothesis Two was retained on two of the six cluster scale mean gain scores at the .10 level. There was not a statistically significant difference in the PHSCS pretest and posttest mean scores on the School and Physical Appearance cluster scale scores between the Experimental and Control groups.

3. Null Hypothesis Three was retained at the .10 level. There was not a statistically significant difference in the mean scores on the analysis of variance procedure testing the self-concept of residential abused children based on the demographic characteristic of sex.

4. Null Hypothesis Four was rejected at the .10 level. There was a statistically significant difference in the mean gain scores on the analysis of variance procedure testing the self-concept of residential abused children based on the demographic characteristic of age. A further analysis of this data using the Scheffe test for multiple comparisons revealed that a significant difference in the mean scores of the younger aged subjects (8 to 11 years old) from the mean scores of the middle aged subjects (12–14 years old) and the older aged subjects (15–17 years old) existed. No significant difference in the mean scores between the middle-aged subjects and the older aged subjects was found.

5. Null Hypothesis Five was retained at the .10 level. There was no statistically significant difference in the mean scores on the analysis of variance procedure testing the self-concepts of residential abused children based on the demographic characteristic of lapse of time since the last reported incidence of abuse.

CONCLUSIONS

The study supports others, in that the overall mean scores on the PHSCS of the children in this study (44.78), all of whom had been the victims of abuse, are lower than the average score of the group used to normalize the PHSCS (51.84). The first major finding of this study reinforces previous research that indicates in terms of positive self-concept that abuse is detrimental.

The self-concept is learned, may be changed, and may be enhanced. This study supports the self-concept enhancement theory because the self-concepts of both the experimental group and the control group were enhanced during the 28-day treatment program, with the enhancement of the experimental group being statistically significant.

Effectiveness of the Treatment Program

1. From the results of the study and literature cited earlier, it can be concluded that the study supported the use of an adventure games program (as described) to enhance the self-concept of abused children. The adventure games program was a combination of non-competitive, initiative, and challenge games that included a debriefing session at the end of each game's program. The debriefing session gave the game participants the opportunity to express their feelings about the games and their role in the games, and the interaction among the games' participants.

2. Using the results of the study it can be concluded that it supported the use of an adventure games program (as described) to enhance the self-concept of abused children—especially in the areas of behavior, anxiety, popularity, and happiness. Findings from the study do not support the conclusion that an adventure games program will enhance the self-concept of abused children in the areas of school and personal appearance. This conclusion might be partially explained by the fact that the study took place during a time when school was not in session and none of the games or debriefing sessions related directly to school performance or personal appearance. All of the games and debriefing discussions related either directly or indirectly to the subjects' behavior, day-to-day relationships or by providing fun experiences, excitement, cooperativeness, and happiness.

3. Results of the study suggest that differences in self-concept are not related to the demographic characteristic of sex. Other studies investigating sex differences in self-concept have generally found no differences (Wylie, 1974). Based on the low mean scores on the PHSCS pretest for both boys (43.65) and girls (45.96) it can be concluded that abuse is destructive to the self-concept of both males and females.

4. The results support that differences in self-concept related to age are significant. This finding may not be conclusive, because other studies show that younger aged subjects tend to have a higher self-concept than middle or older aged subjects. Harter (1983) found that self-concept may be less stable and subject to unreliability in measurement among younger children whose sense of self is still under development. Generally, Wylie (1974) found no relationship between age and self-concept between the ages of 8 and 23 years. While this study concludes abuse is not as harmful to the self-concept of younger children that abuse is to older

children, the researcher noted that this conclusion is not supported by the majority of the literature on this subject.

5. Results from the study suggest that differences in self-concept are not related to the demographic characteristic of lapse of time since the last incidence of abuse. This finding led to the conclusion that since self-concept is tied to the children's opinion of themselves in light of what children perceive significant others in their lives feel toward them, abuse by the parents create emotional scars that do not fade with time. They would indicate that the removal of the child from the abusive environment might not be enough in the way of treatment for abuse. Perhaps additional steps other than removal and time are necessary to help overcome at least the lowered self-concept caused by an abusive home background.

APPLICATIONS OF THE FINDINGS

Studies concerning the enhancement of self-concept in abused children by the use of adventure games have many applications for recreation leaders. Since a positive self-concept is related to many success experiences in children (McFern, 1973) and is the starting point in the success of children in social settings (Brothers, 1975), any activity that promotes the self-concept of any child should be considered in program planning. With the evidence that too much emphasis on competitive games can actually hurt the self-concept of children not highly skilled in physical activities (Orlick, 1978), the inclusion of an adventure games program into the recreation agency's physical activity program merits consideration. If this adventure games program cannot be considered as a part of the daily activity, certainly specific programs focused on raising the self-concept in children should be considered as a periodical endeavor.

Because recreators lead children in activities that have so many components related to the development of positive and negative self-concept (group involvement, group identity, problem solving, feeling of importance or feeling of non-importance, availability of significant others, playful environment, and the abundance of opportunities for both failure and success), these professionals should explore every method possible to use their program environments to enhance self-concept. This adventure games approach would be helpful in any environment where children and adults develop "significant others" relationships.

APPENDICES

Appendix A

SELECTED NATIONAL ORGANIZATIONS SERVING CHILDREN AND YOUTH

The following listing of private non-profit organizations should prove helpful to Recreation and Leisure Services personnel seeking additional information or assistance pertaining to child abuse issues. Such organizations provide a multitude of direct and non-direct services to families, child care employees, and families.

American Association for Protecting Children
9725 E. Hampden
Denver, CO 80231
Phone: (303) 695-0811

American Bar Association
Family Law Section
750 N. Lake Shore Drive
Chicago, IL 60611
Phone: (312) 988-5636

Association of Junior Leagues
825 *3rd* Avenue
New York, NY 10022
Phone: (212) 355-4380

Big Brothers/Big Sisters of America
230 N. 13*th* Street
Philadelphia, PA 19107
Phone: (215) 567-2748

C. Henry Kempe National Center for the Prevention and Treatment of Child Abuse and Neglect
1205 Oneida Street
Denver, CO 80220
Phone: (303) 321-3963

Childhelp USA
  6463 Independence Avenue
  Woodland Hills, CA 91367
  Phone: (818) 347-7280
  National Child Abuse Hotline: (800) 422-4453 (800) 4-A-CHILD

Child Welfare League of America
  67 Irving Place
  New York, NY
  Phone: (212) 254-7410

Child Welfare League of America
  440 First Street N.W.
  Washington, DC 20001
  Phone: (202) 638-2952

Children's Defense Fund
  122 C Street, N.W.
  4th Floor
  Washington, DC 20001
  Phone: (202) 347-0308

Clearinghouse on Child Abuse
  and Neglect Information
  8201 Greensboro Drive
  Suite 600
  McLean, VA 22102

National Association of Black Social Workers
  271 W. 125*th* Street
  New York, NY 10027
  Phone: (212) 749-0470

National Committee for Prevention of
  Child Abuse (NCPCA)
  332 S. Michigan Avenue
  Suite 950
  Chicago, IL 60604
  Phone: (312) 663-3520

National Council on Child Abuse and Family Violence
  1050 Connecticut N.W.
  Suite 300
  Washington, DC 20036
  Phone: (202) 429-6695
  Toll free (except CA): (800) 222-2000

National Council of the YMCA's of USA
101 N. Wacker Drive
14*th* Floor
Chicago, IL 60606
Phone: (312) 977-0031

National Institute for Latchkey Children and Youth
900 Seventeenth Street, N.W.
Washington, DC 20006
Phone: (319) 229-6126

National Legal Resource Center for
Child Advocacy and Protection
1800 M Street, N.W.
2*nd* Floor S
Washington, DC 20036
Phone: (202) 331-2250

Parents Anonymous
22330 Hawthorne Blvd.
Suite 210
Torrance, CA 90505
Phone: (213) 371-3501

The Salvation Army
National Headquarters
799 Bloomfield Avenue
Verone, NJ 07044
Phone: (201) 239-0606

Save The Children National Office
54 Wilton Road
Westport, CT 06880
Phone: (203) 226-7271

U.S. Catholic Conference
1312 Massachusetts Avenue, N.W.
Washington, DC 20005
Phone: (202) 659-6771

SELECT INTERNATIONAL ORGANIZATIONS ADDRESSING CHILD ABUSE AND NEGLECT

The following partial listing of international organizations may be helpful to Recreation and Leisure Services personnel in the quest for additional information and assistance.

Childhelp International, Inc.
6463 Independence Avenue
Woodland Hills, CA 91367
Phone: (818) 347-7280

**The International Society for the
Prevention of Child Abuse and Neglect**
C. Henry Kempe Center
1205 Oneida Street
Denver, CO 80220
Phone: (303) 321-3963

International Society of Child Abuse and Neglect
University of Louvain
Louvain-la-Neuve, Belgium

International Union of Child Welfare
1 Rue de Varembe
1211 Geneve 20, Switzerland

The Salvation Army
101 Queen Victoria Street
London, England EC4P 4EP
Phone: 01-236-5222

World Union for the Safeguard of Youth
28 Plases de St. Georges
F-75009, Paris, France

Appendix C

SELECT STATE LEVEL RESOURCES

The listing which follows is far from being all-inclusive. The governmental agencies which follow should have at their disposal a wide range of information and assistance Recreation and Leisure Services personnel may find helpful in the efforts to intervene in and to assist in the prevention and treatment of child abuse. The agencies should also assist in the networking of the recreation organization with other state, county, and local agencies.

Alabama

Bureau of Family and Children's Services
64 N. Union Street
Montgomery, AL 36130
Phone: (205) 261-3409

Alaska

Division of Family and Youth Services
Department of Health and Social Services
Alaska Office Building, Rm. 204
Pouch H-01
Juneau, AK 99811
Phone: (907) 465-3170

Arizona

Administration for Children, Youth and Families
1717 W. Jefferson Street
P.O. Box 6123
Phoenix, AZ 85005
Phone: (602) 255-3981

Arkansas

Department of Human Services
Division of Social Services
Donaghey Building, Suite 317
7*th* and Main Streets, P.O. Box 1437
Little Rock, AR 72203
Phone: (501) 371-2521

   Statewide Child Abuse Hotline: (800) 482-5946

California
Office of Child Abuse Prevention
Adult and Family Services Division
Department of Social Services
744 P Street
Sacramento, CA 95814
Phone: (916) 323-2888
   Central Registry of Child Abuse: (916) 445-7586

Colorado
Division of Family and Children's Services
Department of Social Services
1575 Sherman Street
Denver, CO 80203
Phone: (303) 866-2551
   Statewide Hotline (other than metro Denver): (800) 842-2288

Connecticut
Division of Children's and Protective Services
Department of Children and Youth Services
170 Sigourney Street
Hartford, CT 06105
Phone: (203) 566-5506
   Statewide Child Abuse Reporting Hotline: (800) 842-2228

Delaware
Division of Child Protective Services
Department of Services for Children, Youth and Their Families
824 Market Street, 7*th* Floor
Wilmington, DE 19801
Phone: (302) 571-6140
   Statewide Child Abuse Reporting Hotline: (800) 292-9582

District of Columbia
Family Services Administration
Commission on Social Services
Randall Building
1*st* and Eye Streets, S.W.
Washington, DC 20024
Phone: (202) 727-5947
   Child Abuse and Neglect Reporting: (202) 727-0995

Florida

Children, Youth and
Family Services Programs Office
Department of Health and Rehabilitation Services
1317 Winewood Blvd.,
Building 8, Room 317
Tallahassee, FL 33609
Phone: (904) 488-8762

Statewide Child Abuse Reporting Hotline: (800) 342-9152

Georgia

Office of Child Protective Services
Division of Family and Children Services
Department of Human Resources
47 Trinity Avenue, S.W.
Atlanta, GA 30334
Phone: (404) 894-2287

Hawaii

Family and Children's Services
Public Welfare Division
Department of Social Services and Housing
P.O. Box 339
Honolulu, HI 96809
Phone: (808) 548-5846

Idaho

Division of Welfare, Child Protection
Department of Health and Welfare
Statehouse
Boise, ID 83720
Phone: (208) 384-3340

Illinois

Division of Child Protection
Department of Children and
Family Services
1 N. Old State Capitol Plaza
Springfield, IL 62706
Phone: (217) 785-2513

Statewide Child Abuse Reporting Hotline: (800) 252-2873

Indiana

Division of Child Welfare-Social Services
Field Services (Child Abuse)
141 South Meridian Street
Indianapolis, IN 46225
Phone: (317) 232-4431

Statewide Child Abuse Reporting Hotline: (800) 562-2407

Iowa

Protection Services
Division of Social Services
Department of Human Services
Hoover State Office Building
Des Moines, IA
Phone: (515) 281-5583

Statewide Child Abuse Reporting Hotline: (800) 362-2178

Kansas

Family Services Section,
Youth Services
Department of Social and
Rehabilitation Services
2700 W. 6*th*
Smith-Wilson Building
Topeka, KS 66606
Phone: (913) 296-4657

Kentucky

Department of Social Services
Cabinet of Human Resources
275 E. Main Street
Frankfort, KY 40204
Phone: (502) 564-4650

Louisiana

Protective Services
Office of Human Development
Department of Health and Human Resources
P.O. Box 44367
Baton Rouge, LA 70804
Phone: (504) 342-4049

Maine

Protective Services for Children
Office of Social and Rehabilitation Services
State House
Augusta, ME 04333
Phone: (207) 289-2971
  Statewide Child Abuse Reporting Hotline: (800) 452-1999

Maryland

Protective Services
Office of Child Welfare Services
300 W. Preston Street
Baltimore, MD 21202
Phone: (301) 576-5242

H.E.L.P./Resource Project
Office of Child Welfare Services
300 W. Preston Street
Baltimore, MD 21202
Phone: (301) 576-5245

Massachusetts

Department of Social Services
150 Causeway Street
Boston, MA 02114
Phone: (617) 727-0900
  Statewide Child Abuse Reporting Hotline: (800) 792-5200

Michigan

Children's Protective Services
Office of Children and Youth Services
Department of Social Services
300 S. Capitol Avenue, P.O. Box 30037
Lansing, MI 48909
Phone: (517) 373-7580

Minnesota

Child Abuse and Neglect
Social Services Division
Department of Human Services
Centennial Office Building, 4*th* Floor
St. Paul, MN 55155
Phone: (612) 296-8337

Mississippi

Adult and Child Protective Services
Division of Social Services
Department of Public Welfare
P.O. Box 352
Jackson, MS 39205
Phone: (601) 354-0341

  Statewide Child Abuse Reporting Hotline: (800) 222-8000

Missouri

Division of Family Services
Department of Social Services
Broadway State Office Building
P.O. Box 1527
Jefferson City, MO 65102
Phone: (314) 751-4247

  Statewide Child Abuse Reporting Hotline: (800) 392-3738

Montana

Community Services Division
Department of Social and
Rehabilitation Services
P.O. Box 4210
Helena, MT 59604
Phone: (406) 444-5622

Nebraska

Child Protective Services
Human Services
Department of Social Services
301 Centennial Mall South
5th Floor, P.O. Box 95026
Lincoln, NE 68509-5026
Phone: (402) 471-3121

Nevada

Welfare Division, Protective Services
Department of Human Resources
Capitol Complex, 251 Jeanell Drive
Carson City, NV 89710
Phone: (702) 885-4730

Youth Services Division
Department of Human Resources
505 E. King Street, Room 603
Carson City, NV 89710
Phone (702) 885-5982

New Hampshire

Protective Services
Bureau of Child and Family Services
Department of Health and Welfare
Hazen Drive
Concord, NH 03301
Phone: (603) 271-4405
    Child Abuse Reporting, Info-Line: (800) 852-3311

New Jersey

Division of Youth and Family Services
Department of Human Services
CN 717, P.O. Box 510
Trenton, NJ 08625
Phone: (609) 292-6920

Office of Child Abuse Control/Hotline
1230 Whitehouse-Mercerville Road
Trenton, NJ 08625
Phone: (800) 792-8610

New Mexico

Family Protective Services
Social Services Division
Human Services Department
P.O. Box 2348
Santa Fe, NM 87503-2348
Phone: (505) 827-4372
    Statewide Child Abuse Reporting Hotline: (800) 432-6217

New York

Division of Children and Family Services
Department of Social Services
40 N. Pearl Street
Albany, NY 12243
Phone: (518) 474-9428
    State Operations/Child Protective Services Hotline: (518) 474-9607
    Statewide Child Abuse Reporting Hotline: (800) 342-3720

North Carolina
Protective Services Unit
Family Services Section
Department of Human Resources
325 N. Salisbury Street
Raleigh, NC 27611
Phone: (919) 733-2580

North Dakota
Children and Family Services
Department of Human Services
State Capitol
Bismarck, ND 58505
Phone: (701) 224-2316

Ohio
Bureau of Children's Protective Services
Division of Family and Children's Services
Department of Human Services
30 E. Broad Street
Columbus, OH 43215
Phone: (614) 466-2146

Oklahoma
Child Welfare Services
Department of Human Services
P.O. Box 25352
Oklahoma City, OK 73125
Phone: (405) 521-3778
   Statewide Child Abuse Reporting Hotline: (800) 522-3511

Oregon
Children's Services Division
Department of Human Resources
318 Public Service Building
Salem, OR 97310
Phone: (503) 378-4374 (503) 378-3016

Pennsylvania
Office of Children, Youth and Families
Department of Public Welfare
P.O. Box 2675
Harrisburg, PA 17120
Phone: (717) 787-4756
   Statewide Child Abuse Reporting Childline: (800) 932-0313

Rhode Island

Child Protective Services
Department of Children and Their Families
610 Mount Pleasant Avenue
Providence, RI 02908
Phone: (401) 861-6000 Ext. 2332

Statewide Child Abuse Reporting Hotline: (800) RI–CHILD

South Dakota

Child Protection Services
Department of Social Services
Richard F. Kneip Building
700 N. Illinois Street
Pierre, SD 57501
Phone: (605) 773-3227

South Carolina

Child Protective and
Preventative Services Division
Department of Social Services
P.O. Box 1520
Columbia, SC 29202-1520
Phone: (803) 758-8593

Tennessee

Child Protective Services,
Office of Social Services
Department of Human Services
111-7*th* Avenue, N.
Nashville, TN 37203
Phone: (615) 741-5929

Texas

Office of Services to
Families and Children
Department of Human Services
P.O. Box 2960
Austin, TX 78769
Phone: (512) 450-3448

Statewide Child Abuse Reporting Hotline: (800) 252-5400

Utah

Protective Services,
Child Abuse Registry
Division of Family Services
Department of Social Services
150 W. North Temple Street
Salt Lake City, UT 84110
Phone: (801) 533-7128

Vermont

Protective Services
Department of Social and
Rehabilitation Services
Agency of Human Services
103 S. Main Street
Waterbury, VT 05676
Phone: (802) 241-2142

Virginia

Child Protective Services
Bureau of Child Welfare Services
Department of Social Services
8007 Discovery Drive
Richmond, VA 23288
Phone: (804) 281-9081

   Statewide Child Abuse Reporting Hotline: (800) 552-7096

Washington

Child Protection Services
Division of Community Program Development
Department of Social and Health Services
State Office Building 2
Olympia, WA 98504
Phone: (206) 753-0206

West Virginia

Children's Protective Services
Division of Social Services
Department of Human Services
1900 Washington Street, E.
Charleston, WV 25305
Phone: (304) 348-7980

   Statewide Child Abuse Reporting Hotline: (800) 352-6313

Wisconsin

Protective Services
Office for Children, Youth and Families
Department of Health and Social Services
State Office Building
1 W. Wilson Street, P.O. Box 7850
Madison, WI 53707
Phone: (608) 267-2245

Wyoming

Child Protective Services
Division of Public Assistance and Social Services
Department of Health and Social Services
Hathaway Building
Cheyenne, WY 82002
Phone: (307) 777-7892

Appendix D

NCPCA REGIONAL RESOURCE CENTERS

The centers listed below are funded by the U.S. Department of Health and Human Services. Each center has a child abuse and neglect component, and each provides a wide range of information, including programs, materials, services, and possible volunteer opportunities in the community.

Region I (serving Connecticut, Maine, Massachusetts, New Hampshire, Rhode Island, Vermont): Resource Center for Children and Families, Judge Baker Guidance Center, 295 Longwood Ave., Boston, MA 02115, (617) 232-8390.

Region II (serving New Jersey, New York, Puerto Rico, Virgin Islands): Resource Center for Children and Youth Services, Cornell University, Family Life Development Center, College of Human Ecology, E 200 MVR, Ithaca, NY 14853, (607) 256-7794.

Region III (serving Delaware, District of Columbia, Maryland, Pennsylvania, Virginia, West Virginia): Resource Center for Children, Youth, and Families, Virginia Commonwealth University, School of Social Work, 1001 W. Franklin St., Richmond, VA 23284, (804) 257-6231.

Region IV (serving Alabama, Florida, Georgia, Kentucky, Mississippi, North Carolina, South Carolina, Tennessee): Resource Center for Children and Youth Services, University of Tennessee, School of Social Work, 1838 Terrace Ave., Knoxville, TN 37996, (615) 974-2308.

Region V (serving Illinois, Indiana, Michigan, Minnesota, Ohio, Wisconsin): Resource Center on Children and Youth Services, University of Wisconsin-Milwaukee, School of Social Welfare, P.O. Box 786, Milwaukee, WI 53201, (414) 963-4184.

Region VI (serving Arkansas, Louisiana, New Mexico, Oklahoma, Texas): Resource Center for Children, Youth, and Families, University of Texas at Austin, 2609 University, Austin, TX 78712, (512) 471-4067.

Region VII (serving Iowa, Kansas, Missouri, Nebraska): Children, Youth, and Family Resource Center, University of Iowa Oakdale Campus, Institute of Child Behavior and Development, Oakdale, IA 52319, (319) 353-4791.

Region VIII (serving Colorado, Montana, North Dakota, South Dakota, Utah, Wyoming): Family Resource Center, University of Denver, Graduate School of Social Work, Denver, CO 80208, (303) 753-3464.

Region IX (serving Arizona, California, Guam, Hawaii, Nevada, Pacific Trust Territories): Resource Center for Children, Youth and Families, California State University at Los Angeles, 5151 State University Dr., Los Angeles, CA 90032, (213) 224-3283.

Region X (serving Alaska, Idaho, Oregon, Washington): Northwest Resource Center for Children, Youth and Families, University of Washington, School of Social Work, 4101 15*th* Ave., N.E., Seattle, WA 98195, (206) 543-1517.

CHILD ABUSE PREVENTION AND TREATMENT ACT (PL93-247)

AN ACT

To provide financial assistance for a demonstration program for the prevention, identification, and treatment of child abuse and neglect, to establish a National Center on Child Abuse and Neglect, and for other purposes.

Be it enacted by the Senate and House of Representatives of the United States of America in Congress assembled, That this Act may be cited as the "Child Abuse Prevention and Treatment Act."

THE NATIONAL CENTER ON CHILD ABUSE AND NEGLECT

SEC. 2. (a) The Secretary of Health, Education, and Welfare (hereinafter referred to in this Act as the "Secretary") shall establish an office to be known as the National Center on Child Abuse and Neglect (hereinafter referred to in this Act as the "Center").

(b) The Secretary, through the Center, shall—

(1) compile, analyze, and publish a summary annually of recently conducted and currently conducted research on child abuse and neglect;

(2) develop and maintain an information clearinghouse on all programs, including private programs, showing promise of success, for the prevention, identification, and treatment of child abuse and neglect;

(3) compile and publish training materials for personnel who are engaged or intend to engage in the prevention, identification, and treatment of child abuse and neglect;

(4) provide technical assistance (directly or through grant or contract) to public and non-profit private agencies and organizations to assist them in planning, improving, developing, and carrying out programs and activities relating to the prevention, identification, and treatment of child abuse and neglect;

(5) conduct research into the causes of child abuse and neglect, and into the prevention, identification, and treatment thereof; and

(6) make a complete and full study and investigation of the national incidence of child abuse and neglect, including a determination of the extent to which incidents of child abuse and neglect are increasing in number of severity.

DEFINITION

SEC. 3. For purposes of this Act the term "child abuse and neglect" means the physical or mental injury, sexual abuse, negligent treatment, or maltreatment of a child under the age of eighteen by a person who is responsible for the child's welfare under circumstances which indicate that the child's health or welfare is harmed or threatened thereby, as determined in accordance with regulations prescribed by the Secretary.

DEMONSTRATION PROGRAMS AND PROJECTS

SEC. 4. (a) The Secretary, through the Center, is authorized to make grants to, and enter into contracts with, public agencies or non-profit private organizations (or combinations thereof) for demonstration programs and projects designed to prevent, identify, and treat child abuse and neglect. Grants or contracts under this subsection may be —

(1) for the development and establishment of training programs for professional and paraprofessional personnel in the fields of medicine, law, education, social work, and other relevant fields who are engaged in, or intend to work in, the field of the prevention, identification, and treatment of child abuse and neglect; and training programs for children, and for persons responsible for the welfare of children, in methods of protecting children from child abuse and neglect;

(2) for the establishment and maintenance of centers, serving defined geographic areas, staffed by multidisciplinary teams of personnel trained in the prevention, identification, and treatment of child abuse and neglect cases, to provide a broad range of services related to child abuse and neglect, including direct support and supervision of satellite centers and attention homes, as well as providing advice and consultation to individuals, agencies, and organizations which request such services;

(3) for furnishing services of teams of professional and paraprofessional personnel who are trained in the prevention, identification, and treatment of child abuse and neglect cases, on a consulting basis to small communities where such services are not available; and

(4) for such other innovative programs and projects, including programs and projects for parent self-help, and for prevention and treatment of

drug-related child abuse and neglect, that show promise of successfully preventing or treating cases of child abuse and neglect as the Secretary may approve. Not less than 50 per centum of the funds appropriated under this Act for any fiscal year shall be used only for carrying out the provisions of this sub-section.

(b) (1) Of the sums appropriated under this Act for any fiscal year, not less than 5 per centum and not more than 20 per centum may be used by the Secretary for making grants to the States for the payment of reasonable and necessary expenses for the purpose of assisting the States in developing, strengthening, and carrying out child abuse and neglect prevention and treatment programs.

(2) In order for a State to qualify for assistance under this subsection, such State shall—

(A) have in effect a State child abuse and neglect law which shall include provisions for immunity for persons reporting instances of child abuse and neglect from prosecution, under any State or local law, arising out of such reporting;

(B) provide for the reporting of known and suspected instances of child abuse and neglect;

(C) provide that upon receipt of a report of known or suspected instances of child abuse or neglect an investigation shall be initiated promptly to substantiate the accuracy of the report, and, upon a finding of abuse or neglect, immediate steps shall be taken to protect the health and welfare of the abused or neglected child, as well as that of any other child under the same care who may be in danger of abuse or neglect;

(D) demonstrate that there are in effect throughout the State, in connection with the enforcement of child abuse and neglect laws and with the reporting of suspected instances of child abuse and neglect, such administrative procedures, such personnel trained in child abuse and neglect prevention and treatment, such training procedures, such institutional and other facilities (public and private), and such related multi-disciplinary programs and services as may be necessary or appropriate to assure that the State will deal effectively with child abuse and neglect cases in the State;

(E) provide for methods to preserve the confidentiality of all records in order to protect the rights of the child, his parents or guardians;

(F) provide for the cooperation of law enforcement officials, courts of competent jurisdiction, and appropriate State agencies providing human services;

(G) provide that in every case involving an abused or neglected child which results in a judicial proceeding a guardian ad litem shall be appointed to represent the child in such proceedings;

(H) provide that the aggregate of support for programs or projects related to child abuse and neglect assisted by State funds shall not be reduced below the level provided during fiscal year 1973, and set forth policies and procedures designed to assure that Federal funds made available under this Act for any fiscal year will be so used as to supplement and, to the extent practicable, increase the level of State funds which would, in the absence of Federal funds, be available for such programs and projects;

(I) provide for dissemination of information to the general public with respect to the problem of child abuse and neglect and the facilities and prevention and treatment methods available to combat instances of child abuse and neglect; and

(J) to the extent feasible, insure that parental organizations combating child abuse and neglect receive preferential treatment. (3) Programs or projects related to child abuse and neglect assisted under part A or B of title IV of the Social Security Act shall comply with the requirements set forth in clauses (B), (C), (E), and (F) of paragraph (2).

(c) Assistance provided pursuant to this section shall not be available for construction of facilities; however, the Secretary is authorized to supply such assistance for the lease or rental of facilities where adequate facilities are not otherwise available, and for repair or minor remodeling or alteration of existing facilities.

(d) The Secretary shall establish criteria designed to achieve equitable distribution of assistance under this section among the States, among geographic areas of the Nation, and among rural and urban areas. To the extent possible, citizens of each State shall receive assistance from at least one project under this section.

AUTHORIZATIONS

SEC. 5. There are hereby authorized to be appropriated for the purposes of this Act $15,000,000 for the fiscal year ending June 30, 1974, $20,000,000 for the fiscal year ending June 30, 1975, and $25,000,000 for the fiscal year ending June 30, 1976, and for the succeeding fiscal year.

ADVISORY BOARD ON CHILD ABUSE AND NEGLECT

SEC. 6. (a) The Secretary shall, within sixty days after the date of enactment of this Act, appoint an Advisory Board on Child Abuse and Neglect (hereinafter referred to as the "Advisory Board"), which shall be composed of representatives from Federal agencies with responsibility for programs and activities related to child abuse and neglect, including the Office of

Child Development, the Office of Education, the National Institute of Education, the National Institute of Mental Health, the National Institute of Child Health and Human Development, the Social and Rehabilitation Service, and the Health Services Administration. The Advisory Board shall assist the Secretary in coordinating programs and activities related to child abuse and neglect administered or assisted under this Act with such programs and activities administered or assisted by the Federal agencies whose representatives are members of the Advisory Board. The Advisory Board shall also assist the Secretary in the development of Federal standards for child abuse and neglect prevention and treatment programs and projects.

(b) The Advisory Board shall prepare and submit, within eighteen months after the date of enactment of this Act, to the President and to the Congress a report on the programs assisted under this Act and the programs, projects, and activities related to child abuse and neglect administered or assisted by the Federal agencies whose representatives are members of the Advisory Board. Such report shall include a study of the relationship between drug addiction and child abuse and neglect.

(c) Of the funds appropriated under section 5, one-half of 1 per centum, or $1,000,000, whichever is the lesser, may be used by the Secretary only for purposes of the report under subsection (b).

COORDINATION

SEC. 7. The Secretary shall promulgate regulations and make such arrangements as may be necessary or appropriate to ensure that there is effective coordination between programs related to child abuse and neglect under this Act and other such programs which are assisted by Federal funds.

Approved January 31, 1974.

Appendix F

PL93-247, AS AMENDED—INCLUDING
CHILD ABUSE AMENDMENTS OF 1984 (PL98-457)

AN ACT

To provide financial assistance for a demonstration program for the prevention and treatment of child abuse and neglect, to establish a National Center on Child Abuse and Neglect, and for other purposes.

Be it enacted by the Senate and House of Representatives of the United States of America in Congress assembled, That this Act may be cited as the "Child Abuse Prevention and Treatment Act," as amended.

THE NATIONAL CENTER ON CHILD ABUSE AND NEGLECT

SEC. 2. (a) The Secretary of Health and Human Services (hereinafter referred to in this Act as the "Secretary") shall establish an office to be known as the National Center on Child Abuse and Neglect (hereinafter referred to in this Act as the "Center").

(b) The Secretary, through the Center, shall—

(1) compile, analyze, publish, and disseminate a summary annually of recently conducted and currently conducted research on child abuse and neglect;

(2) develop and maintain an information clearinghouse on all programs, including private programs, showing promise of success, for the prevention, identification and treatment of child abuse and neglect;

(3) compile, publish and disseminate training materials for personnel who are engaged or intend to engage in the prevention, identification and treatment of child abuse and neglect;

(4) provide technical assistance (directly or through grant or contract) to public and non-profit private agencies and organizations to assist them in planning, improving, developing and carrying out programs and activities relating to the prevention, identification and treatment of child abuse and neglect;

(5) conduct research into the causes of child abuse and neglect, and into the prevention, identification, and treatment thereof;

(6) study and investigate the national incidence of child abuse and neglect and make findings about any relationship between non-payment of child support and between various other factors and child abuse and neglect, and the extent to which incidents of child abuse and neglect are increasing in number and severity, and, within two years after the date of the enactment of the Child Abuse Amendments of 1984, submit such findings to the appropriate Committees of the Congress together with such recommendations for administrative and legislative changes as are appropriate; and

(7) in consultation with the Advisory Board on Child Abuse and Neglect, annually prepare reports on efforts during the preceding two-year period to bring about coordination of the goals, objectives, and activities of agencies and organizations which have responsibilities for programs and activities related to child abuse and neglect, and, not later than March 1, 1985, and March 1 of each second year thereafter, submit such a report to the appropriate Committees of the Congress. The Secretary shall establish research priorities for making grants or contracts under clause (5) of this subsection and, not less than sixty days before establishing such priorities, shall publish in the Federal Register for public comment a statement of such proposed priorities.

(c) The functions of the Secretary under subsection (b) of this section may be carried out either directly or by way of grant or contract. Grants may be made under subsection (b) (5) for periods of not more than three years. Any such grant shall be reviewed at least annually by the Secretary, utilizing peer review mechanisms to assure the quality and progress of research conducted under such grant.

(d) The Secretary shall make available to the Center such staff and resources as are necessary for the Center to carry out effectively its functions under this Act.

(e) No funds appropriated under this Act for any grant or contract may be used for any purpose other than that for which such funds were specifically authorized.

DEFINITION

SEC. 3. For purposes of this Act—

(1) the term "child abuse and neglect" means the physical or mental injury, sexual abuse or exploitation, negligent treatment, or maltreatment of a child under the age of eighteen, or the age specified by the child protection law of the State in question, by a person (including any employee of a residential facility or any staff person providing out-of-home care) who is responsible for the child's welfare under circumstances which indicate

that the child's health or welfare is harmed or threatened thereby, as determined in accordance with regulations prescribed by the Secretary; and (2)(A) the term "sexual abuse" includes—

(i) the employment, use, persuasion, inducement, enticement, or coercion of any child to engage in, or having a child assist any other person to engage in, any sexually explicit conduct (or any simulation of such conduct) for the purpose of producing any visual depiction of such conduct, or

(ii) the rape, molestation, prostitution, or other such form of sexual exploitation of children, or incest with children, under circumstances which indicate that the child's health or welfare is harmed or threatened thereby, as determined in accordance with regulations prescribed by the Secretary; and (B) for the purpose of this clause, the term "child" or "children" means any individual who has not or individuals who have not attained the age of eighteen.

(3) the term "withholding of medically indicated treatment" means the failure to respond to the infant's life-threatening conditions by providing treatment (including appropriate nutrition, hydration, and medication) which, in the treating physician's or physicians' reasonable medical judgment, will be most likely to be effective in ameliorating or correcting all such conditions, except that the term does not include the failure to provide treatment (other than appropriate nutrition, hydration, or medication) to an infant when, in the treating physician's or physicians' reasonable medical judgment, (A) the infant is chronically and irreversibly comatose; (B) the provision of such treatment would (i) merely prolong dying, (ii) not be effective in ameliorating or correcting all of the infant's life-threatening conditions, or (iii) otherwise be futile in terms of the survival of the infant; or (C) the provision of such treatment would be virtually futile in terms of the survival of the infant and the treatment itself under such circumstances would be inhumane.

DEMONSTRATION OF SERVICE PROGRAMS AND PROJECTS

SEC. 4. (a) The Secretary, through the Center, is authorized to make grants to, and enter into contracts with, public agencies or non-profit private organizations (or combinations thereof) for demonstration or service programs and projects designed to prevent, identify, and treat child abuse and neglect. Grants or contracts under this subsection may be—

(1) for training programs for professional and paraprofessional personnel in the fields of medicine, law, education, social work, and other relevant fields who are engaged in, or intend to work in, the field of prevention, identification, and treatment of child abuse and neglect; and training pro-

grams for children, and for persons responsible for the welfare of children, in methods of protecting children from child abuse and neglect;

(2) for the establishment and maintenance of centers, serving defined geographic areas, staffed by multidisciplinary teams of personnel trained in the prevention, identification, and treatment of child abuse and neglect, including direct support and supervision of satellite centers and attention homes, as well as providing advice and consultation to individuals, agencies and organizations which request such services;

(3) for furnishing services of teams of professional and paraprofessional personnel who are trained in the prevention, identification, and treatment of child abuse and neglect cases, on a consulting basis to small communities where such services are not available; and

(4) for such other innovative programs and projects, including programs and projects for parent self-help, and for prevention and treatment of drug-related child abuse and neglect, that show promise of successfully preventing or treating cases of child abuse and neglect as the Secretary may approve.

(b)(1) The Secretary, through the Center, is authorized to make grants to the States for the purpose of assisting the States in developing, strengthening, and carrying out child abuse and neglect prevention and treatment programs.

(2) In order for a State to qualify for assistance under this subsection, such State shall—

(A) have in effect a State child abuse and neglect law which shall include provisions for immunity for persons reporting instances of child abuse and neglect from prosecution, under any State or local law, arising out of such reporting;

(B) provide for the reporting of known and suspected instances of child abuse and neglect;

(C) provide that upon receipt of a report of known or suspected instances of child abuse or neglect an investigation shall be initiated promptly to substantiate the accuracy of the report, and, upon a finding of abuse or neglect, immediate steps shall be taken to protect the health and welfare of the abused or neglected child, as well as that of any other child under the same care who may be in danger of abuse or neglect;

(D) demonstrate that there are in effect throughout the State, in connection with the enforcement of child abuse and neglect laws and with the reporting of suspected instances of child abuse and neglect, such administrative procedures, such personnel trained in child abuse and neglect prevention and treatment, such training procedures, such institutional and other facilities (public and private), and such related multidisciplinary programs and services as may be necessary or appropriate to assure that the State will deal effectively with child abuse and neglect cases in the State;

(E) provide for methods to preserve the confidentiality of all records in order to protect the rights of the child, and the child's parents or guardians;

(F) provide for the cooperation of law enforcement officials, courts of competent jurisdiction, and appropriate State agencies providing human services;

(G) provide that in every case involving an abused or neglected child which results in a judicial proceeding a guardian ad litem shall be appointed to represent the child in such proceedings;

(H) provide that the aggregate of support for programs or projects related to child abuse and neglect assisted by State funds shall not be reduced below the level provided during fiscal year 1973, and set forth policies and procedures designed to assure that Federal funds made available under this Act for any fiscal year will be so used as to supplement and, to the extent practicable, increase the level of State funds which would, in the absence of Federal funds, be available for such programs and projects;

(I) provide for dissemination of information to the general public with respect to the problem of child abuse and neglect and the facilities and prevention and treatment methods available to combat instances of child abuse and neglect;

(J) to the extent feasible, insure that parental organizations combating child abuse and neglect receive preferential treatment; and

(K) within one year after the date of the enactment of the Child Abuse Amendments of 1984, have in place for the purpose of responding to the reporting of medical neglect (including instances of withholding of medically indicated treatment from disabled infants with life-threatening conditions), procedures or programs, or both (within the State child protective services system), to provide for (i) coordination and consultation with individuals designated by and within appropriate health-care facilities, (ii) prompt notification by individuals designated by and within appropriate health-care facilities of cases of suspected medical neglect (including instances of withholding of medically indicated treatment from disabled infants with life-threatening conditions), and (iii) authority, under State law, for the State child protective service system to pursue any legal remedies, including the authority to initiate legal proceedings in a court of competent jurisdiction, as may be necessary to prevent the withholding of medically indicated treatment from disabled infants with life-threatening conditions. If a State has failed to obligate funds awarded under this subsection within eighteen months after the date of award, the next award under this subsection made after the expiration of such period shall be reduced by an amount equal to the amount of such unobligated funds unless the Secretary determines that extraordinary reasons justify the failure to so obligate.

(3)(A) Subject to subparagraph (B) of this paragraph, any State which on the date of enactment of the Child Abuse Amendments of 1984 does not qualify for assistance under this subsection may be granted a waiver of any requirement under paragraph (2) of this subsection—

(i) for a period of not more than one year, if the Secretary makes a finding that such State is making a good-faith effort to comply with any such requirement, and for a second one-year period if the Secretary makes a finding that such State is making substantial progress to achieve such compliance; or

(ii) for a nonrenewable period of not more than two years in the case of a State the legislature of which meets only biennially, if the Secretary makes a finding that such State is making a good-faith effort to comply with any such requirement.

(B) No waiver under subparagraphs (A) may apply to any requirement under paragraph (2)(K) of this subsection.

(4) Programs or projects related to child abuse and neglect assisted under part B of title IV of the Social Security Act shall comply with the requirements set forth in clauses (B), (C), (E), (F), and (K) of paragraph (2).*

(c)(1) The Secretary is authorized to make additional grants to the States for the purpose of developing, establishing, and operating or implementing—

(A) the procedures or programs required under clause (K) of subsection (b)(2) of this section;

(B) information and education programs or training programs for the purpose of improving the provision of services to disabled infants with life-threatening conditions for (i) professional and paraprofessional personnel concerned with the welfare of disabled infants with life-threatening conditions, including personnel employed in child protective services programs and health-care facilities, and (ii) the parents of such infants; and

(C) programs to help in obtaining or coordinating necessary services, including existing social and health services and financial assistance for families with disabled infants with life-threatening conditions, and those services necessary to facilitate adoptive placement of such infants who have been relinquished for adoption.

(2)(A) The Secretary shall provide, directly or through grants or contracts with public or private nonprofit organizations, for (i) training and technical assistance programs to assist States in developing, establishing, and operating or implementing of programs and procedures meeting the requirements of clause (K) of subsection (b)(2) of this section; and (ii) the establishment and operation of national and regional information and resource clearinghouses for the purpose of providing the most current and complete information regarding medical treatment procedures and resources and community resources for the provision of services and treatment for disabled infants with life-threatening conditions (including compiling, maintaining, updating, and disseminating regional directories of community services and resources, including the names and phone numbers of State and local medical organizations) to assist parents, families, and physicians and seeking to coordinate the availability of appropriate regional education resources for health-care personnel).

(B) Not more than $1,000,000 of the funds appropriated for any fiscal year under section 5 of this Act may be used to carry out this paragraph.

(C) Not later than 210 days after the date of the enactment of the Child Abuse Amendments of 1984, the Secretary shall have the capability of providing and begin to provide the training and technical assistance described in subparagraph (A) of this paragraph.

(d) Assistance provided pursuant to this section shall not be available for construction of facilities; however, the Secretary is authorized to supply such assistance for the lease or rental of facilities where adequate facilities are not otherwise available, and for repair or minor remodeling or alteration of existing facilities.

(e) The Secretary, in consultation with the Advisory Board on Child Abuse and Neglect, shall ensure that a proportionate share of assistance under this Act is available for activities related to the prevention of child abuse and neglect.

(f) For the purpose of this section, the term "State" includes each of the several States, the District of Columbia, the Commonwealth of Puerto Rico, American Samoa, the Virgin Islands, Guam and the Trust Territories of the Pacific.*

(f) The Secretary shall establish criteria designed to achieve equitable distribution of assistance under this section among the States, among geographic areas of the Nation, and among rural and urban areas. To the extent possible, citizens of each State shall receive assistance from at least one project under this section.**

AUTHORIZATIONS

SEC. 5. There are hereby authorized to be appropriated for the purpose of this act $15,000,000 for the fiscal year ending June 30, 1974, $20,000,000 for the fiscal year ending June 30, 1975, $25,000,000 for the fiscal year ending June 30, 1976, and for the succeeding fiscal years, $25,000,000 for the fiscal year ending September 30, 1978, $27,500,000 for the fiscal year ending

September 30, 1979, and $30,000,000 each for the fiscal year ending September 30, 1980, and September 30, 1981, respectively. There are hereby further authorized to be appropriated for the purposes of this Act $33,500,000 for fiscal year 1984, $40,000,000 for fiscal year 1985, $41,500,000 for fiscal year 1986, and $43,100,000 for fiscal year 1987. Of the funds appropriated for any fiscal year under this section except as provided in the succeeding sentence, (A) not less than $9,000,000 shall be available in each fiscal year to carry out section 4(b) of this Act (relating to State grants), (B) not less than $11,000,000 shall be available in each fiscal year to carry out sections 4(a) (relating to demonstration or service projects), 2(b)(1) and 2(b)(3) (relating to information dissemination), 2(b)(5) (relating to research), and 4(c)(2) (relating to training, technical assistance, and information dissemination) of this Act, giving special consideration to continued funding of child abuse and neglect programs or projects (previously funded by the Department of Health and Human Services) of national or regional scope and demonstrated effectiveness, (C) $5,000,000 shall be available in each such year for the purpose of making additional grants to the States to carry out the provisions of section 4(c)(1) of this Act. With respect to any fiscal year in which the total amount appropriated under this section is less than $30,000,000, funds shall first be available as provided in clauses (A) and (B) in the preceding sentence and of the remainder one-half shall be available as provided for in clause (C) and one-half as provided for in clause (D) in the preceding sentence.

ADVISORY BOARD ON CHILD ABUSE AND NEGLECT

SEC. 6.(a) The Secretary shall, within sixty days after the date of enactment of this Act, appoint an Advisory Board on Child Abuse and Neglect (hereinafter referred to as the "Advisory Board"), which shall be composed of representatives from Federal agencies with responsibility for programs and activities related to child abuse and neglect, and not less than three members from the general public with experience or expertise in the field of child abuse and neglect, and not less than three members from the general public with experience or expertise in the field of child abuse and neglect. The Advisory Board shall assist the Secretary in coordinating programs and activities related to child abuse and neglect planned, administered, or assisted by the Federal agencies whose representatives are members of the Advisory Board. The Advisory Board shall also assist the Secretary in the development of Federal standards for child abuse and neglect prevention and treatment programs and projects. The Advisory Board may be available, at the Secretary's request, to assist the Secretary in coordinating adoption-related activities of the Federal Government.

(b) Members of the Advisory Board, other than those regularly employed by the Federal Government, while serving on business of the Advisory Board, shall be entitled to receive compensation at a rate not in excess of the daily equivalent payable to a GS-18 employee under section 5332 of title 5, United States Code, including travel time; and, while so serving away from their homes or regular places of business, they may be allowed travel expenses (including per diem in lieu of subsistence) as authorized by section 5703 of such title for persons in the Government service employed intermittently.

COORDINATION

SEC. 7. The Secretary shall promulgate regulations and make such arrangements as may be necessary or appropriate to ensure that there is effective coordination among programs related to child abuse and neglect under this Act and other such programs which are assisted by Federal funds.

Related Provisions of Public Law 98-457

REGULATIONS AND GUIDELINES

SEC. 124.(a)(1) Not later than 60 days after the date of the enactment of this Act, the Secretary of Health and Human Services (hereinafter in this part referred to as the "Secretary") shall publish proposed regulations to implement the requirements of section 4(b)(2)(K) of the Act (as added by section 122(3) of this Act).

(2) Not later than 180 days after the date of the enactment of this Act and after completion of a process of not less than 60 days for notice and opportunity for public comment, the Secretary shall publish final regulations under this subsection.

(b)(1) Not later than 60 days after the date of the enactment of this Act, the Secretary shall publish interim model guidelines to encourage the establishment within health-care facilities of committees which would serve the purposes of educating hospital personnel and families of disabled infants with life-threatening conditions, recommending institutional policies and guidelines concerning the withholding of medically indicated treatment (as that term is defined in clause (3) of section 3 of the Act (as added by section 121(3) of this Act)) from such infants, and offering counsel and review in cases involving disabled infants with life-threatening conditions.

(2) Not later than 180 days after the date of the enactment of this Act and after completion of a period of not less than 60 days for notice and

opportunity of public comment, the Secretary shall publish the model guidelines.

REPORT ON FINANCIAL RESOURCES

SEC. 125. The Secretary shall conduct a study to determine the most effective means of providing Federal financial support, other than the use of funds provided through the Social Security Act, for the provision of medical treatment, general care, and appropriate social services for disabled infants with life-threatening conditions. Not later than 270 days after the date of the enactment of this Act, the Secretary shall report the results of the study to the appropriate Committees of the Congress and shall include in the report such recommendations for legislation to provide such financial support as the Secretary considers appropriate.

IMPLEMENTATION REPORT

SEC. 126. Not later than October 1, 1987, the Secretary shall submit to the appropriate Committees of the Congress a detailed report on the implementation and the effects of the provisions of this part and the amendments made by it.

STATUTORY CONSTRUCTION

SEC. 127.(a) No provision of this Act or any amendment made by this Act is intended to affect any right or protection under section 504 of the Rehabilitation Act of 1973.

(b) No provision of this Act or any amendment made by this Act may be so construed as to authorize the Secretary or any other governmental entity to establish standards prescribing specific medical treatments for specific conditions, except to the extent that such standards are authorized by other laws.

(c) If the provisions of any part of this Act or any amendment made by this Act or the application thereof to any person or circumstances be held invalid, the provisions of the other parts and their application to other persons or circumstances shall not be affected thereby.

EFFECTIVE DATES

SEC. 128.(a) Except as provided in subsection (b), the provisions of this part or any amendment made by this part shall be effective on the date of the enactment of this Act.

(b)(1) Except as provided in paragraph (2), the amendments made by sections 122 and 123(b) of this Act* shall become effective one year after the date of such enactment.

(2) In the event that, prior to such effective date, funds have not been appropriated pursuant to section 5 of this Act (as amended by section 104 of this Act) for the purpose of grants under section 4(c)(1) of the Act (as added by section 123(a) of this Act), any State which has not met any requirement of section 4(b)(2)(K) of the Act (as added by section 122(3) of this Act) may be granted a waiver of such requirements for a period of not more than one year, if the Secretary finds that such State is making a good-faith effort to comply with such requirements.

Appendix G

OTHER HELPFUL TERMS TO KNOW

Abandonment: Act of a parent or caretaker leaving a child without adequate supervision or provision for his/her needs for an excessive period of time. State laws vary in defining adequacy of supervision and the length of time a child may be left alone or in the care of another before abandonment is determined. The age of a child also is an important factor.

Abdominal Distention: Swelling of the stomach area. The distention may be caused by internal injury or obstruction or by malnutrition.

Abrasion: Wound in which an area of the body surface is scraped of skin or mucous membrane.

Acute Care Capacity: Capacity of a community to respond quickly and responsibly to a report of a child abuse or neglect. It involves receiving the report and providing a diagnostic assessment including both a medical assessment and an evaluation of family dynamics. It also involves rapid intervention, including immediate protection of the child when needed and referral for long-term care or service to the child and his/ her family.

Advocacy: Interventive strategy in which a helping person assumes an active role in assisting or supporting a specific child and/or family or a cause on behalf of children and/or families. This could involve finding and facilitating services for specific cases or developing new services or promoting program coordination. The advocate uses his/her power to meet client needs or to promote causes.

Affidavit: Written statement signed in the presence of a Notary Public who "swears in" the signer. The contents of the affidavit are stated under penalty of perjury. Affidavits are frequently used in the initiation of juvenile court cases and are, at times, presented to the court as evidence.

Alopecia: Absence of hair from skin areas where it normally appears; baldness.

Anomie: A state of anomie is characterized by attitudes of aimlessness, futility, and lack of motivation and results from the breakdown or failure of

---

Source: *Interdisciplinary Glossary on Child Abuse and Neglect.*

standards, rules, norms, and values that ordinarily bind people together in some socially organized way.

Anorexia: Lack or loss of appetite for food.

Apathy-Futility Syndrome: Immature personality type often associated with child neglect and characterized by an inability to feel and to find any significant meaning in life. This syndrome, often arising from early deprivation in childhood, is frequently perpetrated from generation to generation within a family system (Polansky).

Atrophy: Wasting away of flesh, tissue, cell, or organ.

Avitaminosis: Condition due to complete lack of one or more essential vitamins. (See also HYPOVITAMINOSIS)

Battered Child Syndrome: Term introduced in 1962 by C. Henry Kempe, M.D., in the *Journal of the American Medical Association* in an article describing a combination of physical and other signs indicating that a child's internal and/or external injuries result from acts committed by a parent or caretaker. In some states, the battered child syndrome has been judicially recognized as an accepted medical diagnosis. Frequently, this term is misused or misunderstood as the only type of child abuse and neglect.

Bonding: The psychological attachment of mother to child which develops during and immediately following childbirth.

Burn: Wound resulting from the application of too much heat. Burns are classified by the degree of damage caused.

> 1*st* degree: Scorching or painful redness of the skin.
> 2*nd* degree: Formation of blisters.
> 3*rd* degree: Destruction of outer layers of the skin.

Child Protective Services: A specialized child welfare service, usually a part of a county department of public welfare, legally responsible in most states for investigating suspected cases of child abuse and neglect and intervening in confirmed cases.

Children-at-Risk: May refer to the possibility that children in the custody of a state or county will get lost in a series of placements or for other reasons not be returned to their natural homes when these homes are no longer threatening to the children's welfare. May also refer to children in potentially abusive institutions but usually refers to children in families at risk.

Commission, Acts of: Overt acts by a parent or caretaker toward a child resulting in physical or mental injury, including but not limited to beatings, excessive disciplining, or exploitation.

Community Council for Child Abuse and Neglect: Community group, including both professionals and citizens, which attempts to develop and coordinate resources and/or legislation for the prevention, identification, and treatment of child abuse and neglect. It is often the name given to the program coordination component of the community team.

Community Neglect: Failure of a community to provide adequate support and social services for families and children, or lack of community control over illegal or discriminatory activities with respect to families and children.

Community Support Systems: Community resources such as schools, public health services, day-care centers, welfare advocacy (leisure service agencies?) whose utilization can aid in preventing family dysfunction and child abuse and neglect, and aid in treating identified cases of abuse and neglect.

Community Team: Often used incorrectly to refer to a multidisciplinary professional group which only diagnoses and plans treatment for specific cases of child abuse and neglect. More accurately, a community team separates the diagnosis and treatment functions and provides a third component for education training, and public relations. The community team also includes a community task force or council, including citizens as well as professionals from various disciplines, which coordinates the three community team components and advocates for resources and legislation. Citizens on the community team also monitor the professionals and agency participants.

Conjunctiva: Transparent lining covering the white of the eye and eyelids. Bleeding beneath the conjunctiva can occur spontaneously or from accidental or non-accidental injury.

Contusion: A wound producing injury to soft tissue without a break in the skin, causing bleeding into surrounding tissues.

Crisis Intervention: Action to relieve a specific stressful situation or series of problems which are immediately threatening to a child's health and/or welfare. This involves alleviation of parental stress through provision of emergency services in the home and/or removal of the child from the home.

Crisis Nursery: Facility offering short-term relief of several hours to several days' duration to parents temporarily unable or unwilling to care for their children. The primary purposes are child protection, stabilization of the home, and prevention of child abuse and neglect.

Day Care: A structured, supervised place for children to go more or less regularly which parents work or attend school. Experts believe that family stress can be relieved by more extensive provision of day-care services, and day-care providers are increasingly concerned with identification and prevention of child abuse and neglect.

Edema: Swelling caused by excessive amount of fluid in body tissue. It often follows a bump or bruise but may also be caused by allergy, malnutrition, or disease.

Encopresis: Involuntary passage of feces.

Enuresis: Involuntary passage of urine.

Failure to Thrive Syndrome (FTT): A serious medical condition most often seen in children under one year of age. An FTT child's height, weight, and motor development fall significantly short of the average growth rates of normal children. In about 10 percent of FTT cases, there is an organic cause such as serious heart, kidney, or intestinal disease, a genetic error or metabolism, or brain damage. All other cases are a result of a disturbed parent-child relationship manifested in severe physical and emotional neglect of the child.

Guardian: Adult charged lawfully with the responsibility for a child. A guardian has almost all the rights and powers of a natural parent, but the relationship is subject to termination or change. A guardian may or may not also have custody and therefore actual care and supervision of the child.

Hematemesis: Vomiting of blood from the stomach, often resulting from internal injuries.

Hematoma: A swelling caused by a collection of blood in an enclosed space, such as under the skin or the skull.

Hematurea: Blood in the urine.

Hemoptysis: Spitting or coughing blood from the windpipe or lungs.

Hyperactive: More active than is considered normal.

Hyphema: Hemorrhage within the anterior chamber of the eye, often appearing as a bloodshot eye. The cause could be a blow to the head or violent shaking.

Hypoactive: Less active than is considered normal.

Hypovitaminosis: Condition due to the deficiency of one or more essential vitamins.

Impetigo: A highly contagious, rapidly spreading skin disorder which occurs principally in infants and young children. The disease, characterized by red blisters, may be an indicator of neglect and poor living conditions.

Incest: Sexual intercourse between persons who are closely related. Some state laws recognize incest only as sexual intercourse among consanguineous, or blood, relations; other states recognize incest as sexual relations between a variety of family members related by blood and/or law. While incest and sexual abuse are sometimes thought to be synonymous, it should be realized that incest is only one aspect of sexual abuse. Incest can occur within families between members of the same sex, but the most common form is between father and daughter.

Intradermal Hemorrhage: Bleeding within the skin or a bruise. Bruises are common injuries exhibited by battered children and are usually classified by size:

- Petechiae—very small bruise caused by broken capillaries. Petechiae may be traumatic in nature or may be caused by clotting disorders.
- Purpura—petechiae occurring in groups, or a small bruise up to 1 cm in diameter.
- Ecchymosis—large bruise.

Latchkey Children: Working parents' children who return after school to a home where no parent or caretaker is present. This term was coined because these children often wear a house key on chains around their necks.

Lesion: Any injury to any part of the body from any cause that results in damage or loss of structure or function of the body tissue involved. A lesion may be caused by poison, infection, dysfunction, or violence, and may be either accidental or intentional.

Local Authority: Refers to two groups: (1) the social service agency (local) designated by the state department of social services and authorized by state law to be responsible for local child abuse and neglect prevention, identification, and treatment efforts, and (2) the community child protection coordinating council (community council).

Maltreatment: Actions that are abusive, neglectful, or otherwise threatening to a child's welfare. Frequently used as a general term for child abuse and neglect.

Mongolian Spots: A type of birthmark that can appear anywhere on a child's body, most frequently on the lower back. These dark spots usually fade by age five. They can be mistaken for bruises.

Polyphagia: Excessive or voracious eating.

Psychological Parent: Adult who, on a continuing day-to-day basis, fulfills a child's emotional needs for nurturance through interaction, companionship, and mutuality. May be the natural parent or another person who fulfills these functions.

Societal Child Abuse and Neglect: Failure of society to provide social policies and/or funding to support the well-being of all families and children or to provide sufficient resources to prevent and treat child abuse and neglect, particularly for minority populations such as migrant workers and Native Americans.

Appendix H

NEW JERSEY BILL S-2512

EXPLANATION — Matter enclosed in brackets [thus] in the above bill is not enacted and is intended to be omitted in the law.

Matter underlined thus is a new matter.

AN ACT concerning the certification of recreation and leisure service professionals, amending P.L. 1966, c. 293, amending and supplementing P.L. 1966, c. 291 and repealing sections 10, 14, and 18 of P.L. 1966, c. 291.
BE IT ENACTED by the Senate and General Assembly of the State of New Jersey:

1. Section 1 of P.L. 1966, c. 291 (C. 13:1C-1) is amended to read as follows:

1. As used in this act[, unless the context shall otherwise indicate, the following words shall have the following meaning]:

(a) "Board" means the board of recreation examiners established under this act.

(b) ["Recreation administrator"] "Recreation and leisure service professional" means [the executive head or assistant to the executive head administering a major recreation program for the State or a county or municipality, or any agency thereof, or for any public institution] a person engaged in an administrative, supervisory or programming position in either a State, county, municipal or private non-profit department of recreation or parks, or in a clinical or public therapeutic recreation department that provides leisure services as a primary function.

(c) ["Recreation supervisor"] "Public recreation professional" means a person [responsible for the planning, organizing and supervising of a part of a program administered by a recreation administrator] employed to plan, implement and evaluate recreation and park programs and services, or to administer those programs and services in a State, county, municipal or private non-profit department of recreation or parks. A public recreation professional shall have a title such as administrator, director, coordinator, program development specialist, superintendent, manager or supervisor.

(d) "Therapeutic recreation professional" means a person who is concerned with the role of leisure as it contributes to the quality of life of individuals with a physical, cognitive, emotional or social limitation. Specifically, a therapeutic recreation professional seeks to facilitate the development, maintenance and expression of a satisfying leisure life-style

297

through a continuum of services including therapy, leisure education and recreation participation. A therapeutic recreation professional shall have a title such as administrator, director, coordinator, supervisor, recreation therapist, therapeutic recreation specialist, recreation assistant, activity specialist, patient activities coordinator or recreation and social planner, and shall be employed in a clinical or public recreation, recreation therapy, activity therapy, allied clinical therapy or therapy services department.

(e) "Clinical" means a medically based or rehabilitation agency, facility, or institution including hospitals, nursing homes, rehabilitation programs, developmental centers, mental health programs, and intermediate care centers.

(cf: P.L.1966, c. 291, S.1)

2. Section 7 of P.L. 1966, c. 291 (C. 13:1C-7) is amended to read as follows:

7. It shall be the duty of the board to:

(a) Administer a plan of [permissive] professional certification [and registration for recreation administrators and recreation supervisors] which is mandatory for employment of professionals in State, county or municipal recreation and leisure services and in clinical or public therapeutic recreation agencies, and to administer a plan of professional certification which is permissive for employment of professionals in private non-profit agencies.

(b) Make such rules and regulations as may be necessary for the enforcement of the plan.

(c) Establish and modify qualifications and hold examinations for certification [and registration] of recreation [administrators and recreation supervisors] and leisure science professionals.

(d) Keep, or cause to be kept, an accurate record of all its proceedings, including a register of all applicants for certificates and of all individuals to whom certificates are issued.

(e) Conduct, or assist in conducting, research and studies of problems relating to professional standards among those engaged in recreation work and recommend changes and improvements therein.

(f) Formulate proper application forms, certificates, and other materials pertinent to the plan.

(g) Make annually to the Governor a full and true report of all its activities with recommendations.

(h) Establish fees which are necessary for the administration of the certification plan.

(cf: P.L. 1966, c. 291, s.7)

3. Section 9 of P.L. 1966, c. 291 (C.13:1C-9) is amended to read as follows:

9. Every applicant for certification [and registration] as a recreation [administrator] and leisure service professional who may be designated as a public recreation professional or a therapeutic recreation professional shall, in order to be eligible to take an examination therefor:

(a) hold a baccalaureate degree in recreation from an accredited [college and have a minimum total of 12 months' successful recreation experience] institution of higher education, file an application to take an oral and written examination administered by the board, and, upon successful completion of the examination, serve a 12-month probationary period in full-time recreation and leisure service employment, or

(b) hold a baccalaureate degree in a field [related to] other than recreation[, such as group work, sociology, or physical education] from an accredited [college and have a minimum total of 24 months' successful recreation experience] institution of higher education, file an application to take an oral and written examination administered by the board, and, upon successful completion of the examination, serve a 36-month probationary period in full-time recreation or leisure service employment[, or]

(c) hold a baccalaureate degree from an accredited college and have a total of 36 months' successful recreation experience, or] (Deleted by amendment, P. L. ____ , c. ____ .)

(d) [have 6 or more years' successful administrative and supervisory recreation experience.

In meeting the above designated qualifications an applicant may substitute an additional year of specialized graduate training in recreation for 1 year of successful recreation experience.] (Deleted by amendment, P.L. ____ , c. ____ .) (cf: P.L. 1966, c.791, s.9)

4. Section 11 of P.L. 1966, c. 791 (C. 13:1C-11) is amended to read as follows:

11. Each applicant for [examination] certification shall file an application with the board on a form provided by the board for that purpose, which application must contain such information that the board may determine therefrom whether or not the applicant has the qualifications, required [by this act] pursuant to P.L. 1966, c. 291 (C. 13:1C-1 et seq.) and sections 9 and 11 of P.L. ____ , c. ____ (C. and C.) (now pending before the Legislature as this bill), in order to qualify to take [such] the examination, and each application shall be accompanied by an application fee [of $5.00] as prescribed by the board which shall not be returnable [in event that] if the applicant is not admitted to examination or, if admitted, fails to pass the same. (cf: P.L. 1966, c. 291, s.11)

5. Section 16 of P.L. 1966, c. 291 (C. 13:1C-16) is amended to read as follows:

16. The board may refuse the application of an applicant for an examination or, after due notice and public hearing, refuse to issue or reissue a certificate, or revoke any certificate issued by it, if the applicant for, or holder of, [such] a certificate—

(a) has been convicted of [an offense] a crime involving moral turpitude, violence, sexual assault or neglect which relates to the exploitation of any child or adult, is a drug addict or alcoholic or is mentally incompetent, or

(b) advocates the overthrow of the Government of the United States by force and violence or other unlawful means, or

(c) has made any willful statement or impersonated any other person or permitted or aided any other person to impersonate him in connection with any application or examination for certification [and registration], or

(d) has been found to be inefficient in performing the duties of any position held by him, on the basis of the holding of which experience qualifications are offered on his behalf, or

(e) has been found to be associated with conduct or activities which in the board's opinion establish him as unfit for the responsibilities of a recreation and leisure service professional.

(cf: P.L.1966, c. 291, s.16)

6. Section 17 of P.L. 1966, c. 291 (C. 3:1C-17) is amended to read as follows:

17. Every certificate shall expire upon [March 1] May 30 of the [second] first calendar year following the issuance thereof, or September 30 of the first calendar year following the issuance thereof, but may be renewed upon payment of a renewal fee [of $7.00] as prescribed by the board for one year or for three years prior to the expiration thereof. Any certificate holder may apply for renewal of his certificate at any time during [12] the six months following the date of the expiration thereof, and shall be entitled to renewal thereof except for cause, upon payment of a fee [of $5.00] as prescribed by the board.

If any person holding [one type of] a certificate of one designation makes application for and is granted [another type of] a certificate of another designation through successful passage of the examination, he shall pay a certification fee [of $5.00] as prescribed by the board for that purpose. (cf: P.L.1966, c. 291, s.17)

7. Section 19 of P.L. 1966, c. 291 (C. 13:1C-19) is amended to read as follows:

19. All sums received by the board shall be paid into [the general funds of the State treasury within 30 days after the receipt thereof] a non-lapsing account in the Department of Community Affairs for use by the board in administering P.L. 1966, c. 291 (C. 13:1C-1 et seq.). (cf: P.L. 1966, c. 291, s.19)

8. Section 3 of P.L. 1966, c. 293 (C. 52:27D-3) is amended to read as follows:

3. The commissioner, as administrator and chief executive officer of the department, shall:

(a) Administer the work of the department;

(b) Appoint and remove officers and other personnel employed within the department, subject to the provisions of Title 11A (Civil Service) of the [Revised] New Jersey Statutes, [Civil Service,] and other applicable statutes, except as herein otherwise specifically provided;

(C) Perform, exercise and discharge the functions, powers and duties of the department through such divisions as may be established by this act or otherwise by law;

(d) Organize the work of the department in such divisions, not inconsistent with the provisions of this act, and in such bureaus and other organizational units as he may determine to be necessary for efficient and effective operation;

(e) Adopt, issue and promulgate, in the name of the department, such rules and regulations as may be authorized by law;

(f) Formulate and adopt rules and regulations for the efficient conduct of the work and general administration of the department, its officers and employees;

(g) Institute or cause to be instituted such legal proceedings or processes as may be necessary properly to enforce and give effect to any of his powers or duties;

(h) Make an annual report to the Governor and to the Legislature of the department's operations, and render such other reports as the Governor shall from time to time request or as may be required by law;

(i) Co-ordinate the activities of the department, and the several divisions and other agencies therein, in a manner designed to eliminate overlapping and duplicating functions;

(j) Integrate within the department, so far as practicable, all staff services of the department and of the several divisions and other agencies therein;

(k) Maintain suitable headquarters for the department and such other quarters as he shall deem necessary to the proper functioning of the department; [and]

(l) Perform such other functions as may be prescribed in this act or by any other law; and

(m) Submit to the State Bureau of Identification, and exchange with and receive from the Federal Bureau of Investigation, criminal history record data and fingerprint data at the request of the Board of Recreation Examiners for use in considering applicants for certification or authorization to sit at an examination. The commissioner may collect an appropriate fee from each applicant to cover the costs of the fingerprinting, processing and data exchange. (cf: P.L. 1967, c. 42, s.2)

9. (New section) In addition to the qualifications for certification required by the board pursuant to sections 9, 11, and 13 of P.L. 1966, c. 291 (C. 13:1C-9; c. 13:1c-11 and C. 13:1C-13), the board may require additional standards of

education and experience necessary for examination, certification and renewal of certification. These additional requirements shall be prescribed by regulation and shall be consistent with the appropriate requirements established by the National Recreation and Park Association, the New Jersey Recreation and Park Association and the National Council for Therapeutic Recreation Certification.

10. (New section) Prior to granting initial certification or authorization to sit at an examination, the board shall make a request to the Commissioner of Community Affairs to submit to the State Bureau of Investigation a criminal history background check, cause each applicant to be fingerprinted, and exchange with the Federal Bureau of Investigation criminal history record data and fingerprint data for use in considering applicants for certification or examination.

11. (New section) Any person currently certified pursuant to P.L. 1966, c. 291 (C. 13:1c-1 et seq.) on the effective date of this 1988 amendatory and supplementary act shall be eligible for renewal of certification without examination for a period of 365 days from the effective date of this 1988 amendatory and supplementary act.

12. There is appropriated $95,000 from the General Fund to the Department of Community Affairs for use by the Board of Recreation Examiners in the administration of this 1988 amendatory and supplementary act, and to fund research and studies of problems relating to the professional standards of recreation and leisure service professionals.

13. Sections 10, 14, and 18 of P.L. 1966, c. 291 (C. 13:1C-10; C. 13:1C-14 and C. 13:1C-18) are repealed.

14. This act shall take effect on the 90*th* day following enactment, but section 9 shall remain inoperative until December 31, 1990.

STATEMENT

This bill amends and supplements current law to mandate the certification of recreation and leisure service professionals who work within State, county or municipal recreation and leisure services and in clinical or public therapeutic recreation agencies. Currently, such certification is voluntary. The bill does provide, however, that certification of recreation and leisure service professionals who are employed in private non-profit agencies shall remain voluntary.

The bill also changes the current statutory designations of Recreation and Leisure Service professionals and revises the requirements necessary for certification. In addition, the bill gives to the Board of Recreation Examiners the authority to establish fees for certification and other services it performs, to determine educational and examination requirements in addition to those established within the bill, and to require a criminal history background check prior to certification and examination. The bill also expands the causes for which the board may revoke registration.

The bill appropriates $95,000 to the Department of Community Affairs for use by the Board of Recreation Examiners in the administration of the act, and to fund research and studies of problems relating to the professional standards of Recreation and Leisure Service professionals.

The mandatory certification of recreation and leisure service professionals is necessary to protect the many individuals within the State who receive such services by identifying to them those persons who meet the requirements for certification and are therefore qualified to provide professional and high-quality services. This bill will safeguard and promote the emotional, social, physical and intellectual growth of the people of this State.

REGULATED PROFESSIONS

Parks and Forests

Mandates the certification of Recreation and Leisure Service professionals.

MARYLAND H.B. 528—CRIMINAL BACKGROUND INVESTIGATION—CHILD CARE FACILITIES

EXPLANATION: CAPITALS INDICATE MATTER
ADDED TO EXISTING LAW.

[Brackets] indicate matter deleted from existing law.

HOUSE OF DELEGATES

61r1653   No. 528

CF 61r1652

By: The Speaker (Administration)
Introduced and read first time: January 17, 1986
Assigned to: Judiciary

A BILL ENTITLED

AN ACT concerning

Criminal Background Investigation—Child Care Facilities

FOR the purpose of requiring criminal background investigations for employees and employers of certain child care facilities; permitting criminal background investigations for employees and volunteers at certain child care facilities; requiring disclosure of certain criminal convictions or pending criminal charges by certain employees and employers; providing for the confidentiality of certain information in certain circumstances; providing for a certain procedure for applying for a criminal background investigation; providing immunity from civil and criminal liability for certain persons and agencies; requiring the Department of Public Safety and Correctional Services to conduct the criminal background investigation and to adopt certain rules and regulations; defining certain terms; providing for the prospective application of this Act; providing for a certain penalty under certain circumstances; generally relating to criminal background investigations for certain employees and employers; and providing for the prospective application of this Act.

BY adding to

Article—Family Law

Section 5-560 through 5-568 to be under the new part "Part VI. Criminal Background Investigations for Employees of Facilities that Care for or Supervise Children"

Annotated Code of Maryland

1984 Volume and 1985 Supplement)

SECTION 1. BE IT ENACTED BY THE GENERAL ASSEMBLY OF MARYLAND, That the Laws of Maryland read as follows:

Article—Family Law

PART VI. CRIMINAL BACKGROUND INVESTIGATIONS FOR EMPLOYEES OF FACILITIES THAT CARE FOR OR SUPERVISE CHILDREN

5-560.

(A) IN THIS PART VI OF THIS SUBTITLE, THE FOLLOWING WORDS HAVE THE MEANINGS INDICATED.

(B) "CONVICTION" MEANS A PLEA OR VERDICT OF GUILTY OR A PLEA OF NOLO CONTENDERE.

(C) "DEPARTMENT" MEANS THE DEPARTMENT OF PUBLIC SAFETY AND CORRECTIONAL SERVICES.

(D) "EMPLOYEE" MEANS A PERSON THAT FOR COMPENSATION IS EMPLOYED TO WORK IN A FACILITY IDENTIFIED IN § 5-561 OF THIS ARTICLE AND WHO:

(1) CARES FOR OR SUPERVISES CHILDREN IN THE FACILITY; OR

(2) HAS ACCESS TO CHILDREN WHO ARE CARED FOR OR SUPERVISED IN THE FACILITY.

(E) (1) "EMPLOYER" MEANS AN OWNER, OPERATOR, PROPRIETOR, MANAGER, OR SUBSTITUTE WORKER OF A FACILITY IDENTIFIED IN § 5-561.

(2) "EMPLOYER" DOES NOT INCLUDE A STATE OR LOCAL AGENCY RESPONSIBLE FOR THE TEMPORARY OR PERMANENT PLACEMENT OF CHILDREN IN A FACILITY IDENTIFIED IN § 6-561.

(F) "SECRETARY" MEANS THE SECRETARY OF PUBLIC SAFETY AND CORRECTIONAL SERVICES.

5-561.

(A) NOTWITHSTANDING ANY PROVISION OF LAW TO THE CONTRARY, AN EMPLOYEE AND EMPLOYER IN A FACILITY IDENTIFIED IN SUBSECTION (B) OF THIS SECTION SHALL APPLY

FOR A FEDERAL AND STATE CRIMINAL BACKGROUND INVESTIGATION AT ANY DESIGNATED LAW ENFORCEMENT OFFICE IN THIS STATE.

(B) THE FOLLOWING FACILITIES SHALL REQUIRE EMPLOYEES AND EMPLOYERS TO OBTAIN A CRIMINAL BACKGROUND INVESTIGATION UNDER THIS PART VI:

(1) A GROUP DAY CARE CENTER REQUIRED TO BE LICENSED UNDER TITLE 14 OF THE HEALTH—GENERAL ARTICLE;

(2) A CHILD CARE HOME REQUIRED TO BE LICENSED UNDER TITLE 5 OF THIS ARTICLE OR UNDER TITLE 6 OF THE HEALTH—GENERAL ARTICLE;

(3) A CHILD CARE INSTITUTION REQUIRED TO BE LICENSED UNDER TITLE 5 OF THIS ARTICLE OR UNDER TITLE 6 OF THE HEALTH—GENERAL ARTICLE;

(4) A JUVENILE DETENTION, CORRECTION, OR TREATMENT FACILITY PROVIDED FOR IN TITLE 6 OF THE HEALTH— GENERAL ARTICLE;

(5) A PUBLIC SCHOOL AS DEFINED IN TITLE 1 OF THE EDUCATION ARTICLE;

(6) A PRIVATE OR NONPUBLIC SCHOOL REQUIRED TO REPORT ANNUALLY TO THE STATE BOARD OF EDUCATION UNDER TITLE 2 OF THE EDUCATION ARTICLE;

(7) A FOSTER CARE FAMILY HOME OR GROUP FACILITY AS DEFINED UNDER TITLE 5 OF THIS ARTICLE;

(8) A RECREATION CENTER OR RECREATION PROGRAM OPERATED BY STATE OR LOCAL GOVERNMENT PRIMARILY SERVING MINORS; OR

(9) A DAY OR OVERNIGHT CAMP, AS DEFINED IN TITLE 10, SUBTITLE 16 OF THE CODE OF MARYLAND REGULATIONS, PRIMARILY SERVING MINORS.

(C) AN EMPLOYER AT A FACILITY UNDER SUBSECTION (B) OF THIS SECTION MAY REQUIRE A VOLUNTEER AT THE FACILITY TO OBTAIN A CRIMINAL BACKGROUND INVESTIGATION UNDER THIS PART VI.

(D) AN EMPLOYER AT A FACILITY NOT IDENTIFIED IN SUBSECTION (B) OF THIS SECTION WHO EMPLOYS INDIVIDUALS TO WORK WITH CHILDREN MAY REQUIRE EMPLOYEES, INCLUDING VOLUNTEERS, TO OBTAIN A CRIMINAL BACKGROUND INVESTIGATION UNDER THIS PART VI.

(E) AN EMPLOYEE OR EMPLOYER WHO IS REQUIRED TO HAVE A CRIMINAL BACKGROUND INVESTIGATION UNDER THIS PART VI OF THIS SUBTITLE SHALL PAY FOR:

(1) THE MANDATORY PROCESSING FEE REQUIRED BY THE FEDERAL BUREAU OF INVESTIGATION FOR CONDUCTING THE CRIMINAL BACKGROUND INVESTIGATION; AND

(2) REASONABLE ADMINISTRATIVE COSTS TO THE DEPARTMENT, NOT TO EXCEED 10 PERCENT OF THE PROCESSING FEE.

(F) AN EMPLOYER OR OTHER PARTY MAY PAY FOR THE COSTS BORNE BY THE EMPLOYEE UNDER SUBSECTION (E) OF THIS SECTION.

5-562.

(A) (1) ON OR BEFORE THE FIRST DAY OF ACTUAL EMPLOYMENT, AN EMPLOYEE SHALL APPLY TO THE DEPARTMENT FOR A PRINTED STATEMENT.

(2) ON OR BEFORE THE FIRST DAY OF ACTUAL OPERATION OF A FACILITY IDENTIFIED IN § 5-561, AN EMPLOYER SHALL APPLY TO THE DEPARTMENT FOR A PRINTED STATEMENT.

(B) AS PART OF THE APPLICATION FOR A CRIMINAL BACKGROUND INVESTIGATION, THE EMPLOYEE AND EMPLOYER SHALL SUBMIT:

(1) A COMPLETE SET OF LEGIBLE FINGERPRINTS TAKEN ON STANDARD FINGERPRINT CARDS AT ANY DESIGNATED STATE OR LOCAL LAW ENFORCEMENT OFFICE IN THE STATE OR OTHER LOCATION APPROVED BY THE DEPARTMENT;

(2) THE DISCLOSURE STATEMENT REQUIRED UNDER § 5-563 OF THIS PART IV; AND

(3) PAYMENT FOR THE COSTS OF THE CRIMINAL BACKGROUND INVESTIGATION.

5-563.

(A) AS PART OF THE APPLICATION PROCESS FOR A CRIMINAL BACKGROUND INVESTIGATION, THE EMPLOYEE AND EMPLOYER SHALL COMPLETE AND SIGN A SWORN STATEMENT OR AFFIRMATION DISCLOSING THE EXISTENCE OF A CONVICTION OR PENDING CHARGES WITHOUT A FINAL DISPOSITION FOR ANY OF THE FOLLOWING CRIMINAL OFFENSES, ATTEMPTED CRIMINAL OFFENSES, OR A CRIMINAL OFFENSE WHICH IS EQUIVALENT TO ANY OF THE FOLLOWING:

(1) MURDER;

(2) CHILD ABUSE;

(3) RAPE;

(4) A SEXUAL OFFENSE INVOLVING A MINOR, NONCONSENTING ADULT, OR A PERSON WHO IS MENTALLY DEFECTIVE, MENTALLY INCAPACITATED, OR PHYSICALLY HELPLESS;

(5) CHILD PORNOGRAPHY;

(6) KIDNAPPING OF A CHILD; OR

(7) CHILD ABDUCTION.

(B) (1) THE DEPARTMENT OR ITS DESIGNEE SHALL MAIL A COPY OF AN EMPLOYEE'S DISCLOSURE STATEMENT TO THE EMPLOYER WITHIN 3 DAYS OF THE APPLICATION.

(2) THE DEPARTMENT OR ITS DESIGNEE SHALL MAIL A COPY OF AN EMPLOYER'S DISCLOSURE STATEMENT TO THE APPROPRIATE STATE OR LOCAL LICENSING, REGISTERING, OR CERTIFYING AGENCY, WITHIN 3 DAYS OF THE APPLICATION.

5-564.

(A) THE DEPARTMENT SHALL CONDUCT THE CRIMINAL BACKGROUND INVESTIGATION AND ISSUE THE PRINTED STATEMENT PROVIDED FOR UNDER THIS PART VI.

(B) SUBJECT TO THE PROVISIONS OF SUBSECTION (C) OF THIS SECTION, THE DEPARTMENT SHALL RECORD ON THE PRINTED STATEMENT THE EXISTENCE OF A CONVICTION OR PENDING CHARGES FOR ANY OF THE FOLLOWING CRIMES, ATTEMPTED CRIMES, OR A CRIMINAL OFFENSE THAT IS EQUIVALENT TO ANY OF THE FOLLOWING:

(1) MURDER;

(2) CHILD ABUSE;

(3) RAPE;

(4) A SEXUAL OFFENSE, AS DEFINED UNDER ARTICLE 27, § 464, 464A, 464B, AND 464C OF THE CODE;

(5) CHILD PORNOGRAPHY;

(6) KIDNAPPING OF A CHILD; OR

(7) CHILD ABDUCTION.

(C) (1) EXCEPT FOR ANY NECESSARY ADMINISTRATIVE OR PERSONAL IDENTIFICATION INFORMATION OR THE DATE ON WHICH THE CRIMINAL BACKGROUND INVESTIGATION WAS CONDUCTED OR COMPLETED, THE PRINTED STATEMENT SHALL CONTAIN THE FOLLOWING INFORMATION ONLY, STATED IN THE AFFIRMATIVE OR NEGATIVE:

(I) THAT THE DEPARTMENT HAS OR HAS NOT CONDUCTED THE CRIMINAL BACKGROUND INVESTIGATION AS REQUIRED UNDER THIS PART VI; AND

(II) THAT THE EMPLOYEE IS OR IS NOT THE SUBJECT OF ANY PENDING CHARGES WITHOUT A FINAL DISPOSITION, OR HAS OR HAS NOT BEEN CONVICTED OF A CRIME OR ATTEMPTED CRIME IDENTIFIED IN SUBSECTION (B) OF THIS SECTION.

(2) THE PRINTED STATEMENT MAY NOT IDENTIFY OR DISCLOSE THE SPECIFIC CRIME OR ATTEMPTED CRIME THAT IS THE SUBJECT OF THE EMPLOYEE'S OR EMPLOYER'S CRIMINAL BACKGROUND INVESTIGATION.

(D) (1) UPON COMPLETION OF THE CRIMINAL BACKGROUND INVESTIGATION OF AN EMPLOYEE, THE DEPARTMENT SHALL SUBMIT THE PRINTED STATEMENT TO:

(I) THE EMPLOYEE'S CURRENT OR PROSPECTIVE EMPLOYER AT THE FACILITY OR PROGRAM; AND

(II) THE EMPLOYEE.

(2) UPON COMPLETION OF THE CRIMINAL BACKGROUND INVESTIGATION OF AN EMPLOYER, THE DEPARTMENT SHALL SUBMIT THE PRINTED STATEMENT TO:

(I) THE APPROPRIATE STATE OR LOCAL AGENCY RESPONSIBLE FOR THE LICENSURE, REGISTRATION, OR CERTIFICATION OF THE EMPLOYER'S FACILITY; AND

(II) THE EMPLOYER.

(E) EXCEPT IN THE CASE WHERE A PERSON WHO IS THE SUBJECT OF AN OUTSTANDING ARREST WARRANT OR CRIMINAL SUMMONS HAS BEEN IDENTIFIED, ALL INFORMATION OBTAINED BY THE DEPARTMENT REGARDING ANY CRIMINAL CHARGES AND THEIR DISPOSITION:

(1) SHALL BE CONFIDENTIAL;

(2) MAY NOT BE TRANSMITTED OUTSIDE THE DEPARTMENT, EXCEPT AS EXPRESSLY AUTHORIZED UNDER THIS PART VI; AND

(3) MAY NOT BE TRANSMITTED TO ANYONE WITHIN THE DEPARTMENT EXCEPT AS NEEDED FOR THE PURPOSE OF EVALUATING THE APPLICATION.

5-565.

(A) IN CONFORMITY WITH THE FOLLOWING PROCEDURES, AN INDIVIDUAL MAY CONTEST THE FINDING OF A CRIMINAL CONVICTION OR PENDING CHARGE REPORTED IN A PRINTED STATEMENT.

(B) IN CONTESTING THE FINDING OF A CONVICTION OR A PENDING CHARGE, THE INDIVIDUAL SHALL CONTACT THE OFFICE OF THE SECRETARY, OR A DESIGNEE OF THE SECRETARY, AND A HEARING SHALL BE CONVENED WITHIN 20 WORKDAYS, UNLESS SUBSEQUENTLY WAIVED BY THE INDIVIDUAL. THE SECRETARY, OR A DESIGNEE OF THE SECRETARY, SHALL RENDER A DECISION REGARDING THE APPEAL WITHIN 5 WORKDAYS OF THE HEARING.

(C) FOR PURPOSES OF THIS PART VI, THE RECORD OF A CONVICTION FOR A CRIME IDENTIFIED IN § 5-564 OF THIS PART VI, OR A COPY THEREOF CERTIFIED BY THE CLERK OF THE COURT OR BY A JUDGE OF THE COURT IN WHICH THE CONVICTION OCCURRED, SHALL BE CONCLUSIVE EVIDENCE OF THE CONVICTION. IN A CASE WHERE A PENDING CHARGE IS RECORDED, DOCUMENTATION PROVIDED BY A COURT TO THE SECRETARY, OR A DESIGNEE OF THE SECRETARY, THAT A PENDING CHARGE FOR A CRIME IDENTIFIED IN § 5-564 OF THIS PART VI WHICH HAS NOT BEEN FINALLY ADJUDICATED SHALL BE CONCLUSIVE EVIDENCE.

(D) FAILURE OF THE INDIVIDUAL TO APPEAR AT THE SCHEDULED HEARING SHALL BE CONSIDERED GROUNDS FOR DISMISSAL OF THE APPEAL.

5-566.

AN INDIVIDUAL WHO FAILS TO DISCLOSE A CONVICTION OR THE EXISTENCE OF PENDING CHARGES FOR A CRIMINAL OFFENSE OR ATTEMPTED CRIMINAL OFFENSE AS REQUIRED UNDER § 5-563 OF THIS PART VI, SHALL BE GUILTY OF PERJURY AND UPON CONVICTION IS SUBJECT TO THE PENALTY PROVIDED BY LAW.

5-567.

(A) THE FOLLOWING PERSONS OR AGENCIES SHALL BE IMMUNE FROM CIVIL OR CRIMINAL LIABILITY IN CONNECTION WITH THE CONDUCTING OF A CRIMINAL BACKGROUND INVESTIGATION UNDER THIS PART VI:

(1) AN EMPLOYER THAT IN GOOD FAITH RELIES ON A CRIMINAL BACKGROUND INVESTIGATION TO DENY OR TERMINATE AN INDIVIDUAL'S EMPLOYMENT OR PARTICIPATION IN A FACILITY;

(2) A STATE OR LOCAL AGENCY THAT IN GOOD FAITH RELIES ON A CRIMINAL BACKGROUND INVESTIGATION OF AN EMPLOYER TO DENY, SUSPEND, OR REVOKE LICENSURE, REGISTRATION, OR CERTIFICATION OF A FACILITY; AND

(3) A STATE OR LOCAL AGENCY THAT IN GOOD FAITH PARTICIPATES IN THE MAKING OF A CRIMINAL BACKGROUND INVESTIGATION OF AN EMPLOYEE OR EMPLOYER.

(B) THE FAILURE OF AN EMPLOYER TO REQUIRE A CRIMINAL BACKGROUND INVESTIGATION OF AN INDIVIDUAL WHEN NOT MANDATED UNDER THIS PART VI, MAY NOT GIVE RISE TO CIVIL OR CRIMINAL LIABILITY ON THE PART OF THE EM-

PLOYER FOR FAILURE TO CONDUCT A CRIMINAL BACKGROUND INVESTIGATION.

5-568.

ON OR BEFORE AUGUST 15, 1986, THE SECRETARY SHALL:

(1) PROVIDE FOR THE ADOPTION OF A SPECIFIED FORM OR FORMS TO BE USED IN APPLYING FOR THE CRIMINAL BACKGROUND INVESTIGATION TO BE ISSUED BY THE DEPARTMENT, INCLUDING AN APPROPRIATE DISCLOSURE STATEMENT;

(2) DESIGNATE THE APPROPRIATE STATE OR LOCAL LAW ENFORCEMENT OFFICES IN THE STATE, OR OTHER APPROVED LOCATIONS, WHERE FINGERPRINTS MAY BE OBTAINED AND APPLICATION FOR A CRIMINAL BACKGROUND INVESTIGATION MAY BE MADE; AND

(3) ADOPT RULES AND REGULATIONS NECESSARY AND REASONABLE TO ADMINISTER THIS PART VI OF THIS SUBTITLE.

SECTION 2. AND BE IT FURTHER ENACTED, That the provisions of this Act are prospective and shall apply only to an employee who is initially employed on or after October 1, 1986 and to an employer who operates a facility on or after October 1, 1986.

SECTION 3. AND BE IT FURTHER ENACTED, That this Act shall take effect July 1, 1986.

Appendix J

GUIDELINE FOR INTERVIEWING THE SUSPECTED ABUSED AND/OR NEGLECTED CHILD*

When Talking to the Child:
Do:

- Make sure the interviewer is someone the child trusts
- Conduct the interview in private
- Sit near the child, not across the table or desk
- Tell the child the interview will be shared only with people who will help protect the child, like CPS or law enforcement
- Ask the child to clarify words, terms, which are not understood
- Tell the child if any future action will be required
- Reassure the child that he/she is not responsible

Don't:

- Allow the child to feel in "trouble" or at "fault"
- Disparage or criticize the child's choice of words or language
- Suggest answers to the child which probe or press for answers the child is unwilling to give
- Display horror, shock or disapproval of parents, child or the situation
- Conduct the interview with additional professionals
- Leave the child alone with a stranger
- Ask "why" questions (i.e. "Why did you go with him?")

---

*Source: Harrison and Edwards, p. 115.

Appendix K

AN EXAMPLE OF A RECREATION AND LEISURE SERVICES AGENCY CHILD ABUSE POLICY*

CITY OF YORK DEPARTMENT OF PARKS & RECREATION
POLICY & PROCEDURE MANUAL

authority

section
PARKS & RECREATION

subject
DRAFT POLICY—CHILD ABUSE 8 Oct 1986
STATEMENT OF PRINCIPLE:

It is the firm belief of the City of York that all citizens must do their utmost to ensure that there are no abused children in York. For its part the Municipality has set the following goals for its Parks and Recreation Department:

(1) No individuals in the employ of the City's Parks and Recreation Department will strike or verbally abuse children while on duty. Failure to comply with this edict will be grounds for immediate dismissal. In addition, the Department will report any incident to the Children's Aid Society of Metropolitan Toronto.

(2) Effective training programs will be carried out to ensure that front-line staff who lead children's programs are fully cognizant of their legal responsibilities and that they have sufficient information that they are able to fulfill these responsibilities.

(3) Proper procedures will be in place to ensure immediate investigation of suspected cases by the appropriate Department official and to, where warranted, comply with the Reporting Protocol of the Metropolitan Toronto Children's Aid Society.

(4) Social and recreational programs will be in place that will enhance the quality of family life and reduce tensions that may lead to child abuse.

Provided by the City of York, Ontario Department of Parks and Recreation.

(5) The Parks and Recreation Department will cooperate with other local children's agencies to ensure that there is a coordinated response to child abuse.

STRATEGIES FOR GOAL ATTAINMENT

GOAL 1—STAFF CONTROL:

- All individuals being interviewed for children's or aquatics program positions will be made aware of this directive.
- This directive will be reinforced at all staff training sessions.
- Supervisory staff will investigate promptly any reported cases of staff striking a child and will ensure that there is proper documentation. Staff suspected of child abuse will be suspended from their duties pending results of the investigation. If reasonable grounds exist, a report will be made to the C.A.S. and the individual will be relieved of their duties immediately.

GOAL 2—STAFF TRAINING:

- The Recreation Services Division will ensure that a thorough staff training package is developed.
- This training package will be a component of any training program involving children's program and aquatics staff.
- The Recreation Services Division will ensure that full-time supervisory staff receive the necessary training to ensure that they can provide accurate judgments and support for their front-line staff.

GOAL 3—INVESTIGATION AND REPORTING PROCEDURES:

- A Recreation Supervisor will be assigned the responsibility of developing appropriate procedures in consultation with the Children's Aid Society and the Police.
- These Procedures will be reviewed and evaluated by the Recreation Division who will then assign a staff person to be responsible for all reports to the C.A.S.
- These Procedures will be evaluated periodically to ensure that they remain appropriate.

GOAL 4—PROGRAMS:

- The Department will conduct periodic needs assessments to determine whether service gaps for family oriented programs exist.
- The Department will work cooperatively with other community agencies to ensure that these service gaps are addressed.

GOAL 5 – COORDINATED RESPONSE:

- The Department will assign a staff person to sit on the local child abuse coordinating committee in order to facilitate networking with other agencies.
- Department staff will meet with the C.A.S. Community Development worker to identify methods of cooperation.
- The Department will be open and responsive to initiatives from the community or from other agencies with respect to dealing with child abuse.

REPORTING PROCEDURES

In order to allow staff to comply with Section 68 (3) of the Child and Family Services Act of 1985 a set of procedures has been identified as the best way for the Parks and Recreation Department to respond to suspected incidences of child abuse or neglect.

For purposes of clarity the Department will use the following definition of child abuse as presented in the Handbook *The Abused Child: A Shared Responsibility* (page 6):

Child abuse is any form of physical harm, emotional deprivation, sexual mistreatment or neglect which can result in injury or psychological damage to a child. Child abuse can be active (hitting or verbal abuse) or passive (withdrawal of affection or failure to provide reasonable protection from physical harm). A child, according to Ontario law, is someone under sixteen years of age or up to eighteen years if under the care of the Children's Aid Society.

These procedures apply specifically to Department staff who have responsibility for the delivery of children's programs. While all individuals have the legal responsibility to report what they "believe" to be cases where children are "in need of protection" (Section 68 [2]), these staff have a responsibility to report "suspected" cases of child abuse. This responsibility is articulated in the Child and Family Services Act of 1985 section 68 "Duty to Report" subsection (3):

A person ... who, in the course of his/her professional or official duties, has reasonable grounds to suspect that a child is or may be suffering or may have suffered abuse shall forthwith report the suspicion and the information on which it is based to a society.

Failure to comply with this edict will be construed as an offense and on conviction an individual is liable to a fine of not more than $1000, or to imprisonment for a term of not more than one year, or to both. (Section 81)

Individuals who make a report based on reasonable grounds and without malicious intent will be protected by laws from civil liability as per Section 68 subsection (7).

(*A*) *INTERNAL REPORTING PROCEDURE:*

(1) INITIAL SUSPICION THAT A CHILD MAY BE A VICTIM OF ABUSE

Staff person completes "Record of Abuse Form" immediately and ensures that the appropriate Recreation Supervisor receives Form within 24 hours (keen judgment will be required to determine the degree of immediate danger faced by the child. If very serious an immediate phone call to the Supervisor is the proper response). In addition, the immediate supervisor (Playground Coordinator, Day Camp Director, Senior Instructor/Head Guard, Pool Manager, Youth Center Coordinator, etc.) will be notified immediately so that a second opinion may be gained. If there are other Department staff on site they will also complete a Record of Abuse Form independently.

(2) FOLLOW–UP INVESTIGATION

The line Recreation Supervisor, upon receipt of a report of suspected child abuse, will meet immediately with the reporting staff to verify details of the report. If possible the Supervisor should attempt to make an independent observation of the child and then complete a Record of Abuse Form.

(3) DECISION TO REPORT

If reasonable grounds are established in the mind of the Supervisor, then the Metropolitan Toronto Children's Aid Society will be notified as per the External Reporting Procedures. Supervisors will be aware that their names may be revealed to the parents of the child and that there may be communications with the parent. The front-line staff who made the initial report will be notified of any action taken on the matter.

(4) DECISION NOT TO REPORT

If reasonable grounds are not established, the Recreation Supervisor will:

(a) notify staff who made initial report

(b) ensure Department support if staff chooses to report

(c) prepare a written report documenting all aspects of the case and file same with the Recreation Supervisor within 48 hours. (These reports will stay on confidential file for 5 years. One copy to staff who made initial report).

NOTE: The burden of proving that an incident of abuse has taken place lies with the Children's Aid Society and not with Department Staff, therefore, only reasonable grounds need to be established.

(*B*) *EXTERNAL REPORTING PROCEDURES:*

The Parks and Recreation Department has determined that the following individual has been designated as the one staff person to make all reports to the C.A.S.: _____. This "Reporting Supervisor" will follow the following procedures when making reports:

(1) The reporting supervisor will ensure that all documentation is completed before the call is placed. It is important that prompt follow-up is made on suspected incidences of child abuse; therefore, there is an expectation that no more than 24 hours will expire between the time of initial suspicion and the decision to report. The Documentation will include the initial Record of the Abuse Form as well as other Forms that may have been completed, as well as a summary from the line supervisor that includes the names, addresses and telephone numbers of the observing staff. These names will be given to the C.A.S. and the Police only if required to proceed with prosecution. To the extent possible the Department will be named as the reporting agency. In most cases this will be sufficient.

(2) The reporting supervisor will notify the Commissioner of Parks and Recreation (or his designate), in writing, of the impending report.

(3) The reporting supervisor will then telephone the intake worker for the C.A.S. at 924-4646. The intake worker will require all details of the alleged abuse; therefore, the reporting supervisor should have information readily at hand. Specifically, the worker will need to know:

- name, address, telephone number and age of the child
- name and phone number of the reporting agency
- date, time and location of the incident
- a detailed chronological description of the incident, or
- a detailed description of why abuse is suspected
- the identity of the individual responsible for the alleged abuse
- any other information the reporting staff feel is important.

The reporting supervisor will then indicate that the Department wishes to know of the outcome of the abuse investigation.

(4) The reporting supervisor will then complete a final summary of the incident, including the name of the intake worker.

(5) When the results of the investigation are known the reporting supervisor will add this information to the documentation and then the entire case will be filed under a confidential label in the Superintendent of Recreation Services office.

SYNOPSIS OF PIERS HARRIS
CHILDREN'S SELF-CONCEPT SCALE

The *Piers-Harris Children's Self-Concept Scale*, subtitled "The Way I Feel About Myself," is a brief, self-report measure designed to aid in the assessment of self-concept in children and adolescents. The Piers-Harris is an 80-item, self-report questionnaire designed to assess how children and adolescents feel about themselves. Children are shown a number of statements that tell how some people feel about themselves, and are asked to indicate whether each statement applies to them using dichotomous yes-or-no responses.

As an aid to more detailed clinical interpretation, the *Piers-Harris* also provides six "cluster scales": Behavior, Intellectual and School Status, Physical Appearance and Attributes, Anxiety, Popularity, and Happiness and Satisfaction. Below are given a selected three items from each of the six cluster scales to give the reader a flavor of the scale.*

Item Number	Item
	I. Behavior (16 Items)
12	I am well behaved in school.*
13	It is usually my fault when something goes wrong.
59	My family is disappointed in me.
	II. Intellectual and School Status (17 Items)
5	I am smart.*
49	My classmates in school think I have good ideas.*
66	I forget what I learn.

III. Physical Appearance and Attributes (13 Items)

8	My looks bother me.*
15	I am strong.
41	I have nice hair.

8	My looks bother me.*
15	I am strong.
41	I have nice hair.

IV. Anxiety (14 Items)

4	I am often sad.
43	I wish I were different.*
74	I am often afraid.

V. Popularity (12 Items)

1	It is hard for me to make friends.
40	I am among the last to be chosen for games.
51	I have many friends.

VI. Happiness and Satisfaction (10 Items)

2	I am a happy person.
36	I am lucky.
39	I like being the way I am.*

Note: Asterisks (*) indicate items which load significantly on more than one cluster scale.

This synopsis was summarized from pages 1 and 2, *Revised Test Manual 1984: Piers-Harris Children's Self-Concept Scale* by Ellen V. Piers (copyright © 1969 by Ellen V. Piers and Dale B. Harris). Reprinted by permission of the publisher, Western Psychological Services, 12031 Wilshire Boulevard, Los Angeles, California 90025.

LOW BUDGET MATERIALS
FOR PUPPET MAKING*

Basic Supplies

- Scissors
- Masking tape
- Crayons
- Construction paper
  9" by 12"
- Manila paper
  9" by 12"

- Glue
- Sewing needles
- Straight pins
- Heavy-duty thread

Materials

- Fabrics
- Buttons
- Corks
- Feathers
- String
- Toothpicks
- Pipe Cleaners
- Clothespins

- Paper bags
- Paper cups
- Styrofoam cups
- Map tacks
- Paper plates
- Elastic bands
- Pot pie tins
- Wooden spoons
- Old socks, slippers

- Cardboard tubes
- Paper fasteners
- Styrofoam balls
- Old magazine pictures
- Small cereal boxes
- Scrap aluminum foil
- Scrap ribbons & yarn
- Tongue depressors
- Old mittens, gloves

*Source: Peyton and Koenig: *Puppetry — A Tool for Teaching.*

REFERENCES

ABC World News Tonight. (1983, September 12). Interview with David Elkind on Children and Stress.

Barth, I. (1985, January 3). Infant today; criminal tomorrow. *Times-Union*, p. 4A.

Begley, S., & Fitzgerald, K. (1987, April). The effects of pets on people. *Newsweek on Health*, p. 20.

Benson, L.E. (1981). *Self-concept change in an outdoor leadership course using communication skills and debriefings.* Unpublished master's thesis, Whitworth College, Spokane, WA.

Bertolami, C. (1981, November). *Effects of a wilderness program on self-esteem and laws of control orientations of young adults.* Paper presented at the Annual Canadian Conference on the Application of Curriculum Research, Winnipeg, Manitoba, Canada.

Burgess, R., & Conger, R. (1978). Family interaction in abusive, neglectful and normal families. *Child Development, 49,* 1163–1173.

Bosse, M., Durand, J., & Beaumont, C. (1984). The expedition to devil the flies we will return; an intervention experience in the midst of the wilderness with emotionally disturbed children. *Apprentissage et Socialization, June,* 90–99.

Brightbill, C.K. (1960). *The challenge of leisure.* Englewood Cliffs: Prentice-Hall.

Broadhurst, D. (1986). *Educators, schools, and child abuse.* Chicago: National Committee for Prevention of Child Abuse.

Broadhurst, D. (1984). *The educator's role in the prevention and treatment of child abuse and neglect.* Washington, DC: National Center on Child Abuse and Neglect. (OHDS No. 84-30172).

Broadhurst, D., Edmunds, M., & MacDicken, R.A. (1979). *Early childhood programs and the prevention and treatment of child abuse and neglect.* Washington, DC: National Center on Child Abuse and Neglect.

Broadhurst, D., & MacDicken, R.A. (1979). *Training in the prevention and treatment of child abuse and neglect.* Washington, DC: National Center on Child Abuse and Neglect. (OHDS No. 79-30201).

Brothers, J. (1975). *Better than ever.* New York: Simon and Schuster.

Brown, W.K., & Simpson, B.F. (1979). Confrontation of self through outdoor challenge: Pennsylvania's outdoor experience for juvenile offenders. *Behavioral Disorders, 2,* 41–48.

Buckner, R.L. (1986). *A study of abused children in comparison to selected groups of behavior disturbed and non-abused elementary aged children on psychological constructs of self-concept.* Unpublished doctoral dissertation, University of Arkansas, Fayetteville.

Bulkley, J., Ensminger, J., Fontana, V.J., & Summit, R. (1982). *Dealing with sexual child abuse.* Chicago: National Committee for Prevention of Child Abuse.

Burch, C.A. (1980). Puppet play in a thirteen-year-old boy: remembering, repeating, and working through. *Clinical Social Work Journal, 8* (2), 79–89.

Buros, O.K. (Ed.). (1971). *Seventh mental measurements yearbook.* Highland Park, NJ: Gyphon Press.

Campbell, D.T., & Stanley, J.C. (1963). *Experimental and quasi-experimental design for research.* Chicago: Rand McNally.

Campbell, J.T. (1988, February). Latchkey children: meeting the need in Tennessee. *Parks and Recreation,* pp. 52–54.

Carlson, R.E., Deppe, T.R., & MacLean, J.R. (1963). *Recreation in American life.* Belmont, CA: Wadsworth.

Caufield, B.A. (1979). *Child abuse and the law.* Chicago: National Committee for Prevention of Child Abuse.

Caulfield, B.A. (1981). *Child abuse and the law: a legal primer for social workers.* Chicago: National Committee for Prevention of Child Abuse.

Chandler, R.A. (1985). *Children under stress.* Springfield, IL: Charles C Thomas.

Chase, N.K. (1981). *Outward bound as an adjunct to therapy.* (Accession No. RC 014601). Denver, CO: Colorado Outward Bound School. (ERIC Document Reproduction Service No. ED 241204).

Child sexual abuse: incest, assault and sexual exploitation. (1978). Washington, DC: National Center on Child Abuse and Neglect.

Clearinghouse on Child Abuse and Neglect Information. (1986). *Child abuse and neglect: an informed approach to a shared concern.* Washington, DC: National Center on Child Abuse and Neglect.

Clearinghouse on Child Abuse and Neglect Information. (1987, Fall). *State statutes 1986: who must report.* Washington, DC: National Center on Child Abuse and Neglect.

Coddington, R.D. (1972). The significance of life events as etiological factors in the disease of children: a survey of professional workers. *Journal of Psychosomatic Research, 16,* 7–18.

Cohn, A.H. (1983). *An approach to preventing child abuse.* Chicago: National Committee for Prevention of Child Abuse.

Cohn, A.H. (1986). *Physical child abuse.* Chicago: National Committee for Prevention of Child Abuse.

Collingwood, T.R. (1972). *Survival camping: a therapeutic mode for rehabilitating problem youth.* Little Rock, AR: Arkansas Rehabilitation Research and Training Center.

Confessed killer of 13 executed. (1985, December 6). *Times-Union,* p. 5A.

Coolsen, P., Seligson, M., & Garbarino, J. (1986). *When school's out and nobody's home.* Chicago: National Committee for Prevention of Child Abuse.

Coopersmith, S. (1967). *The antecedents of self-esteem.* San Francisco: Freeman.

Crosswhite, B.T. (1970). *Size and sample needed to validate findings.* Unpublished doctoral dissertation, University of Northern Colorado, Greeley.

Cytrynbaum, S., & Ken K. (1975). *The Connecticut wilderness program: a preliminary evaluation report.* Submitted to the State of Connecticut Council on Human Services, Hartford, CT.

Darst, P.W., & Armstrong, G.P. (1980). *Outdoor adventure activities for school and recreation programs.* Minneapolis: Burgess.

Davis, A.F. (1973). *American heroine.* New York: Oxford University Press.

Dean, D. (1979). Emotional abuse of children. *Children Today, 8,* 18–20.

Doell, C.E., & Fitzgerald, C.B. (1954). *A brief history of parks and recreation in the United States.* Chicago: Athletic Institute.

Duncan, G.M., Frazier, S.H., Littin, E.M., Johnson, A.M., & Barron, A.J. (1958). Etiological factors in first-degree murder. *JAMA, 168,* 1755–1758.

Edwards, P.B. (1984). The family as leisure counselors. *Journal of Physical Education, Recreation and Dance, 55* (8), 47–49, 58.

Elkind, D. (1984). *All grown up and no place to go: teenagers in crisis.* Reading, MA: Addison-Wesley.

Elkind, D. (1981). *The hurried child.* Reading, MA: Addison-Wesley.

Erickson, E.L., McEvoy, A., & Colucci, N.D. (1984). *Child abuse and neglect.* Holmes Beach, FL: Learning Publications.

Espenak, L. (1981). *Dance therapy: theory and application.* Springfield, IL: Charles C Thomas.

Fabos, J.G., Milde, G.T., & Weinmayr, V.M. (1970). *Frederic Law Olmstead, Sr.* University of Massachusetts Press.

Flugelman, A. (Ed.). (1981). *More new games.* Gordon City: Doubleday.

Flugelman, A. (Ed.). (1971). *The new games book.* Garden City: Doubleday.

Fontana, V.J. (1976). *Somewhere a child is crying.* New York: Mentor.

Garbarino, J., & Garbarino, A.C. (1986). *Emotional maltreatment of children.* Chicago: National Committee for Prevention of Child Abuse.

Garbarino, J., & Garbarino, A.C. (1986). *Maltreatment of adolescents.* Chicago: National Committee for Prevention of Child Abuse.

Gerbner, G., Ross, C.J., & Zigler, E. (Eds.). (1980). *Child abuse.* New York: Oxford University Press.

Gershon, E.S. (1986, May–June). Depression seen in a number of children, adolescents. *The National Health,* newspaper of the American Public Health Association.

Gil, D.G. (1970). *Violence against children.* Cambridge: Harvard University Press.

Gray, D.E., & Greben, S. (1974, July). Future perspectives. *Parks and Recreation,* pp. 26–33, 47–56.

Guadagnolo, F., & Farrell, P. (1985, May). What can you ask an applicant. *Parks and Recreation,* pp. 42–44.

Harrison, R., & Edwards, J. (1983). *Child abuse.* Portland, OR: Edrick Communications.

Harter, S. (1983). Developmental perspectives on the self system. In E.M. Hetherington (Ed.), *Handbook on child psychology: Vol. 4. Socialization, personality, social development.* New York: Wiley.

Hearings, select subcommittee on education. (1974). Proceedings of the Committee on Education and Labor, House of Representatives 93rd Congress. Washington, DC: U.S. Government Printing Office.

Heindl, C., Krall, C.A., Salus, M.K., & Broadhurst, D.D. (1979). *The nurse's role in the prevention and treatment of child abuse and neglect.* Washington, DC: National Center on Child Abuse and Neglect. (OHDS No. 79-30202).

Hjorth, C.W. (1982). Using the offer self-image questionnaire with physically abused adolescents. *Journal of Youth and Adolescence, 11* (2), pp. 61–64.

Hjorth, C.W., & Ostrow, E. (1982). The self-image of physically abused adolescents. *Journal of Youth and Adolescence, 11* (2), pp. 71–76.

Horine, L. (1985). *Administration of physical education and sport programs.* New York: Saunders.

Humphrey, J.H. (Ed.). (1984). *Stress in childhood.* New York: AMS Press.

Humphrey, J.H., & Humphrey, J.N. (Eds.). (1985). *Controlling stress in children.* Springfield, IL: Charles C Thomas.

Interdisciplinary glossary on child abuse and neglect: legal, medical, social work terms. (1980). Washington, DC: National Center on Child Abuse and Neglect. (OHDS No. 80-30137).

Issues update: latchkey children. (1988, February). *Parks and Recreation,* pp. 49–51.

It shouldn't hurt to be a child. (1983). Chicago: National Committee for Prevention of Child Abuse.

It's happening! Project adventure. (1988). Hamilton, MA: Project Adventure.

Jenkins, J.L., MacDicken, R.A., & Ormsby, N.J. (1979). *A community approach: the child protection coordinating committee.* Washington, DC: National Center on Child Abuse and Neglect. (OHDS No. 79-30195).

Jenkins, J.L., Salus, Marsha, K., & Schultze, G.L. (1979). *Child protective services: a guide for workers.* Washington, DC: National Center on Child Abuse and Neglect. (OHDS No. 79-30203).

Jersild, A.T. (1952). *In search of self.* New York: Columbia University Bureau of Publication.

Justice, B., & Justice, R. (1976). *The abusing family.* New York: Human Sciences Press.

Kazdin, A.E., Moser, J., Colbus, D., & Beel, R. (1985). Depressive symptoms among physically abused and psychiatrically disturbed children. *Journal of Abnormal Psychology, 94* (3), 298–307.

Kelly, F., & Baer, D. (1968). *Outward bound schools as an alternative to institutionalization for adolescent delinquent boys.* Boston: Fandel.

Kempe, C.H., & Kempe, R.S. (1978). *Child abuse.* Cambridge: Harvard University Press.

Kempe, C.H., & Helfer, R.E. (Eds.). (1980). *The battered child.* Chicago: University of Chicago Press.

Kimbell, R.O. (1980). *Wilderness adventure programs for juvenile offenders.* (Accession No. RC 012398). Chicago: Chicago University. (ERIC Document Reproduction Services No. ED 196-586).

Kinard, E.M. (1980). Emotional development in physically abused children. *American Journal of Orthopsychiatry, 50* (4), 686–696.

Kirchner, G. (1974). *Physical education for elementary school children.* Dubuque, IA: Wm. C. Brown.

Kliman, G.K. (1986). *Psychological emergencies of childhood.* New York: Grune and Stratton.

Kobasa, S.C. (1985). Stressful life events, personality, and health: an inquiry into hardiness. In A. Monat and R.S. Lazarus (Eds.), *Stress and Coping: An Anthology.* New York: Columbia University Press.

Kraus, R.G. (1985). *Recreation leadership today.* Glenview, IL: Scott, Foresman.

Kraus, R.G. (1971). *Recreation and leisure in modern society.* Pacific Palisades: Goodyear.

Kraus, R.G. (1984). *Recreational leisure in modern society.* Glenview, IL: Scott, Foresman.

Kraus, R.G. (1983). *Therapeutic recreation service.* New York: Saunders.

Kuczen, B. (1982). *Childhood stress—don't let your child be a victim.* New York: Delacorte.

Kuczen, B. (1984, February). Freed up from stress. *Working Parents,* pp. 23–26.

Let's-play-to-grow: Manual for parents and teachers. (1977). Washington, DC: Joseph P. Kennedy, Jr. Foundation.

Levanthal, M.B. (Ed.). (1980). *Movement and growth: dance therapy for the special child.* New York: New York University.

Levitt, R., & Crane, B. (1986). *It's O.K. to say no!* Wellingborough: Thorsons.

Linn, J.W. (1968). *Jane Addams.* New York: Greenwood Press.

Marsh, H.W., & others. (1984). *Multidimensional self-concepts: the effects of participation in an outward bound program.* (Accession No. RC 015060). Sydney: University of Sydney, Dept. of Education. (ERIC Document Reproduction Service No. ED 251271).

Martin, H.P. (1979). *Treatment for abused and neglected children.* Washington, DC: National Center on Child Abuse and Neglect. (OHDS No. 79-30199).

Martin, P.B. (1983). *The effects of an outdoor adventure program on group cohesion and change in self-concept.* Unpublished doctoral dissertation, Boston College, Chestnut Hill, MA.

Mather, C. (1981, May 13). Man's best friend? *Nursing Mirror, 152* (20), 22–23.

May, G. (1984). *Understanding sexual child abuse.* Chicago: National Committee for Prevention of Child Abuse.

Mayhall, P.D., & Norgard, K.E. (1983). *Child abuse and neglect.* NewYork: John Wiley.

McCall, Cheryl. (1984, December). The cruelest crime. *Life,* pp. 35–42, 47–52, 56–62.

McClary, S.D. (1984). *A study of curriculum planning in junior high mini-courses.* Unpublished doctoral dissertation, State University of New York at Buffalo.

McFern, A.R. (1973). *A self-concept study of adolescents in four areas of exceptionality.* Unpublished master's thesis, University of Georgia, Athens.

McKeown, T. (1984). Determinants of health. In P.R. Lee, C.L. Estes, & N.B. Ramsey (Eds.), *The Nation's Health.* San Francisco: Boyd and Frazier.

McPhillips, J., & Murphy, D. (1984, April 15). "Serial" killers are empty men thirsting for power, thrills. *Democrat and Chronicle,* pp. 1A, 8A.

Menninger, K. (1968). *The crime of punishment.* New York: Viking Press.

Menninger, W.W. (1986, September). Child abuse, a critical issue in our society. *Scouting,* pp. 36–37, 64–66.

Meyer, H.D., & Brightbill, C.K. (1964). *Community recreation.* Englewood Cliffs: Prentice-Hall.

Meyer, J.L., & Donaho, M.W. (1979). *Get the right person for the job.* Englewood Cliffs: Prentice-Hall.

Michael, W.B., Smith, R.A., & Michael, J.J. (1975). The factorial validity of the Piers-Harris Children's Self-Concept Scale for each of three samples of elementary, junior high, and senior high students in a large metropolitan high school district. *Education and Psychological Measurement, 35,* 405–414.

Miller, A.C., & others. (1986). *Monitoring children's health: key indicators.* Washington, DC: American Public Health Association.

Miller, M.S. (1982). *Child stress! Understanding and answering stress signals of infants, children, and teenagers.* New York: Doubleday.

Miller, R.A. (1978, Fall/Winter). The development of a positive self-image through resident camping experiences. *Communicator,* pp. 48–50.

Monat, A., & Lazarus, R.S. (Eds.). (1985). *Stress and coping: an anthology.* New York: Columbia University Press.

Newberry, B.H., & others. (1987). Stress and disease: an assessment in human stress. In J.H. Humphrey (Eds.): *Human Stress: Current Selected Research, Vol. 2.* New York: Ams Press.

New York Consolidated Laws Service. (1985). Rochester, NY: The Lawyers Cooperative.

Oates, K. (Ed.). (1982). *Child abuse – a community concern.* New York: Brunner/Mazel.

Oates, R.K., & Peacock, A. (1985, October). Self-esteem of abused children. *Child Abuse and Neglect,* pp. 159–163.

O'Brien, S. (1981). *Child abuse.* Provo: Brigham Young University Press.

O'Conner, S.F. (1983). *An ethnographic investigation on the impact of a residential outdoor education program on self-esteem and attitudes to the outdoors of 5th and 7th grade students.* Unpublished doctoral dissertation, The Catholic University of America, Washington, DC.

Orlick, T. (1978). *The cooperative sports and games book.* New York: Pantheon.

Orlick, T. (1982). *The second cooperative sports and games book.* New York: Pantheon.

Peyton, J., & Koenig, B. (1973). *Puppetry – a tool for teaching.* New Haven: New Haven Foundation.

Phillips, B. (1978). *School stress and anxiety: theory research and intervention.* New York: Human Service.

Philpott, A.R. (1977). *Puppets and therapy.* Boston: Plays, Inc.

Piers, E.V., & Harris, D.B. (1964). Age and other correlates of self-concept in children. *Journal of Educational Psychology, 55,* 81–85.

Piers, E.V., & Harris, D.B. (1969). *The Piers-Harris Self-Concept Scale.* Nashville, TN: Counselor Recordings and Tests.

Piers, E.V. (1977). *The Piers-Harris children's self-concept scale: research monograph #1.* Nashville, TN: Counselor Recordings and Tests.

Pigeon, G. *Towards creative play.* Birmingham, England: Educational Drama Association.

Plato. (1973). *Laches and Charmides.* Rosamond Kent Sprague translates. New York: Bobbs-Merrill.

Polansky, N.A., DeSaix, C., & Sharlino, S.A. (1973). *Child abuse: understanding and reaching the parent.* New York: Child Welfare League of America, Inc.

Porter, W. (1975). *The development and evaluation of a therapeutic wilderness program for problem youth.* Unpublished master's thesis, University of Denver.

Pringle, M.K. (1975). *The needs of children.* New York: Schocken.

Rainwater, C.E. (1922). *The play movement in the United States.* Washington, DC: McGrath.

Ramos, S. (1975). *Teaching your child to cope with stress.* New York: McKay.

Ray-Keil, A. Subscription brochure. Seattle, WA: Committee for Children.

Recruitment & selection of staff: a guide for managers of preschool & child care programs. (1985). Washington, DC: U.S. Department of Health and Human Services. (Publication No. 85-31191).

Renfro, N. (1984). *Puppetry, language and the special child.* Austin, TX: Nancy Renfro Studios.

Richards, G.E., & Richards, M.J.F. (1981). *Outward bound bridging course: 1981.* Sydney, Australia: Australian Outward Bound School. (ERIC Document Reproduction Service No. ED 225799).

Robinson, J.P., & Shaver, P.R. (1973). *Measures of social psychological attitudes* (Rev. Ed.). Ann Arbor: University of Michigan, Institute of Social Research.

Rodney, L.S., & Toalson, R.F. (1981). *Administration of recreation, parks, and leisure services.* New York: John Wiley.

Rohnke, K. (1984). *Silver bullets, a guide to initiative problems, adventure games, stunts and trust activities.* Beverly, MA: Wilks.

Roper, L.W. (1973). *FLO: a bibliography of Frederick Law Olmstead.* Baltimore: Johns Hopkins University Press.

Rousseau, J. (1946). *Discours sur les sciences ed les arts.* New York: George R. Havens (Eds.).

Rutter, M. (1983). Stress, coping and development; some issues and some questions. In N. Garmezy & M. Rutter (Eds.), *Stress, Coping and Development in Children.* New York: McGraw-Hill.

Select Committee on Children, Youth and Families, U.S. House of Representatives. (1987). *Abused children in America: victims of official neglect* (Publication No. 70-353). Washington, DC: U.S. Government Printing Office.

Selye, H. (1978, October). *Stress and the reduction of distress.* Presentation at The Second National Conference on Emotional Stress and Heart Disease, Hilton Head, SC.

Selye, H. (1976). *The stress of life.* New York: McGraw-Hill.

Shanas, B. (1975, March). Child abuse: a killer teachers can help control. *Phi Delta Kappan, 56* (7), 482.

Standards for the administration of juvenile justice. (1980, July). Washington, DC: Advisory Committee for Juvenile Justice and Delinquency Prevention, U.S. Department of Justice.

Stavis, P. (1988, April–May). Sue me? *Quality of Care,* pp. 1–3.

Stevenson, E. (1977). *Park makers: a life of Frederick Law Olmstead.* New York: MacMillan.

Stimpson, D., & Pederson, D. (1970). Effects of a survival training experience upon evaluation of self and others for underachieving high school students. *Perceptual and Motor Skills, 31,* 337–338.

Stogner, J.D. (1979). *The effects of a wilderness experience on self-concept and academic performance.* Unpublished doctoral dissertation, Virginia Polytechnic Institute and State University, Blacksburg.

Straus, M.A., Gelles, R.J., & Steinmetz, S.K. (1981). *Behind closed doors.* Garden City, NY: Anchor Press.

Stroebel, E. (1984, March 15). *Stress management for children.* Presentation at the State University of New York, Brockport, NY.

Thacker, R.T. (1979). *The effect of a two week camping experience on the self-concept of physically handicapped children.* Unpublished doctoral dissertation, University of North Carolina, Chapel Hill.

Trowbridge, N. (1972). Self-concept and socio-economic status in elementary school children. *American Educational Research Journal, 9,* 525–537.

U.S. DHEW. (1979). *Healthy people: the surgeon general's report on health promotion and disease prevention.* Washington, DC: U.S. Public Health Service, Office of Assistant Secretary for Health and Surgeon General. (Publication No. 79-55071).

U.S. DHEW. (1979). *Healthy people: the surgeon general's report on health promotion and disease prevention.* Washington, DC: U.S. Public Health Service, Office of Assistant Secretary for Health and Surgeon General. (Publication No. 79-55071A).

Vroom, W. (1894, July). Playgrounds for children. *The Arena,* p. 286.

Washburn, C.A. (1983). *The effects of participation in high-risk ropes course activities on individual self-concept.* Unpublished doctoral dissertation, Oklahoma State University, Stillwater.

Wayne, J.L., & Avery, N.C. (1980). *Child abuse: prevention and treatment through social group work.* Boston: Charles River Books.

Werner, E.E. (1988). Resilient children. In H.E. Fitzgerald and M.G. Walraven (Eds.), *Annual Editions Human Development.* Guilford, CT: Dushkin.

Werner, E.E., & Smith, R.S. (1982). *Vulnerable but invincible: a longitudinal study of resilent children and youth.* New York: McGraw-Hill.

Wethered, A. (1973). *Movement and drama in therapy.* Boston: Plays.

Williams, L.M., & Holcomb, T.J. (1985, September). Preventing child abuse in parks and recreation areas. *Parks and Recreation,* pp. 58–60, 82.

Winterdyk, J.A. (1980). *A wilderness adventure program as an alternative for juvenile probationers: an evaluation.* Unpublished master's thesis, Simon Fraser University, Toronto, Canada.

Wise, W.E. (1935). *Jane Addams of Hull House.* New York: Harcourt, Brace.

Wolff, S. (1981). *Children under stress.* London: Penguin Books.

Wright, A.N. (1982, March). *The effects of high adventure activities on adolescent self-concept: a comparison of situationally specific self-concept measurements.* Paper presented at the National Convention of the American Camping Association, New York.

Wurman, S., Levy, A., & Katz, J. (1972). *The nature of recreation.* Cambridge: M.I.T. Press.

Wylie, R.C. (1974). *The self-concept (Vol. 1).* (Rev. Ed.). Lincoln: The University of Nebraska Press.

Young, L. (1986). *Physical child neglect.* Chicago: National Committee for Prevention of Child Abuse.

AUTHOR INDEX

SUBJECT INDEX